U2

The Illustrated Biography

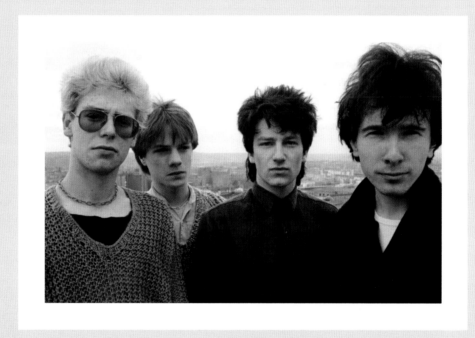

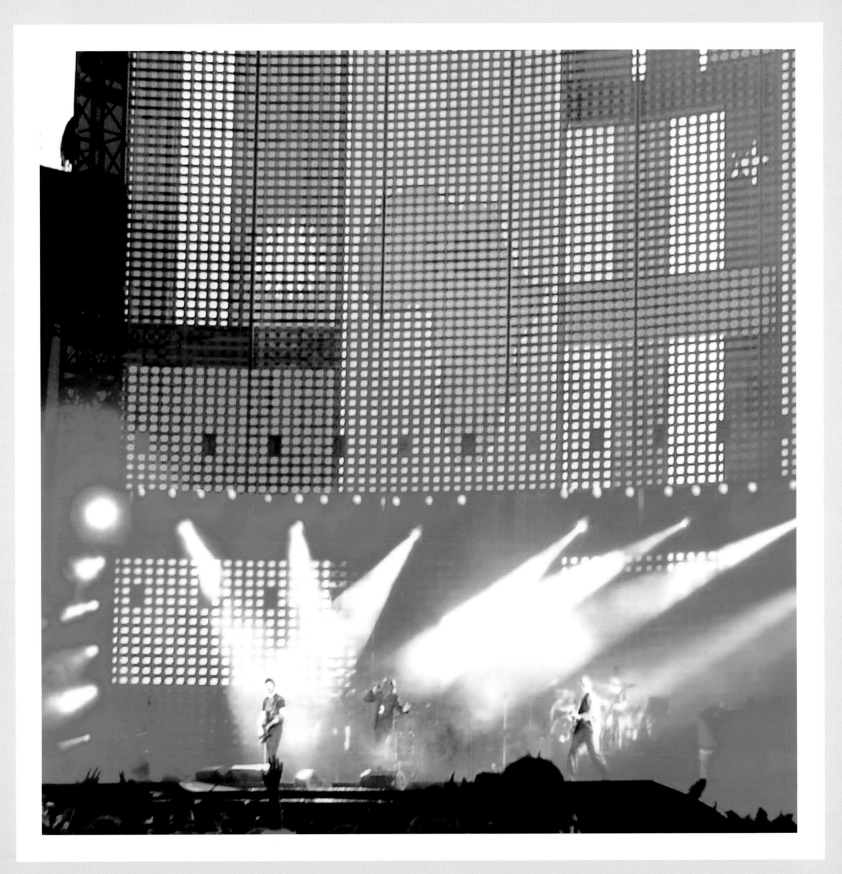

U2

The Illustrated Biography

MARTIN ANDERSEN

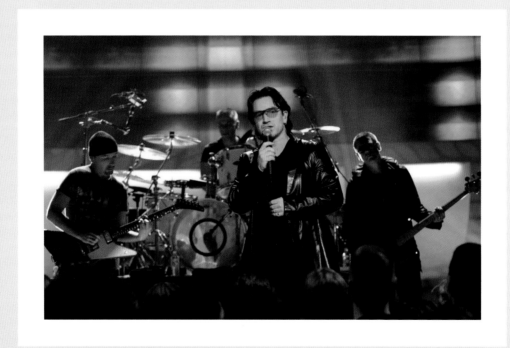

This edition published by Welcome Rain Publishers LLC 2011

First published by Transatlantic Press in 2011

Transatlantic Press
38 Copthorne Road
Croxley Green
Hertfordshire
WD3 4AQ, UK

© Transatlantic Press
Photographs © Getty Images

ISBN 978-1-56649-094-8

Printed and bound in China

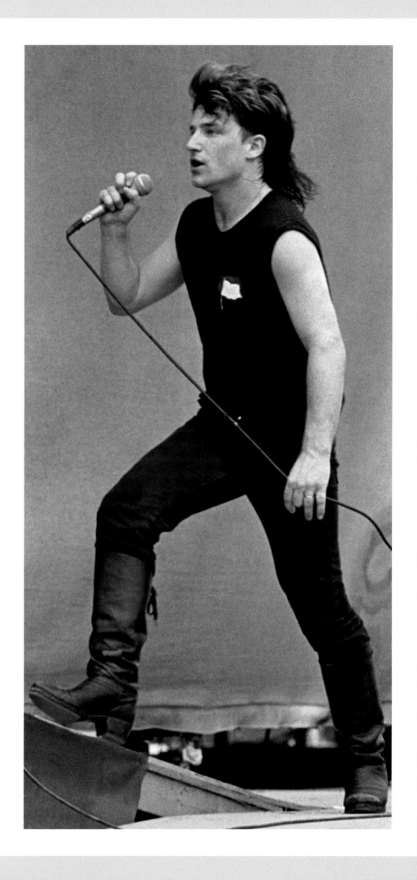

Contents

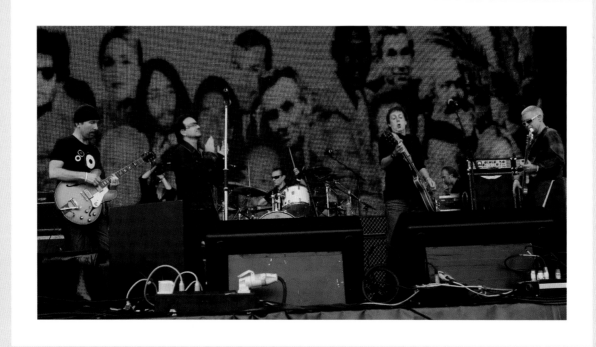

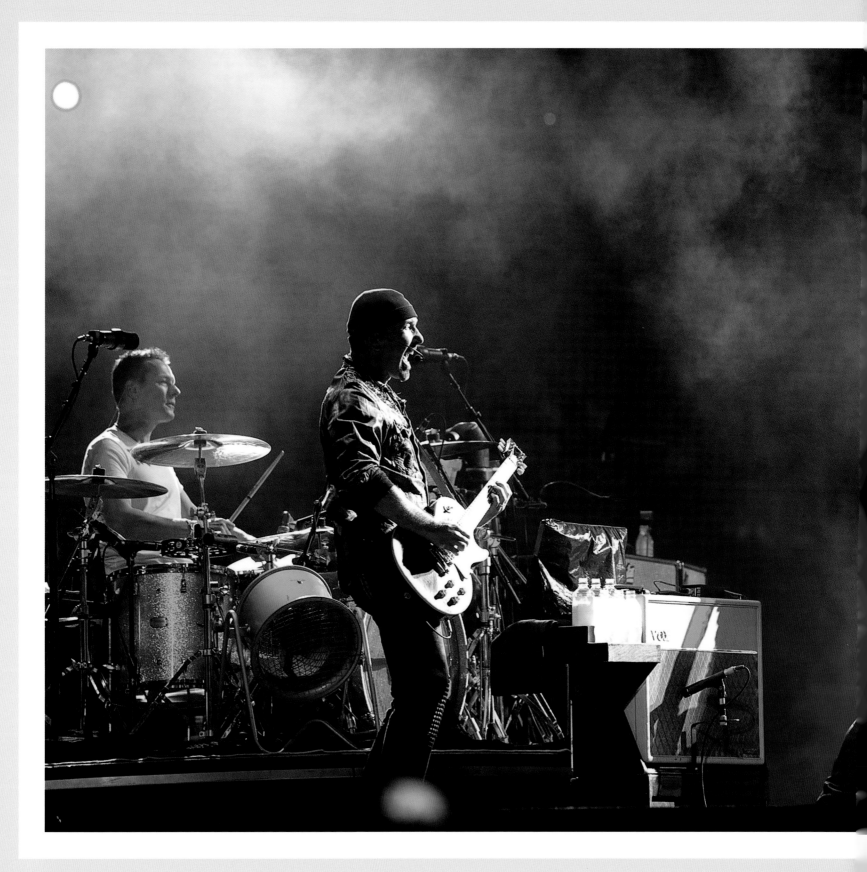

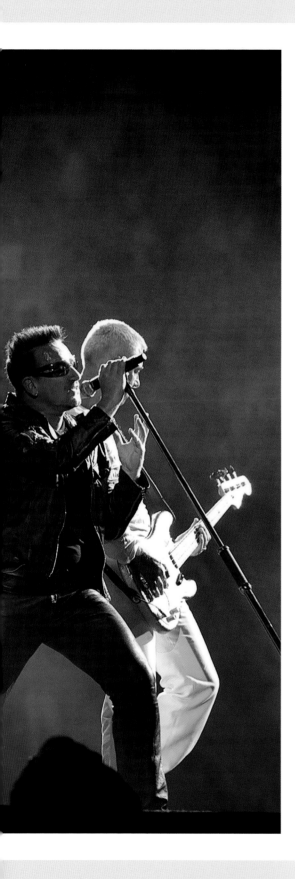

Introduction

"Drummer seeks musicians to form band" was the fateful note young Larry Mullen placed on the school noticeboard one day in 1976. A number of teenage school friends and acquaintances came together in the Mullen family kitchen as a consequence and the nucleus of that group of young, inexperienced musicians from Dublin, Ireland, became one of the most successful and longest-enduring rock 'n' roll bands in the world. The four of them are still together more than thirty years later, having notched up the odd achievement along the way, including winning 22 Grammy awards, selling more than 150 million records and being ranked number 22 in *Rolling Stone* magazine's list of the greatest music artists of all time.

U2 consists of Adam Clayton (bass), Larry Mullen Junior (drums), The Edge (guitar) and Bono (vocals, guitar). Their music took its early influences from punk, but the band learned quickly and the sound developed, without ever losing the distinctive elements of Bono's vocals and The Edge's unique guitar sound. The band's first album, *Boy*, was released on the Island label in 1980. From that release U2 moved slowly from a national to a world stage, their biggest breakthrough coming with their appearance at Bob Geldof's Live Aid concert in 1985, a performance that introduced U2's music to a huge world-wide audience.

Even greater success followed with the release of *The Joshua Tree* in 1987: a number one album on both sides of the Atlantic, the band's first platinum-selling CD and the fastest-selling album of all time in America on its launch. Something of a critical backlash over the subsequent album, *Rattle and Hum* caused U2 to rethink and regroup. 1981's *Achtung Baby* and the Zoo TV tour that followed it were a showcase for new sounds and a more ironic, self-deprecating band image. The rethinking and reinvention have continued ever since.

Religious belief has been a strong influence on the direction the band and its music have taken over the years. Not only does U2 make distinctive music and deliver powerful live shows, but its members have been active – particularly in Bono's case – in both public and private support of numerous social, political and charitable causes.

Most importantly, the band continues to make albums – most recently 2009's *No Line On The Horizon* – and tour in support of them. The 360° Tour continues through 2011 and U2 shows little sign of slowing down: the music still intrigues and astonishes fans old and new; the live shows still thrill.

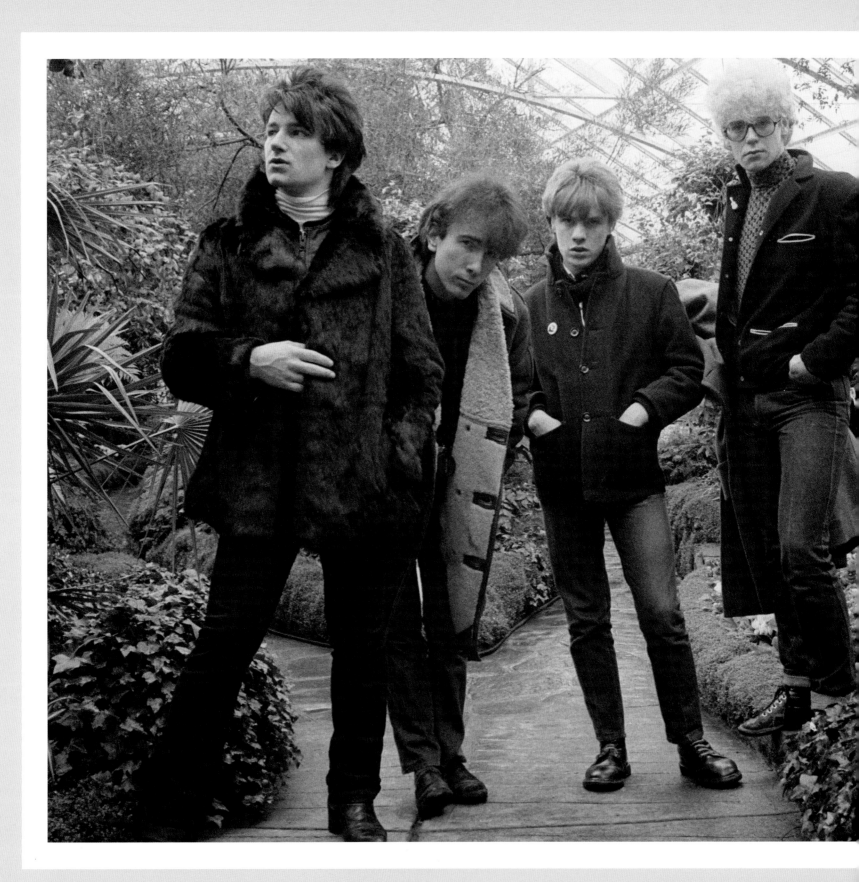

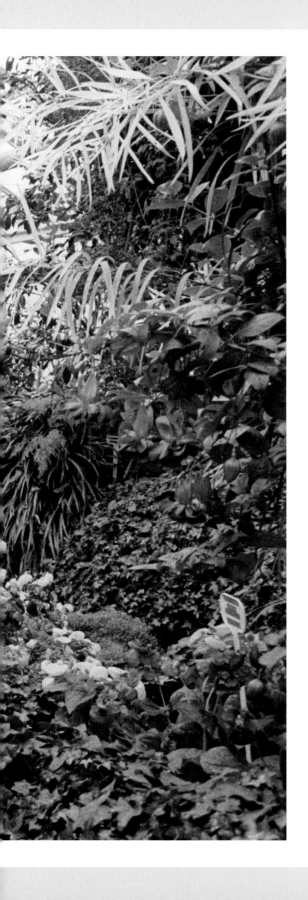

Chapter One
Early Hype

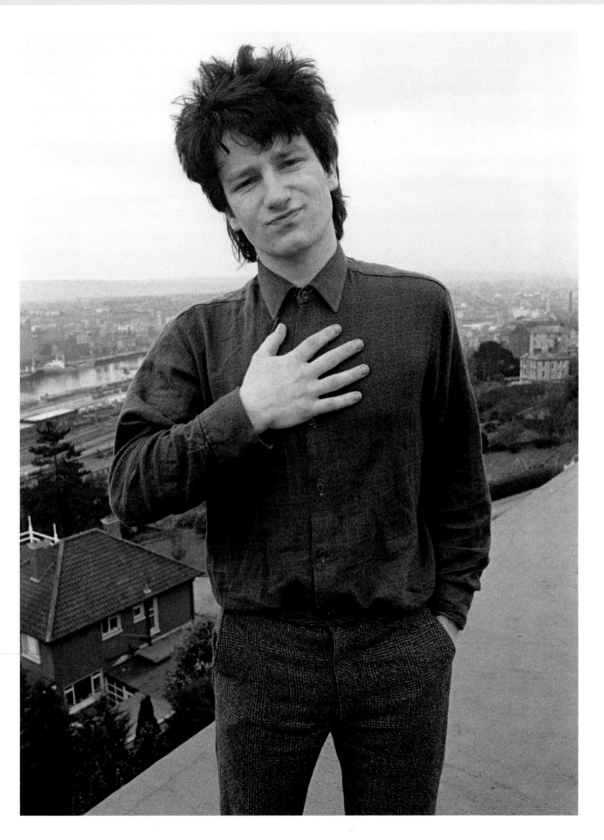

The line-up

Left: Bono, U2's main singer and lyricist, on the roof of the Cork Country Club in the early days of the band. Born Paul David Hewson on 10 May 1960, the nickname Bono, given Paul by teenage friends, is short for Bono Vox, a corruption of the Latin bonavox (the name of a Dublin hearing aid shop!) or "good voice". The young Paul Hewson attended Mount Temple Comprehensive School in Dublin, where he first met both his band mates and his future wife.

Opposite: Larry Mullen Junior, born on 31 October 1961, is U2's drummer. The founder of the band, it was, as he described the first audition, "the Larry Mullen Band for about ten minutes" until Bono walked in the room. Mullen is the quiet member of the band, generally letting the others take the limelight during public appearances.

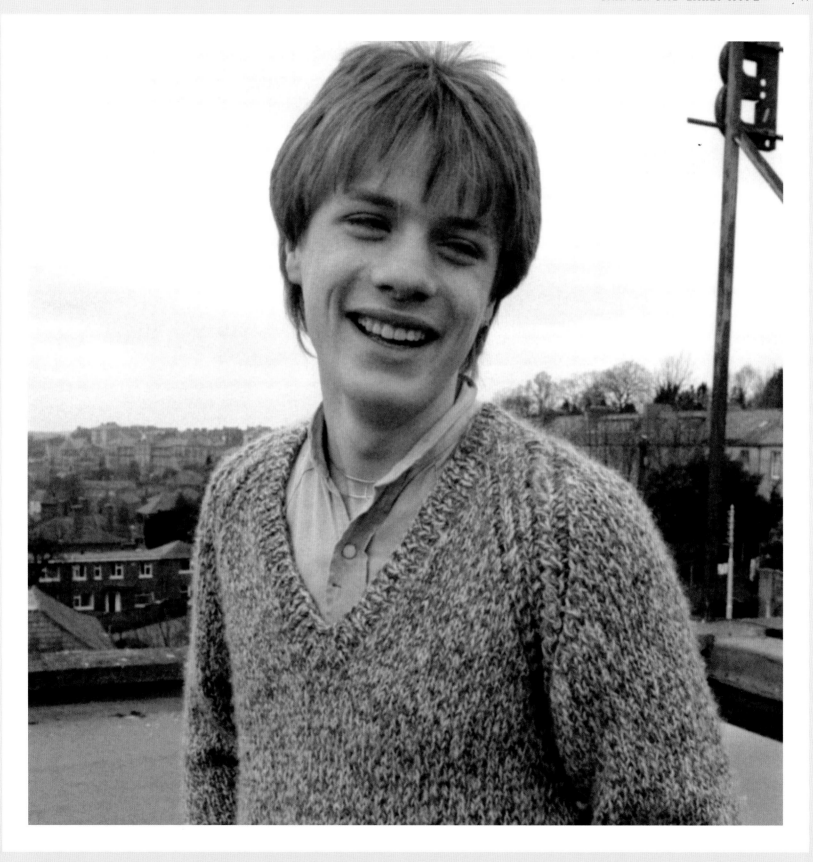

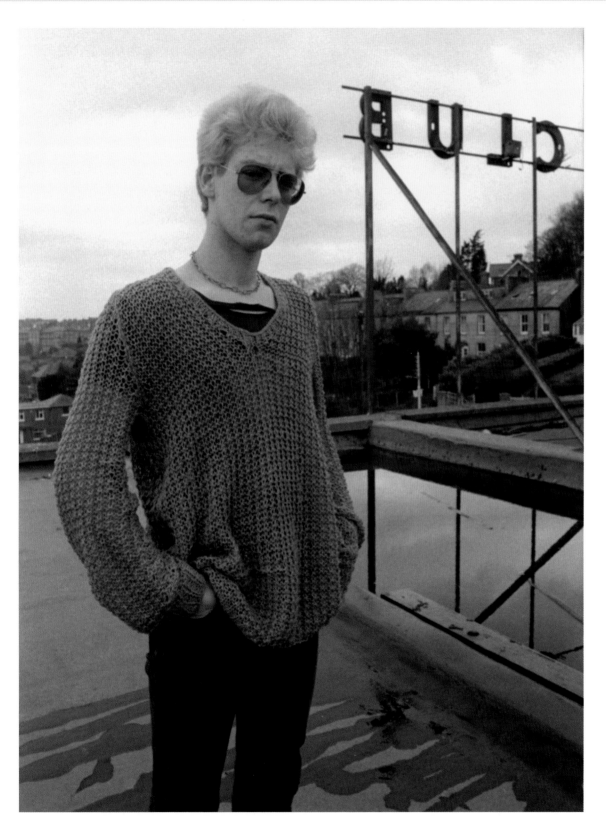

Bass and Lead

Left: Adam Clayton, born on 13 March 1960 in Chinnor, Oxfordshire, England, is U2's bass player. The Claytons moved from the UK to Dublin when Adam was five and became friends there with the Evans family, whose son Dave would later become The Edge. Although his fellow band members found him slightly exotic and were impressed by his knowledge of musical terminology, Adam had in fact had no musical training and his journey towards excellence in bass playing would be a long one.

Opposite: The Edge adopts a pose for the camera.

Born David Evans in England on 8 August 1961, Edge is the band's main guitarist, his "chiming, shimmering sound" being one of the most familiar and distinctive elements of U2's music. The Evans family moved to Ireland when David was one year old. He and his brother Richard (aka Dik) were given music lessons and performed together as children, both attending the first band audition at Larry Mullen's house. Dik stayed with the band until 1978.

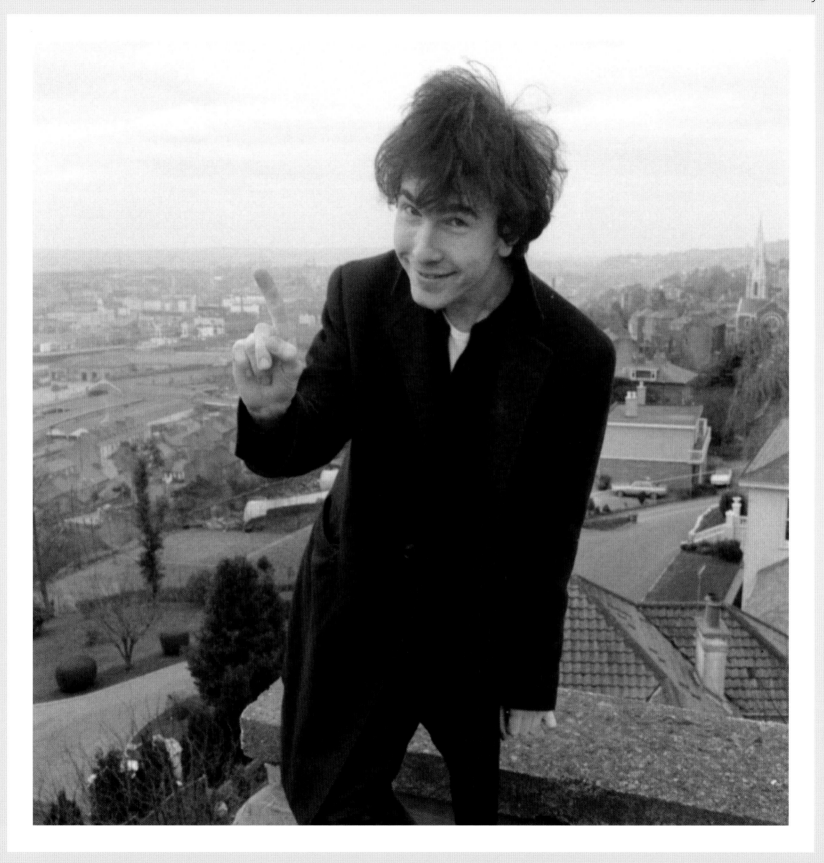

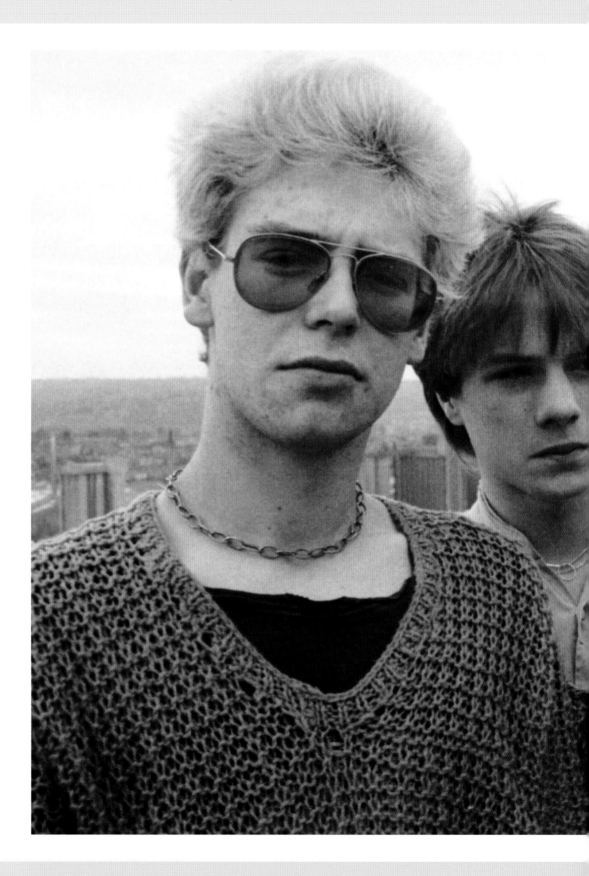

Leaving The Hype

Right: The boys, Adam, Larry, Bono and The Edge. The band they formed following the historic audition in Larry's kitchen on 25 September 1976 was originally called Feedback. They played cover versions of other people's material and weren't, by their own admission, particularly good at first. In March 1977 the band's name was changed to The Hype and then in March 1978, with the departure of Edge's brother Dik from the line-up, it finally became the four-piece U2. On St Patrick's Day 1978, U2 won a talent show in Limerick. The prize was £500 and time in a recording studio to make a demo tape that would be heard by CBS Ireland. The band was on its way...

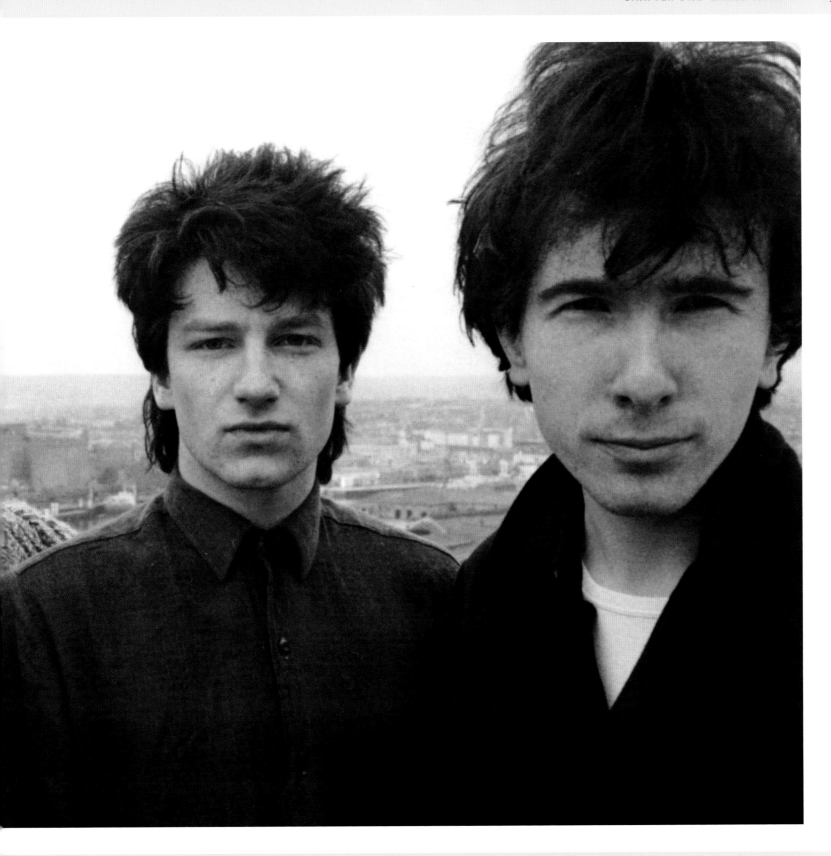

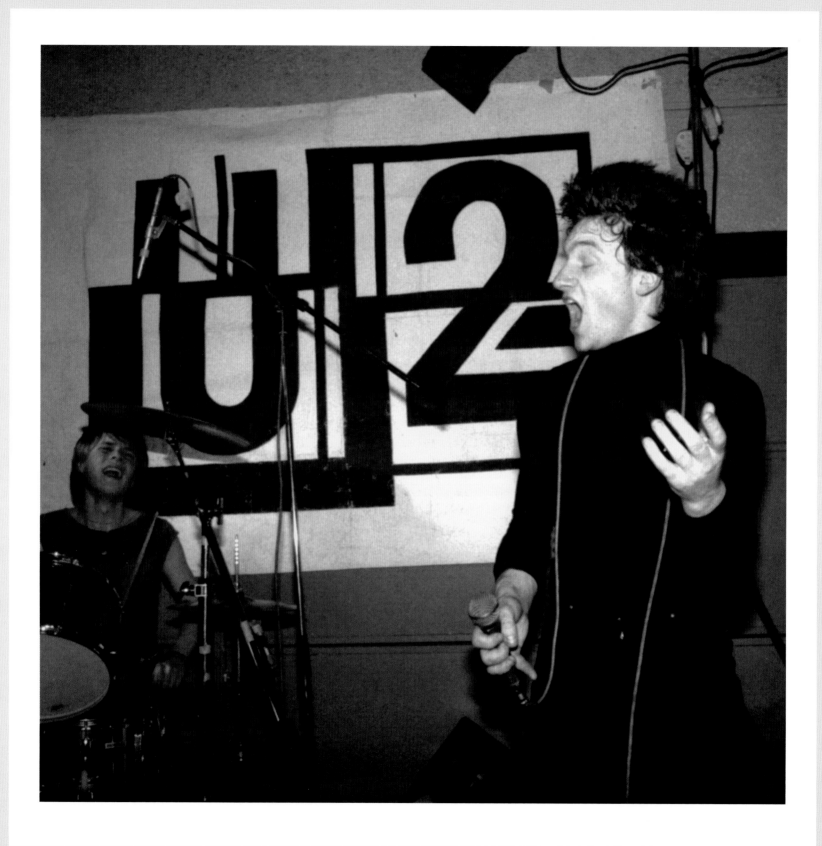

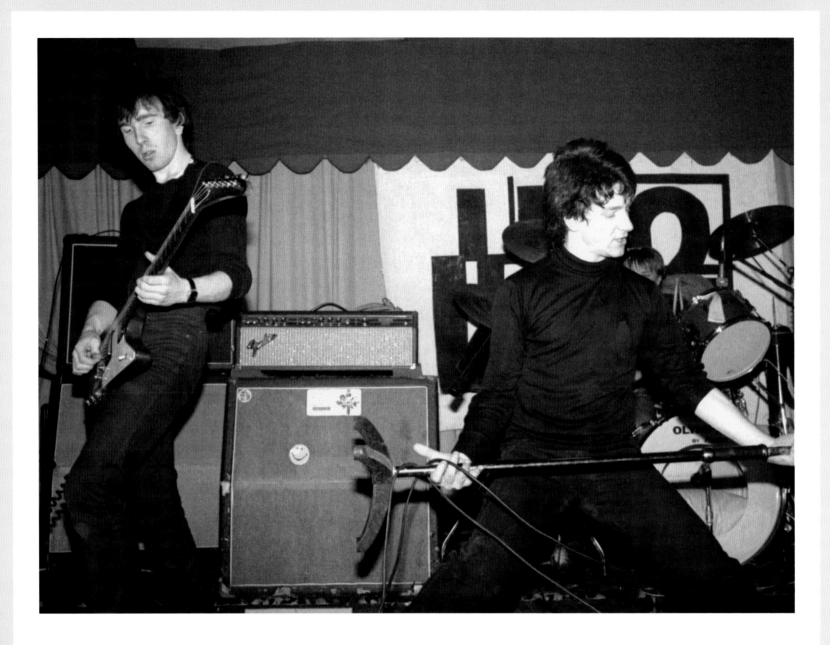

Championed by Hot Press

Opposite: Larry and Bono on stage

The band recorded its first demo in Dublin's Keystone Studios in April 1978. Bill Graham, a writer for music and politics magazine, *Hot Press*, became an early champion of U2 after meeting them and being invited to attend their first recording session; it was he who in May 1978 put them in touch with the man who was to become their manager, Paul McGuinness. Initially reluctant, after watching them perform McGuinness was impressed by Edge's playing and Bono's way with the audience.

Above: Edge and Bono (with Larry partly obscured) on stage. U2 remained with McGuinness and after a couple of months he agreed to manage them. Although Paul had worked as a film technician, theatre director and magazine editor, at this time he had little experience of managing musicians apart from a not-very-successful band called Spud. His stature in the music business has risen with U2's fame and the band acknowledges his important role in furthering their careers under his steady style, which has nonetheless supported almost unlimited artistic freedom.

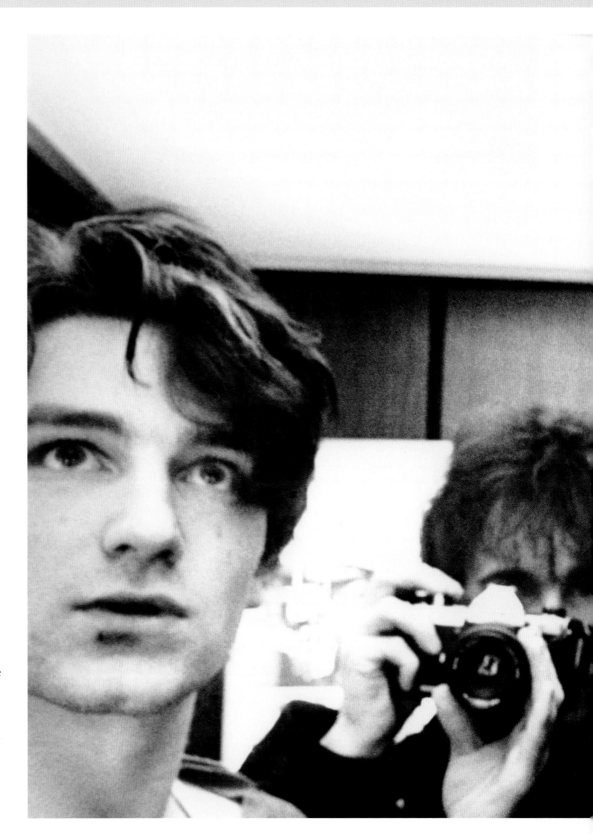

Punk in the rear view mirror

Right: U2, a little more art-house: Bono, Edge (with camera), Larry and Adam (with phone). The band are already looking a little less punk and a little more art-house than in earlier incarnations. As the UK and Irish punk scenes began to evolve towards new wave, U2's sound was still developing, moving from its earlier raw punk sound towards something more sophisticated.

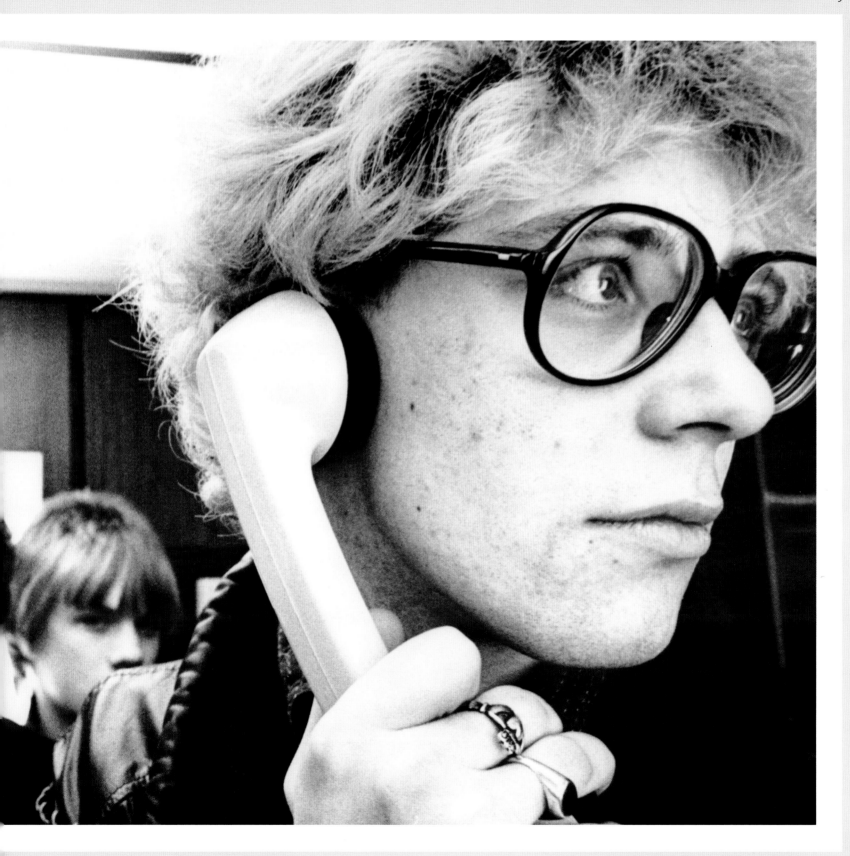

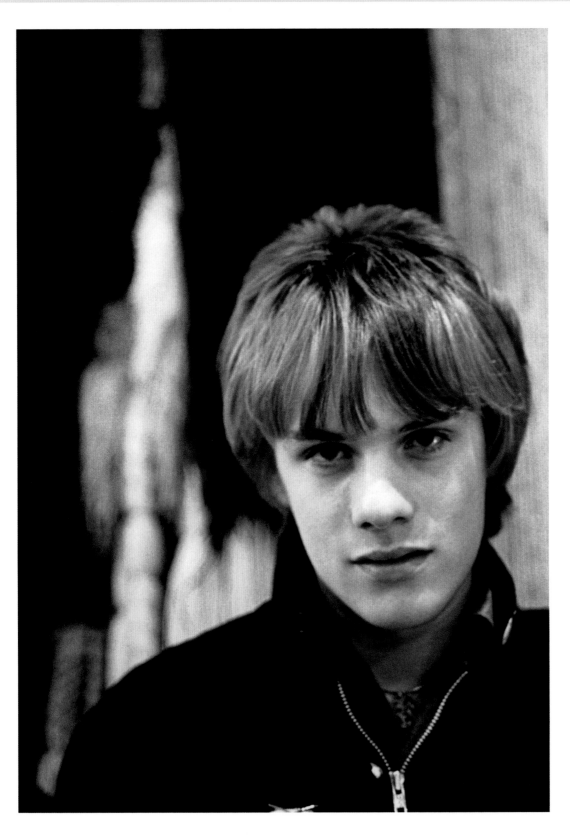

Getting the names right

Left: As the band's popularity increased Larry added the 'Junior' to his name in order to distinguish him from his father and prevent confusion over who needed to pay the increasingly large tax bills the son was beginning to receive. In 1978 Larry's mother was to die in a road accident. He and Bono, whose own mother had died when he was fourteen, were drawn closer together as friends as a result of these losses.

Opposite: Bono at the mic. Bono's nickname, given him by Dublin friends, went through several incarnations: from Steinvic van Huyseman, to Huyseman, to Houseman, to Bon Murray, to Bono Vox of Connell St and, finally, just Bono.

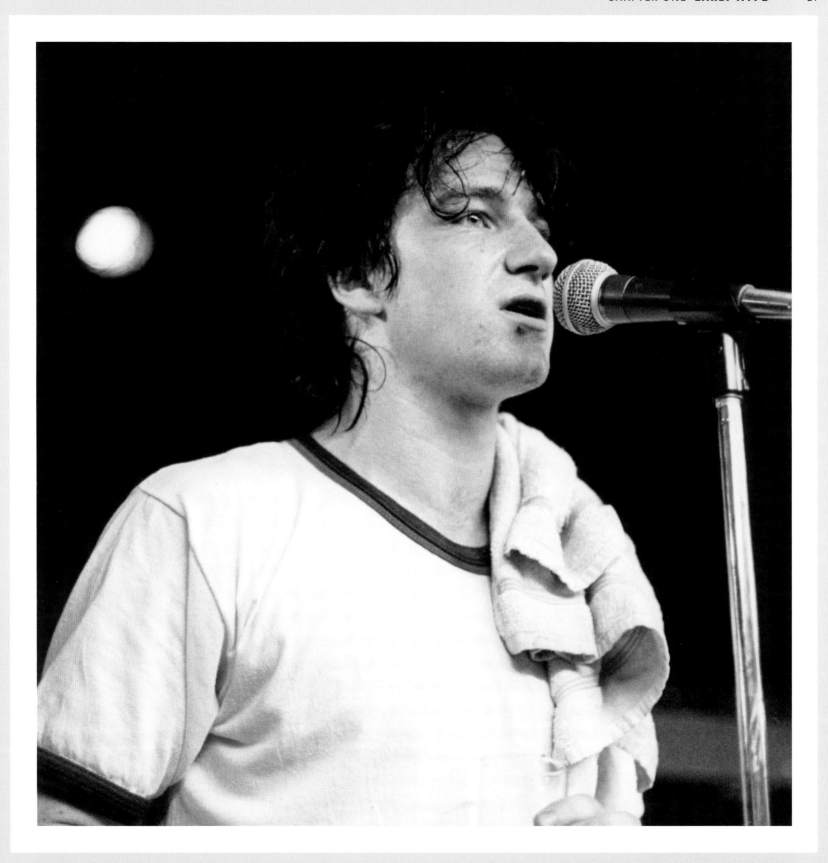

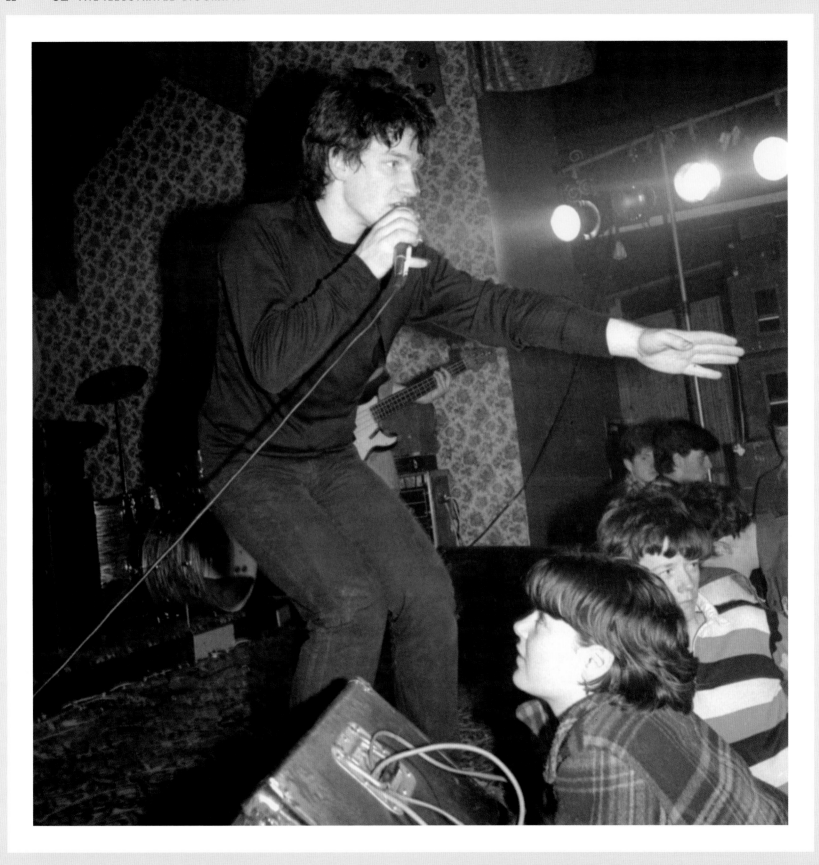

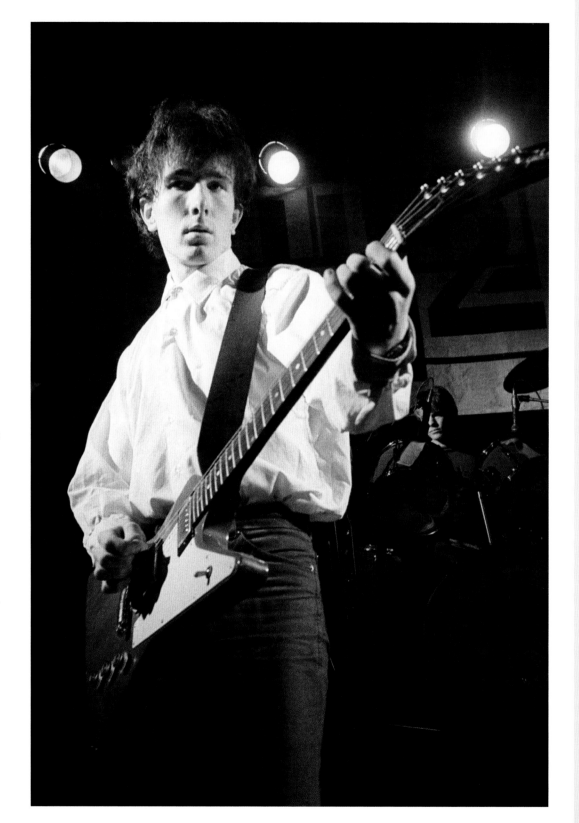

Teenage influences

Opposite: Bono reaches out to fans at an early gig. Bono's stage presence, charisma and extroversion were mainstays of U2's live act; despite this showmanship Bono remains married to his school sweetheart Alison Stewart, Ali, whom he first met at Mount Temple School in Dublin. Their relationship began in 1975 and the two have remained together since.

Right: The nickname Edge was allegedly conferred by Bono in acknowledgement of David Evans' sharp features, with a nod also perhaps to sharpness of intellect. In addition to Bono's vocals the main distinctive element of the U2 sound is The Edge's guitar. Feedback delay gives it a unique texture that runs through much of the band's music. Edge talks of a childhood "visit to a local jumble sale where I purchased a guitar for a pound", at which point his experiments with guitar techniques and technology first began.

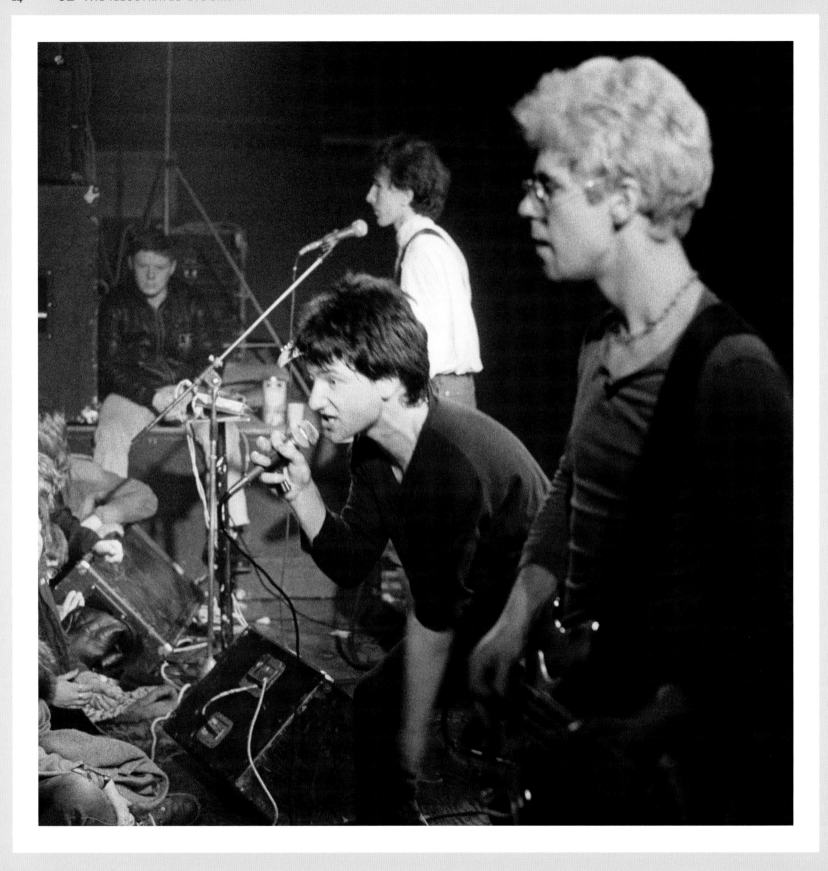

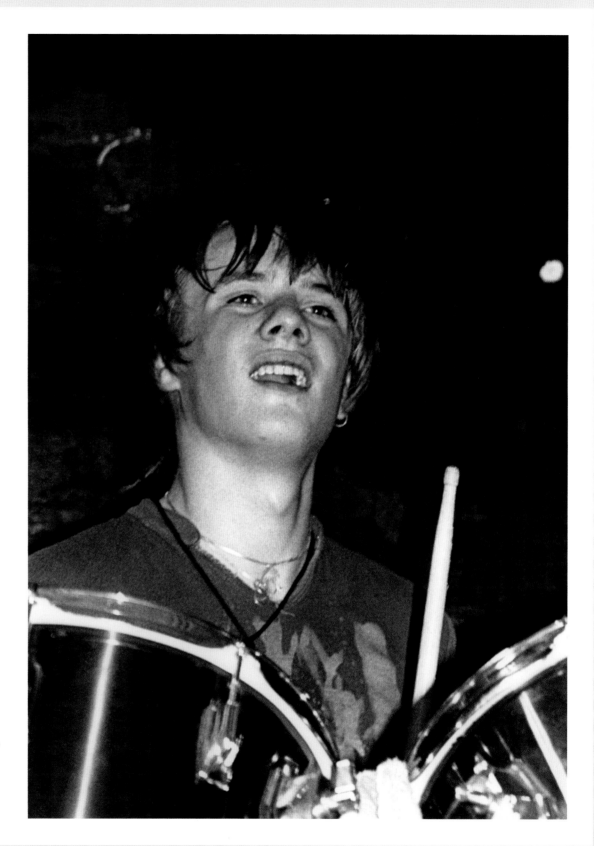

Early gigs

Opposite: Bono, Edge and Adam connect with the fans at Cork Country Club in March 1980.

In September 1978 U2 supported The Stranglers and in December played in Dublin as support act to The Greedy Bastards, a band made of up members of The Sex Pistols and Thin Lizzy. The up-and-coming young band was slightly in awe of the established artists' rock lifestyles.

Right: A sweat-soaked Larry plays live. 1979 was an important year for the band, with TV appearances, demo recording sessions and an increasing level of attention from the music press. In February, Bono and girlfriend Alison travelled to London in a not wholly successful attempt to plug U2 to record company representatives there.

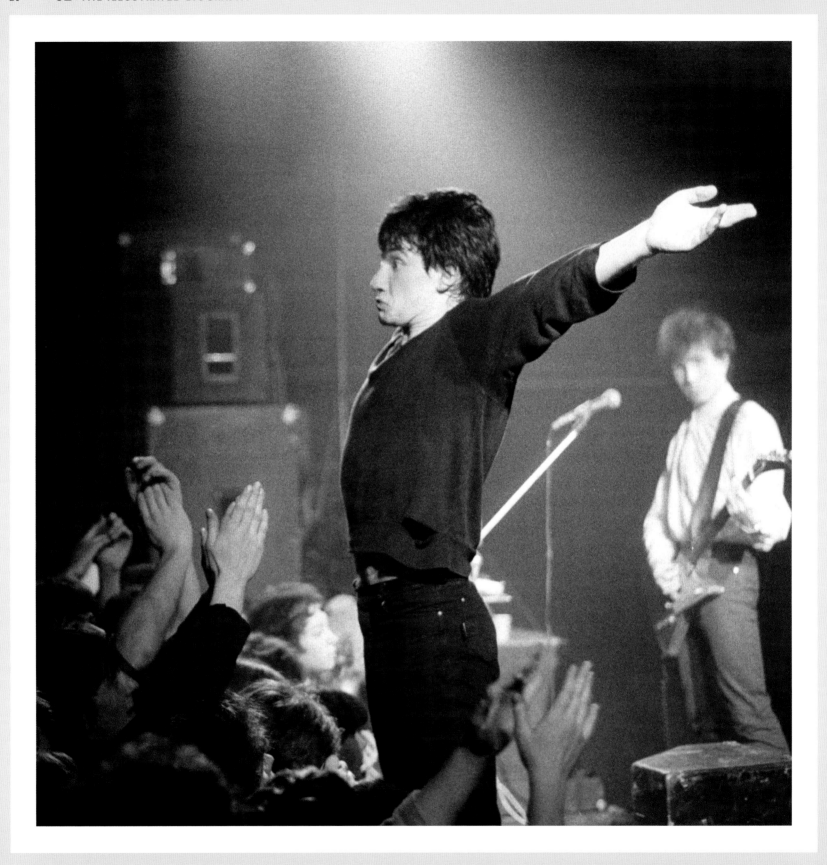

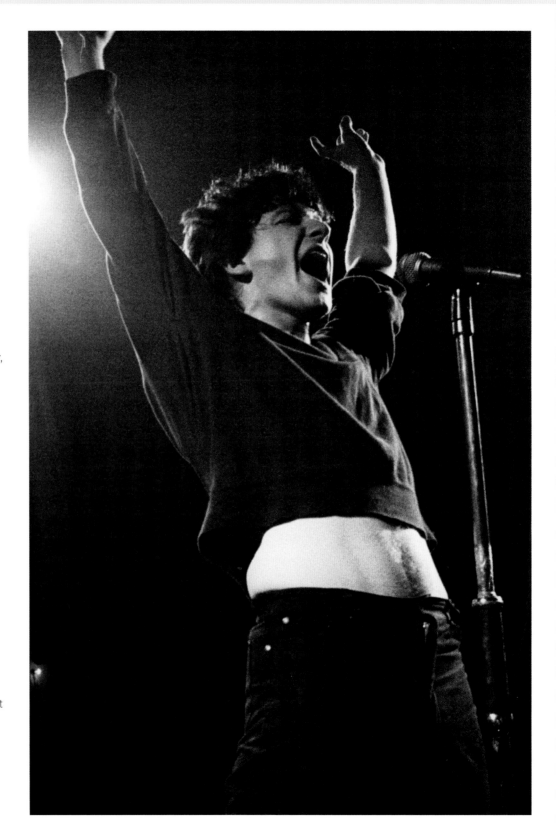

Playing to the audience

Opposite: Bono, always an extrovert performer,
famously suffered a PJ Proby moment at one
of the band's earlier gigs when a leap from a
PA stack left him with a split pair of trousers.
In May 1979 the band played six afternoon
concerts at the Dandelion Market in Dublin,
once again increasing U2's profile with its
growing audience. Around this time, Chris
de Whalley signed an Ireland-only deal
with U2 on behalf of CBS records. Record
label reactions to the band's demo material
were not as positive as those of the A&R
people observing U2 live in performance. A
particularly impressed de Whalley compared
Bono to David Bowie.

Right: Whipping up the crowd, Bono exhorts
his audience.
   An EP entitled *Three* (also known as *U2 3*)
was released in September 1979, becoming
both the band's first official release and its first
Irish chart success. Containing three original
U2 songs from the band's stage repertoire
("Out Of Control", "Boy/Girl" and "Stories
For Boys") the EP had only 1,000 individually
numbered copies produced in its first run and
remains a collectors' rarity.

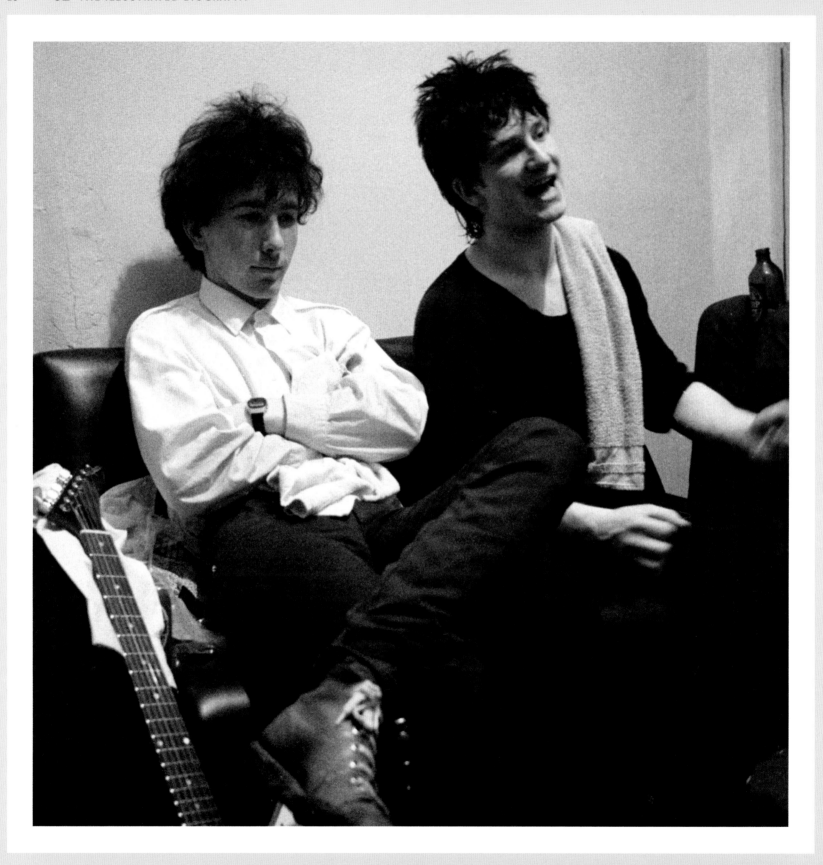

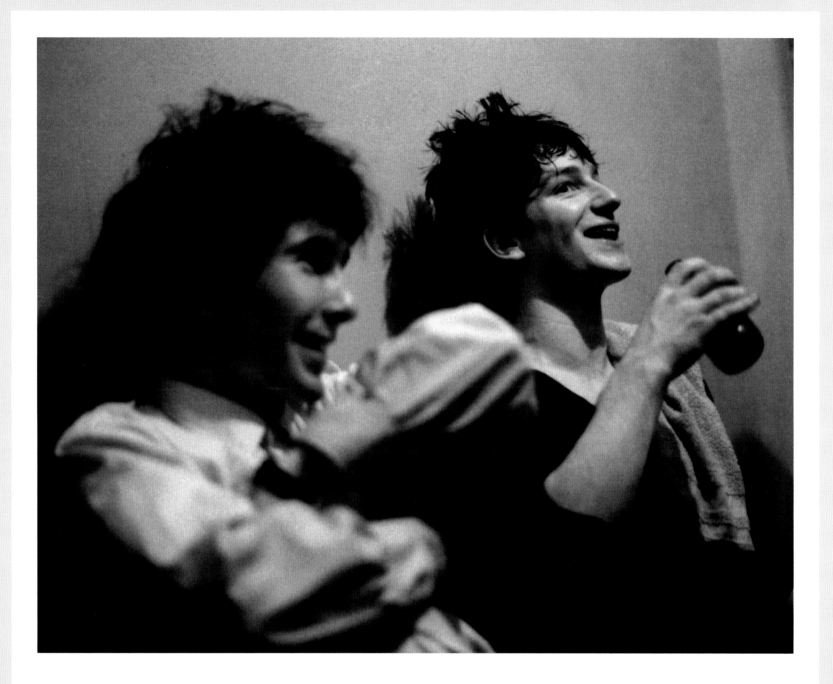

Unwinding backstage

Opposite: Edge and Bono share a cheerful post-gig moment. On 5 october 1979 U2 played its first concert for Irish channel RTE in a televised event from the Cork Opera House.

Above: Enjoying a beer. In October 1979, U2 featured on the cover of *Hot Press* magazine in Ireland, while in November the boys made the cover of *Record Mirror* in the UK. The band's profile continued to grow, but the big break of a record deal still eluded them.

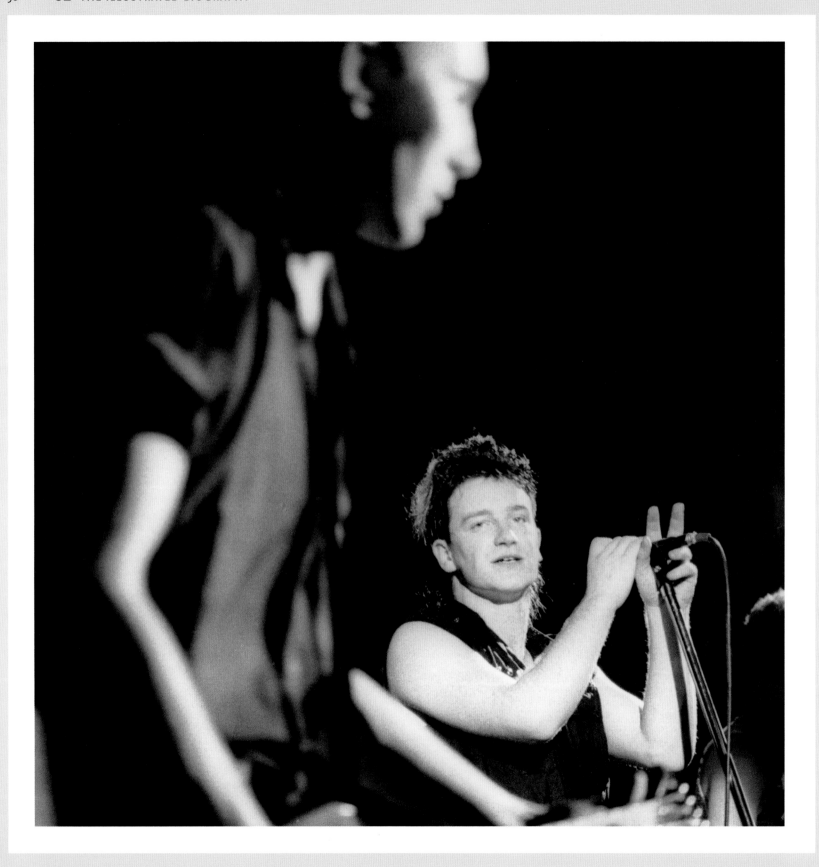

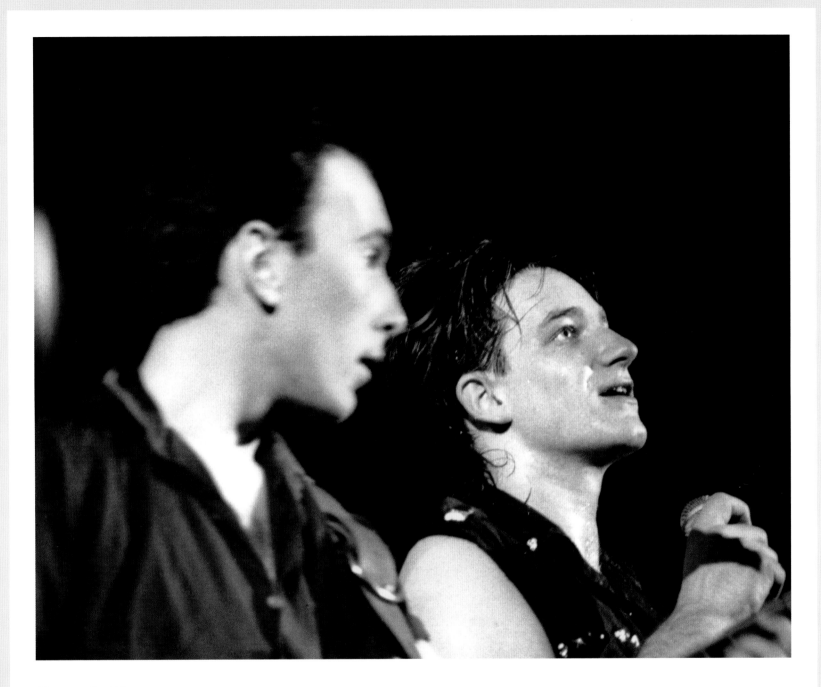

Close to the Edge

Opposite: Bono and The Edge onstage. In late 1979 the band borrowed money from friends and family to finance a UK trip, during which U2 played London clubs (one of them in support of Talking Heads) in an effort to impress British record company executives and get that big break. Although they were to return to Dublin disappointed, they had won the attention of the record companies whose scouts kept track of the band back in their home city.

Above: Bono experiences a revelatory moment, while Edge looks on. From their childhood, three of the band members were strongly committed Christians and at this time U2, with the exception of Adam were devout in their faith, believing that their destiny was in the hands of God. Balancing the demands of being rock stars and the teachings of the Bible would be a recurring issue for Bono, Edge and Larry.

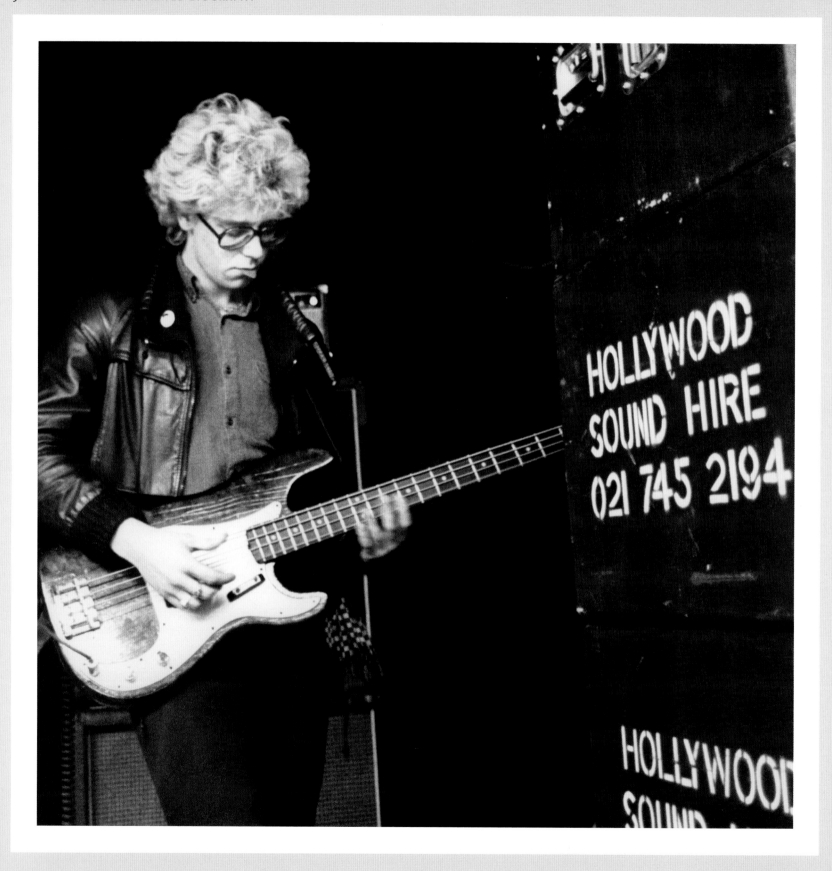

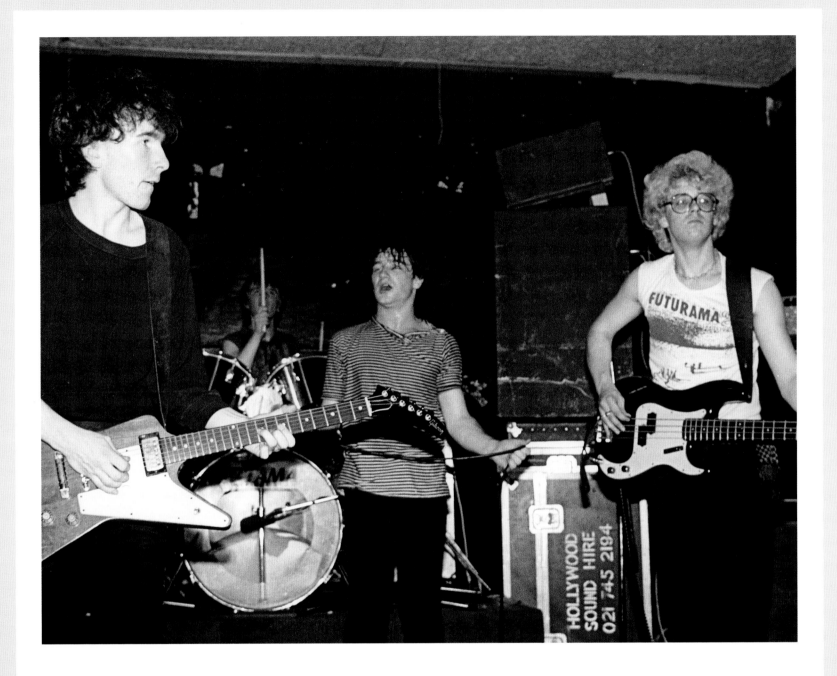

Signed to Island

Opposite: Adam works on his bass-playing technique.

On 15 January 1980 U2 performed the song "Stories for Boys" live on Irish TV channel RTE's *Late Late Show*. In February the band's second single, "Another Day", was released by CBS (although once again only in Ireland).

Above: Edge, Larry, Bono and Adam on stage in the early days of the Boy tour. In March 1980 U2 shared a Dublin music bill with The Virgin Prunes (comprising friends of Bono and Edge's brother Dik) at the Sense of Ireland music festival. Record company talent scouts had continued to look at the band since the British shows and U2 were shortly afterwards signed to Island Records. Their big break had happened.

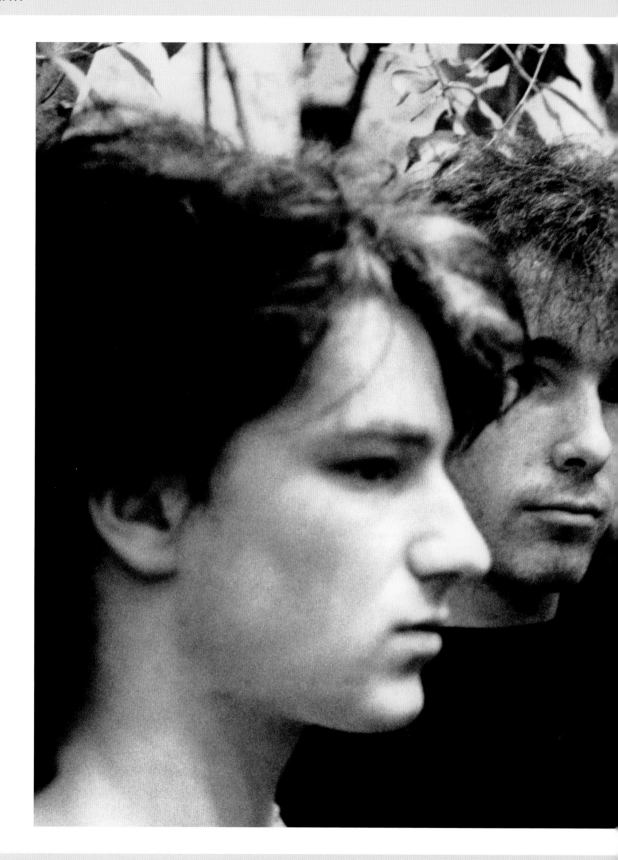

Breaking Europe

Right: Before their October gig at Klacik, Brussels, the band took part in a photoshoot with Virginia Turbett. This was the last night of five which launched the band in Europe with a studio performance for KRO, Dutch radio on the 14th at Hilversum. Here the band look thoughtful in a group shot.

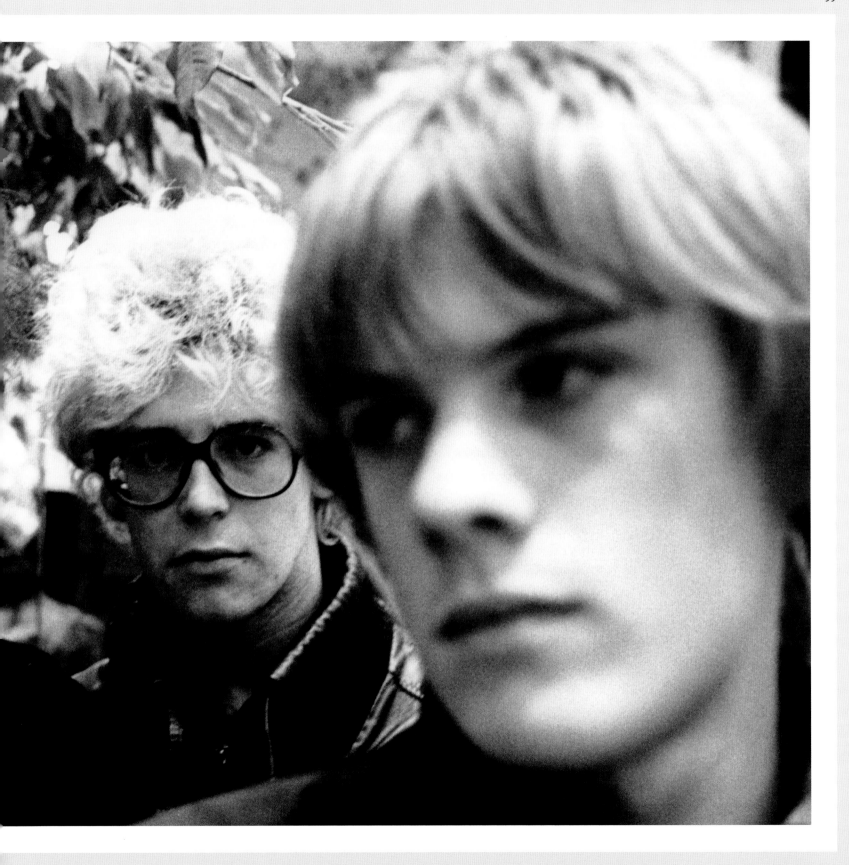

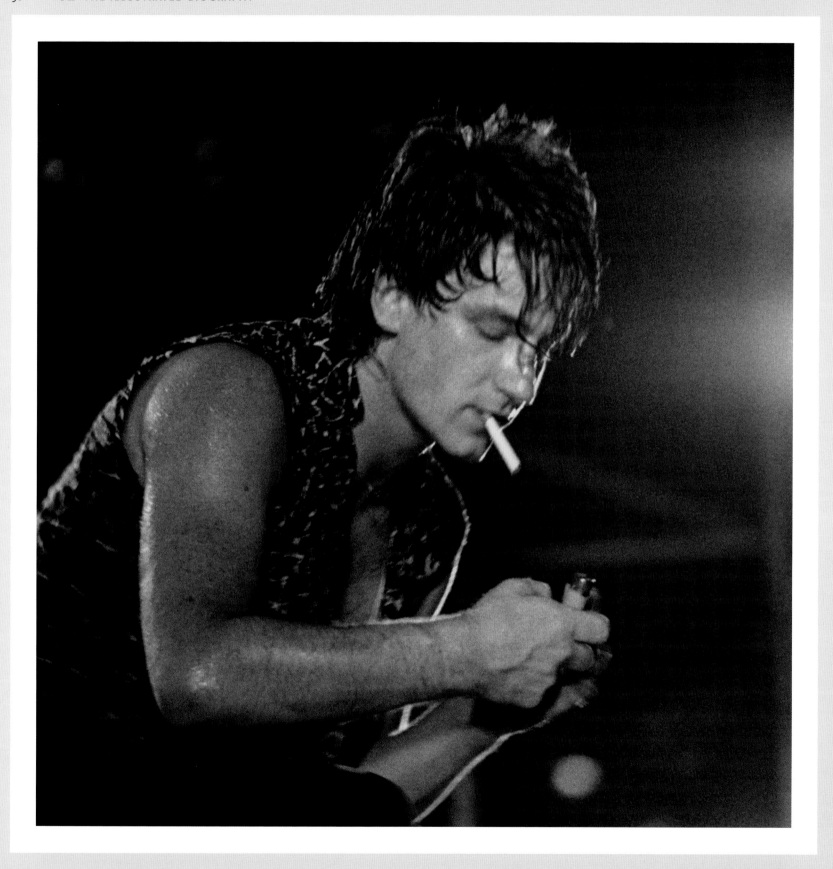

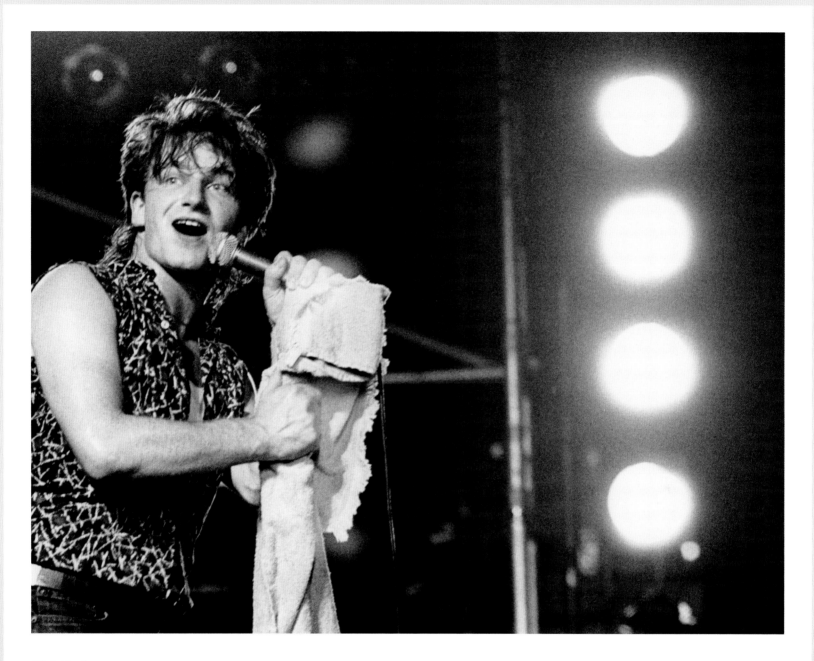

Tick Tock

Opposite: Bono lights up on stage in traditional rock style. Having got their big record deal, U2 were in the studio between March and September 1980 recording their first album, *Boy*. The sessions took place mostly in Windmill Lane Studios, Dublin. They were to have been produced by Martin Hannett of Joy Division production fame, but Ian Curtis's suicide meant Hannett felt unable to proceed and instead Steve Lillywhite, who had already had success with other bands including Siouxsie and the Banshees, was at the controls.

Above: Bono's lively stage act obliges him to keep a towel close to hand. In May 1980 U2 released their new single, "11 O'Clock Tick Tock". This song, a staple of their live act for years to come, was the band's first single to be released both in Ireland and, for the first time, the UK. The band treated itself to a long-wanted van on the strength of how well things were going.

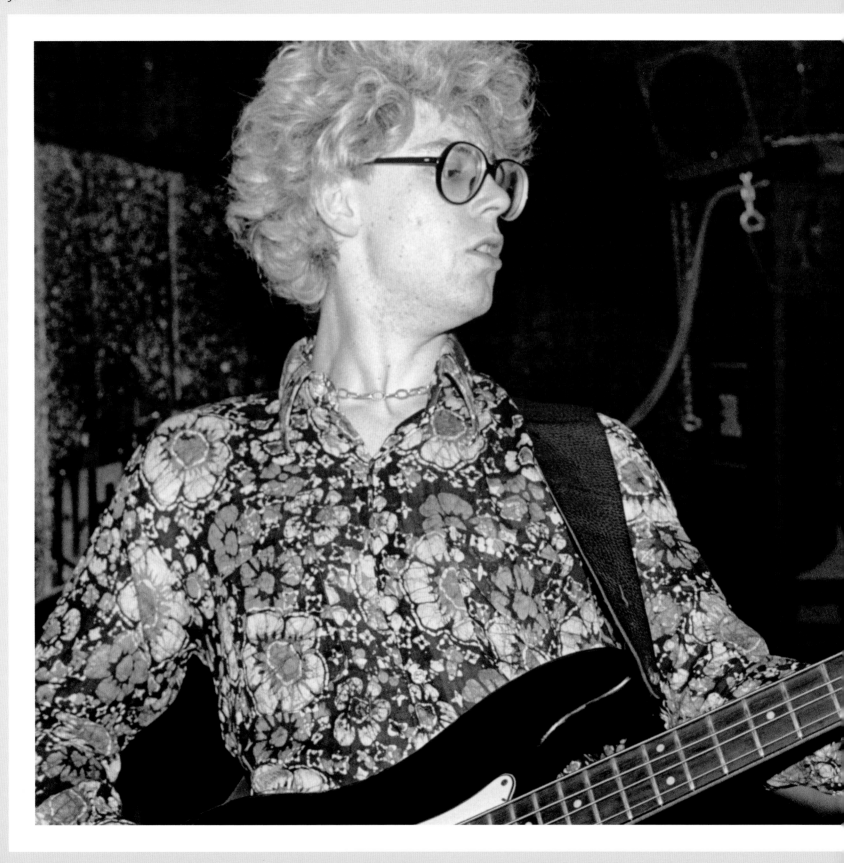

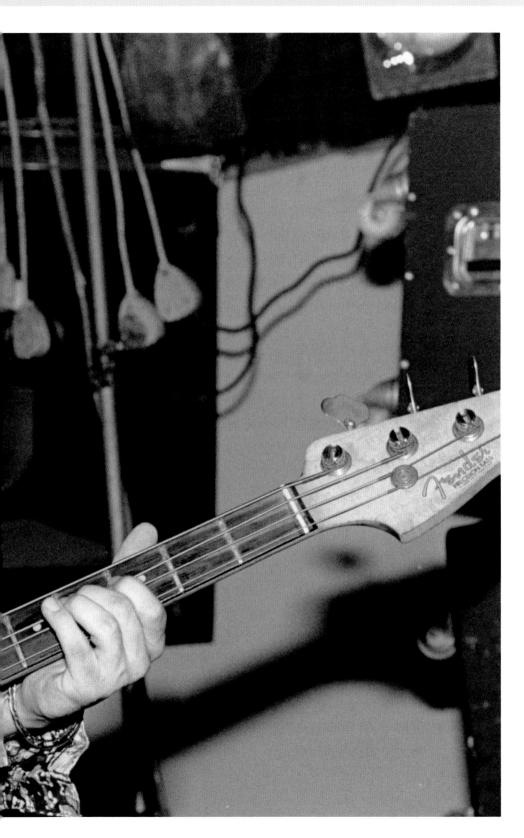

The great outdoors

Left: Adam, pictured during the Boy tour, plays Fender
Precision bass and wears a very loud floral shirt.
U2 played its first outdoor music festival in July 1980
in front of a 15,000 crowd at Lexlip Castle, Kildare. The
Police and Squeeze were also on the bill, higher up the list
than the Dublin boys. U2 have since become one of the
ultimate stadium live acts, eclipsing and outlasting most
other rivals from their early years.

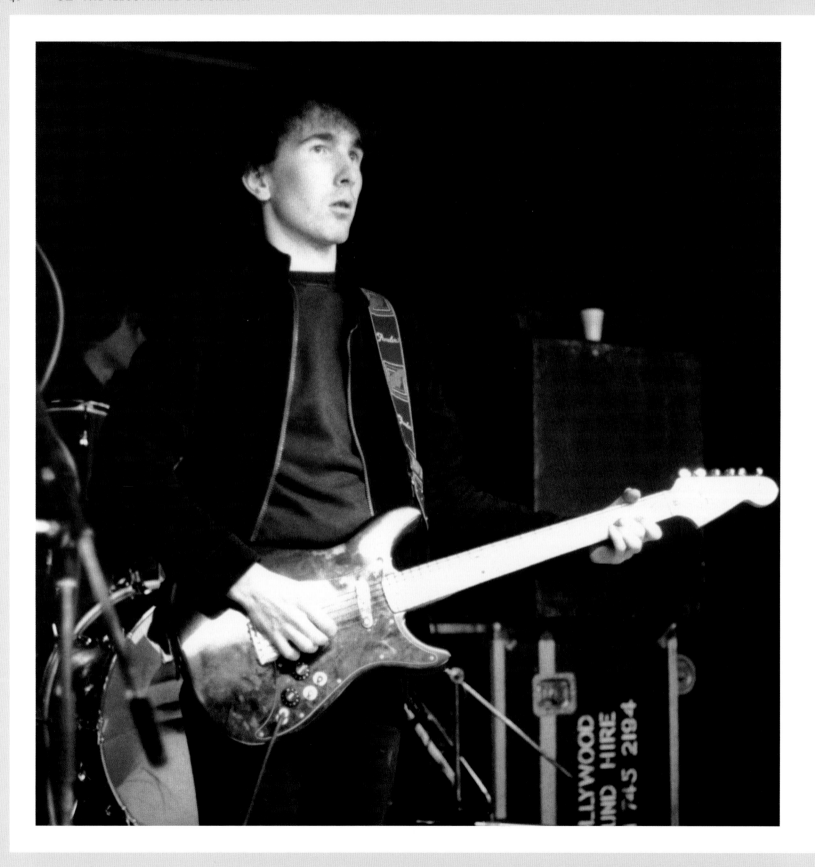

Opening for Talking Heads

Right: Bono on stage at the Hammersmith Palais, London, in December 1980.

U2 opened for Talking Heads on their two dates at the Palais at the beginning of the month. Between September and December 1980 U2 played a 57-date concert tour of the UK and Europe to support the new album. Released on 20 October and called *Boy* it featured the iconic image of a young boy on the cover, the face in fact being that of Bono's young neighbour in Dublin, Peter Rowen.

Opposite: Edge plays the latest Fender Lead II on stage in Belgium during the Boy tour.

In August 1980 the single "A Day Without Me" was released, the band's second on the Island label, produced by Steve Lillywhite; it was the first to be taken from the forthcoming album. Edge's search for a distinctive guitar sound took a huge step forward when earlier in the year he bought an Electro Harmonix Memory Man Deluxe echo box. Bono says: "I remember saying, 'Use this because this will get us to another place.' This will get us outside of the concrete – into the abstract. I just knew that the echo unit would do that. Atmospheres – we were very interested in atmospheric music. Punk started to look incredibly limited."

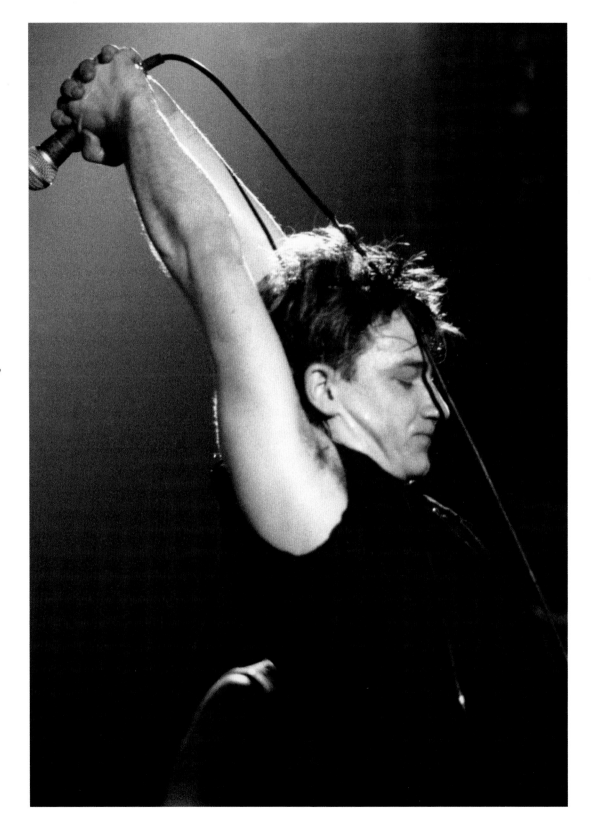

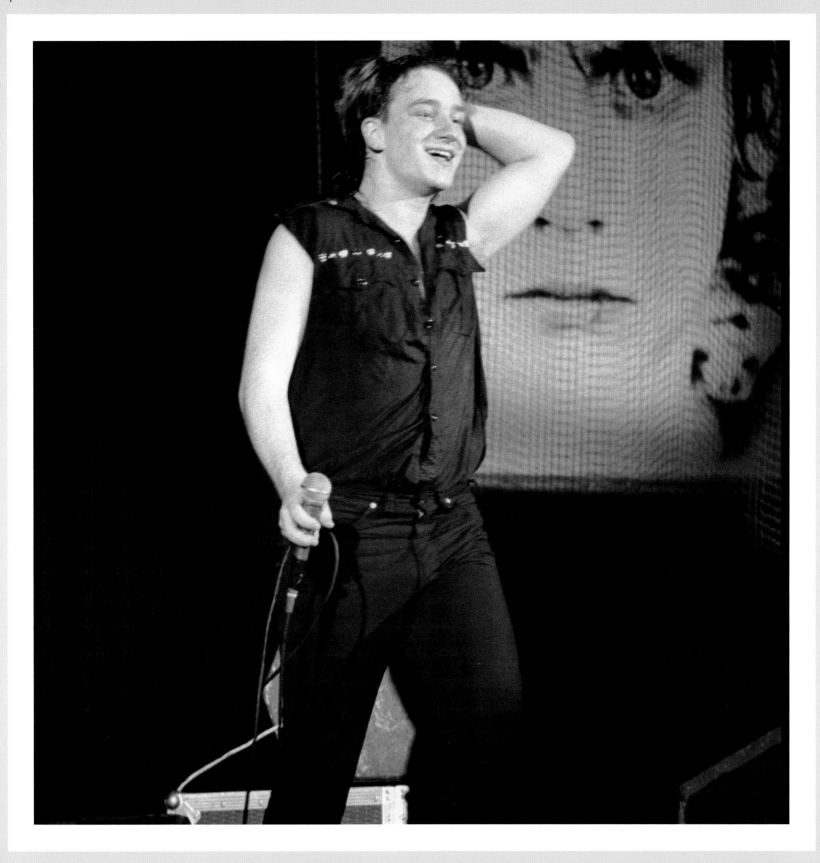

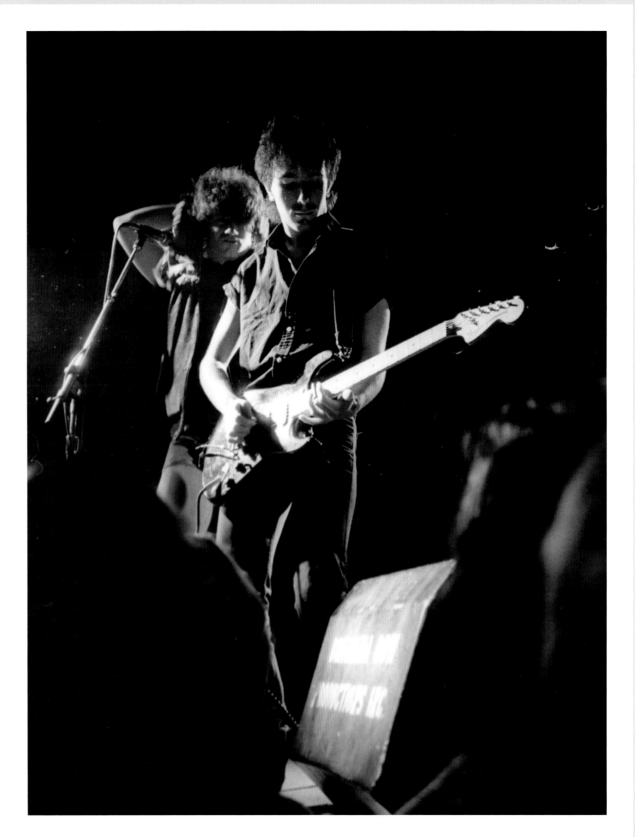

Second single

Opposite: Bono on stage on the Boy tour with that iconic image behind him. In October a second single from the album, "I Will Follow", was released, reaching number 20 in the UK charts. The only one of U2's songs to be played live on every tour since the album's release, it touches on the themes of adolescent frustration and violence that permeated the album; but also confronts some of Bono's emotions around his mother and her death.

Right: Bono and The Edge on stage at The Ritz, New York City. On 6 December U2 played its first concert in the US at the Ritz Club. It was the first in a 14-concert tour to support the new album and to break the band in North America.

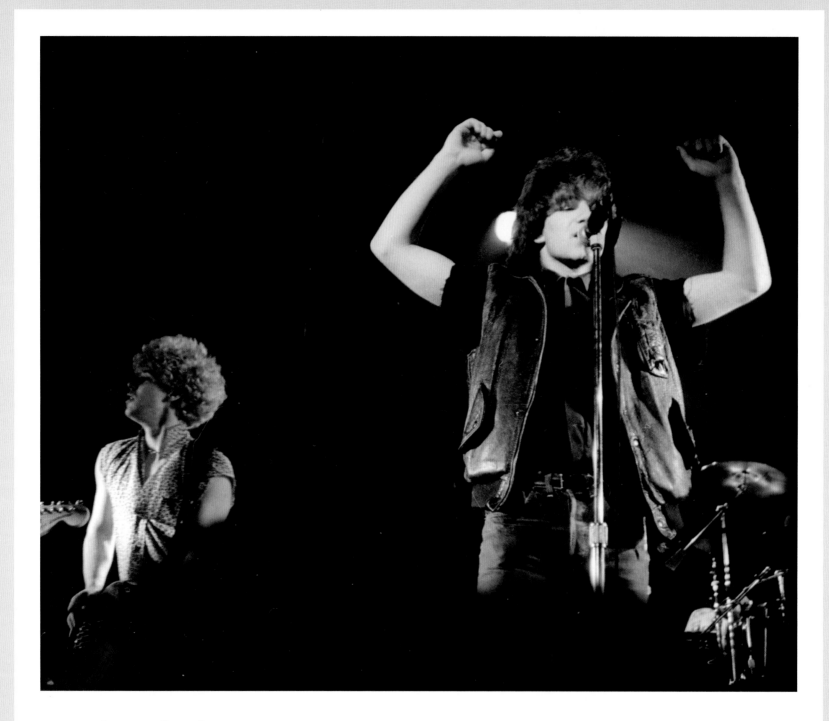

Into the arms of America

Above: Adam and Bono on stage at New York's Ritz Club. Facing an indifferent crowd at best – with some open hostility, the band steadily won the crowd over. Tour promoter Frank Barsalona of Premier Talent, present at the show and watching the band he had hired unseen, later recalled how his response moved from fear of a catastrophic blunder to astonishment when the band performed several encores to the enthused audience; "It was just so exciting, I was choked."

Opposite: A thoughtful-looking Larry.

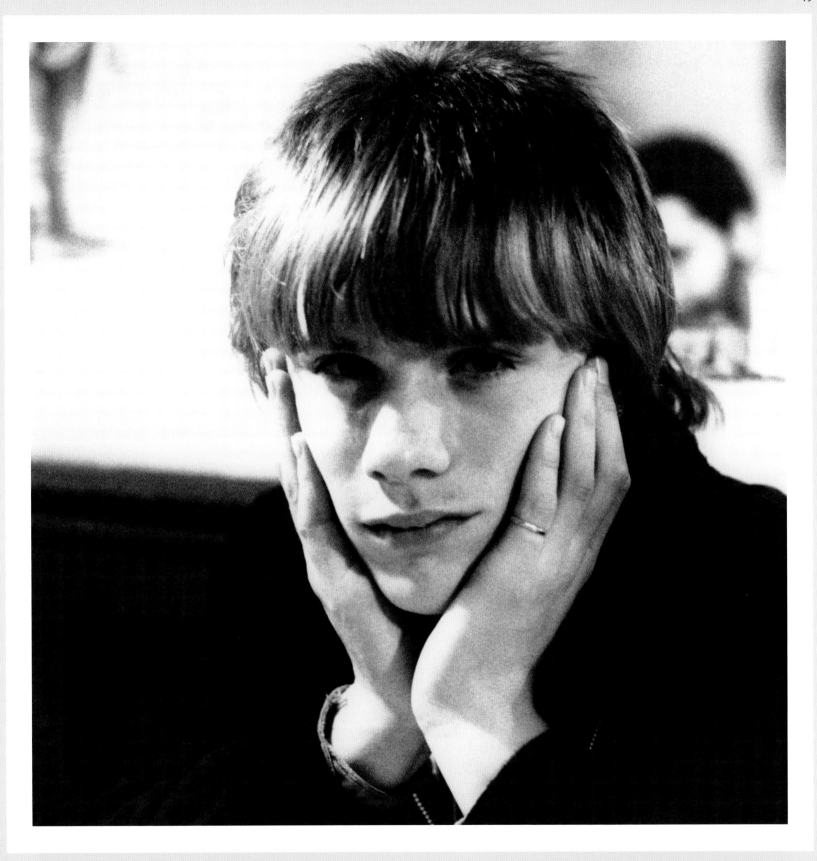

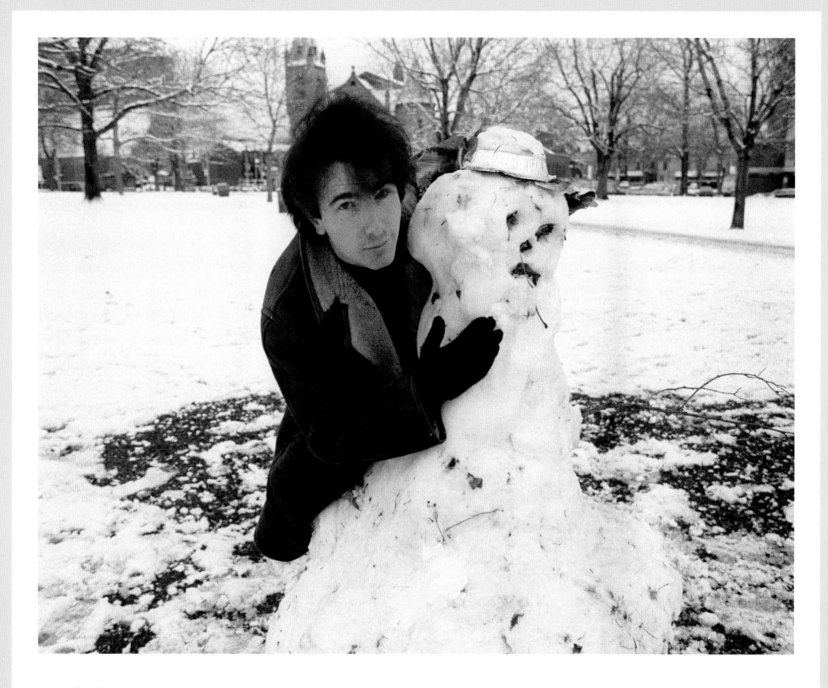

Snow business

Above and opposite: December 1980, U2 pose in a snow-covered playground in Toronto , Canada, during their East Coast tour, breaking them in North America.

Although they were touring in support of *Boy*, the album had been released in Europe only and was available as import-only in North America, though local radio stations, such as Boston's had been supplied with albums for airplay months earlier.

While U2 was embarked on these North American dates John Lennon was shot in New York on 8 December. The following night U2 gave a concert in Toronto where their shock at Lennon's death was converted into a passionate set during which they inserted a few bars of Lennon's "Give Peace A Chance" into the song "Boy" as a tribute. The concert was well-received by the Canadian audience and given rapturous reviews in the local press.

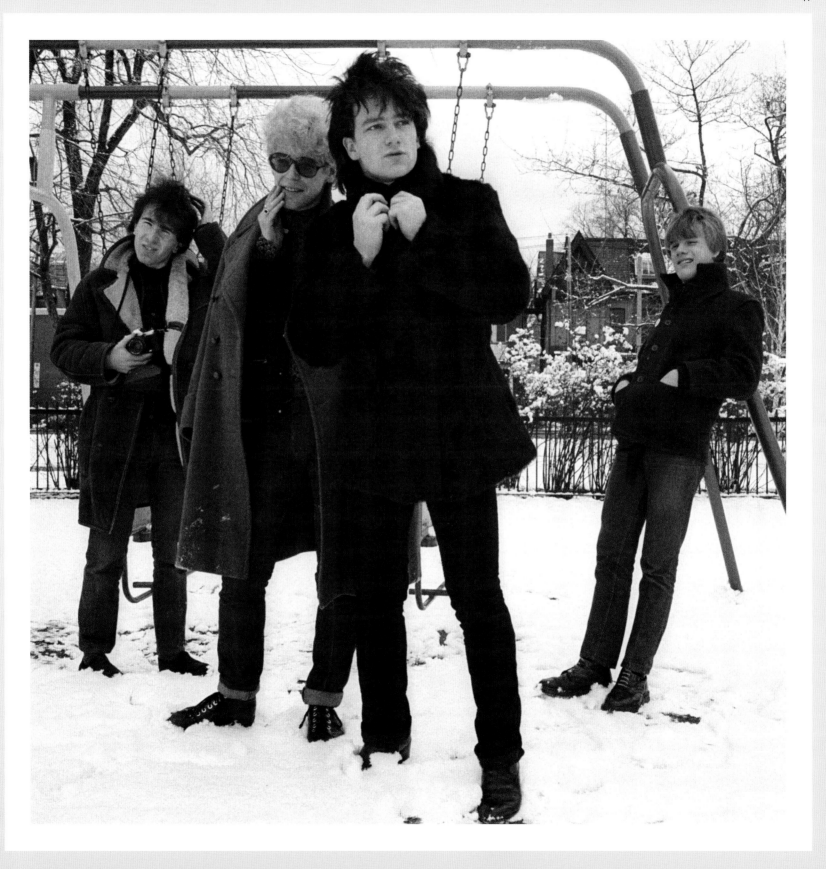

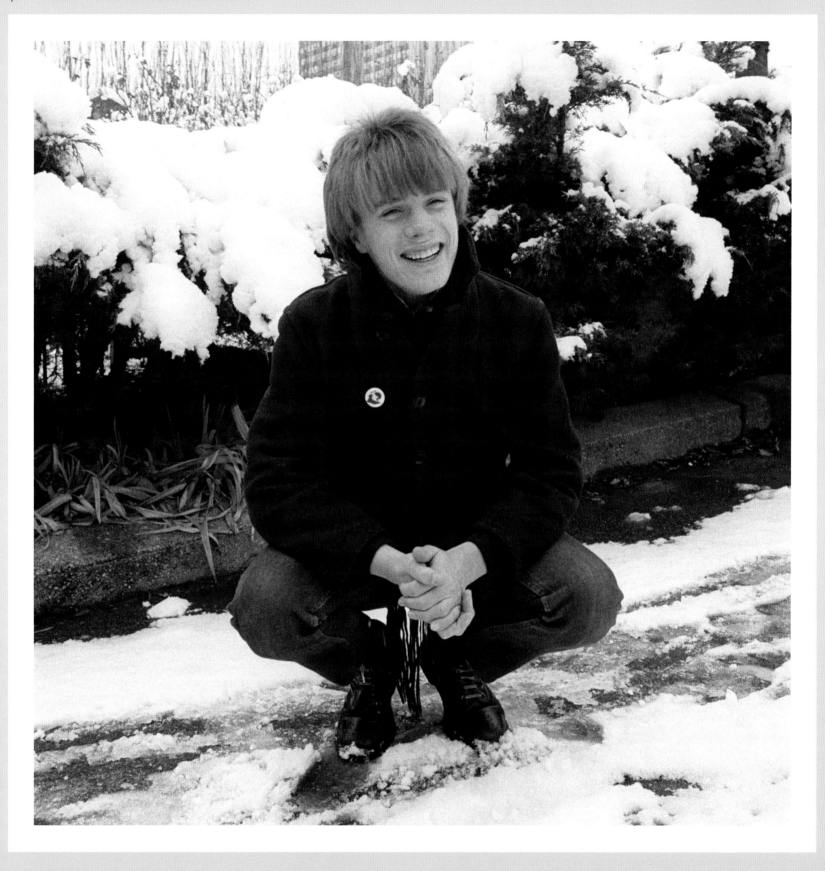

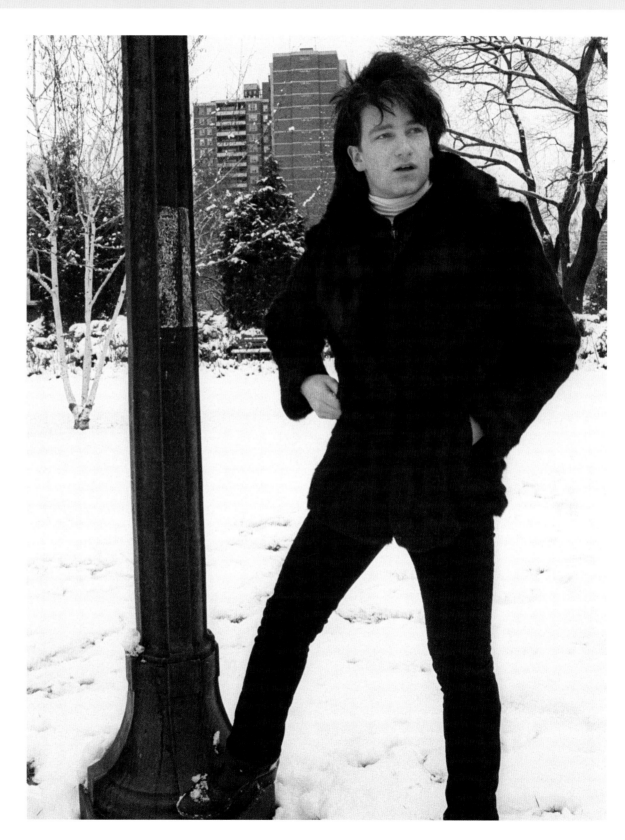

Boys will be boys

Opposite and right:
The success of *Boy* would
not be unqualified, but it took
U2 to a new level of fame
and, importantly, had opened
them up to an American
audience.

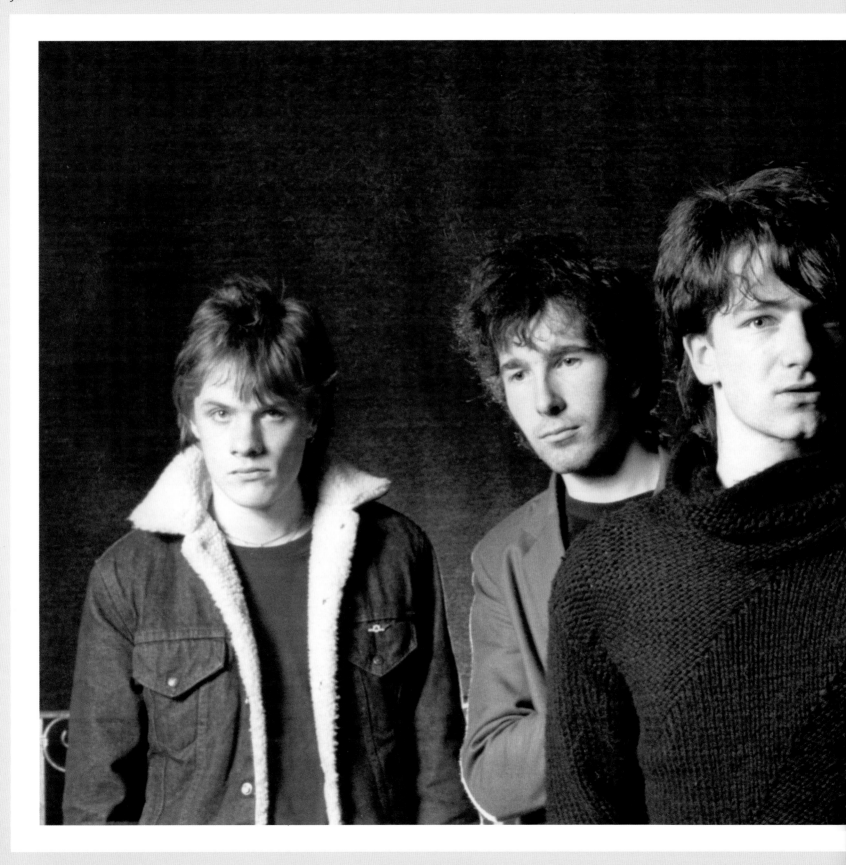

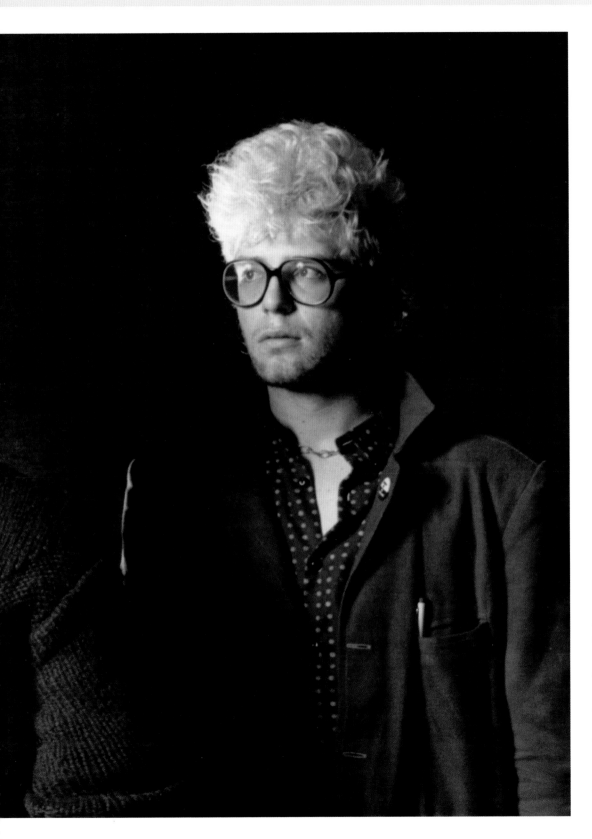

Boy in America

Left: In March U2 resumed touring North America, playing their first gig in the Bayou Club, Washington, DC, on the 3rd – the same day *Boy* was finally released Stateside on Warner Bros label. The previous year's gigs had succeeded in getting the attention of *Rolling Stone* magazine which had assigned journalist Jim Henke to shadow the band since November. His piece was published in the February 1981 edition of *Rolling Stone* – perfect timing for the tour. The single "I Will Follow" was also released in the US in March.

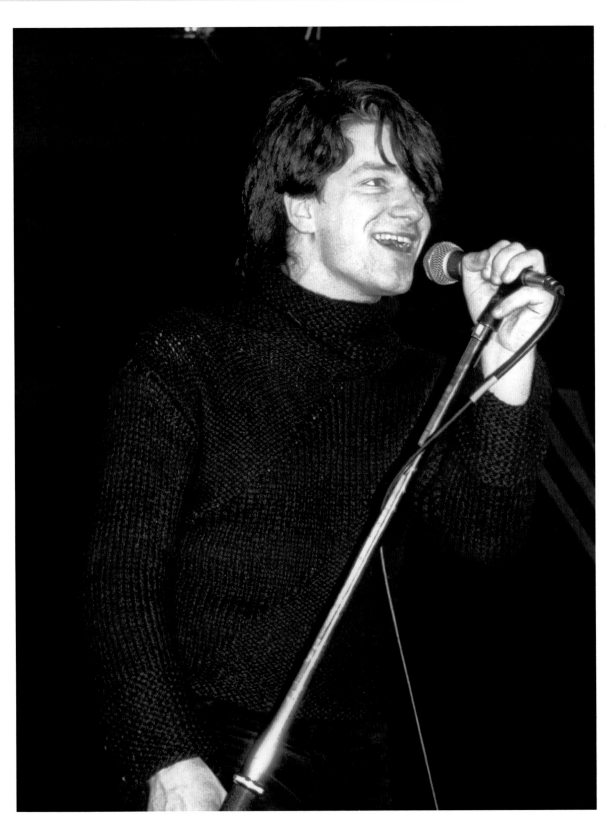

Back to the Ritz

Left: Bono on stage at the Ritz Club, New York City, 7 March 1981.

The band returned to the Ritz and took time out during the following day to go clothes shopping in Manhattan. Bumping into fans from the previous evening's show they visited the World Trade Center.

Opposite: Bono in tartan at the height of the show in the Palladium, New York City on 29 May.

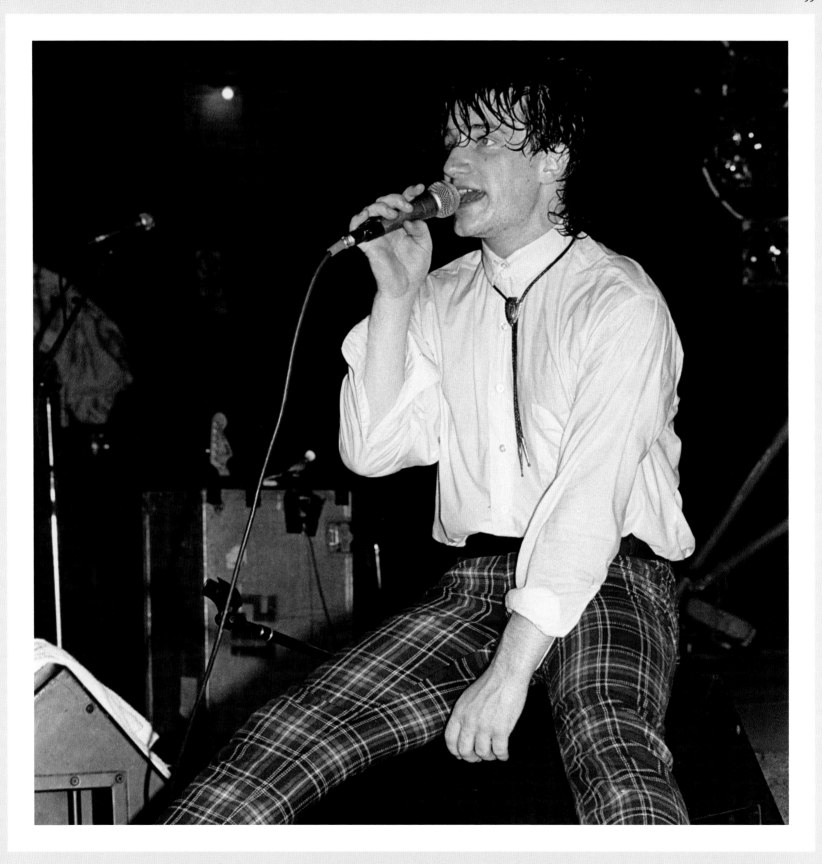

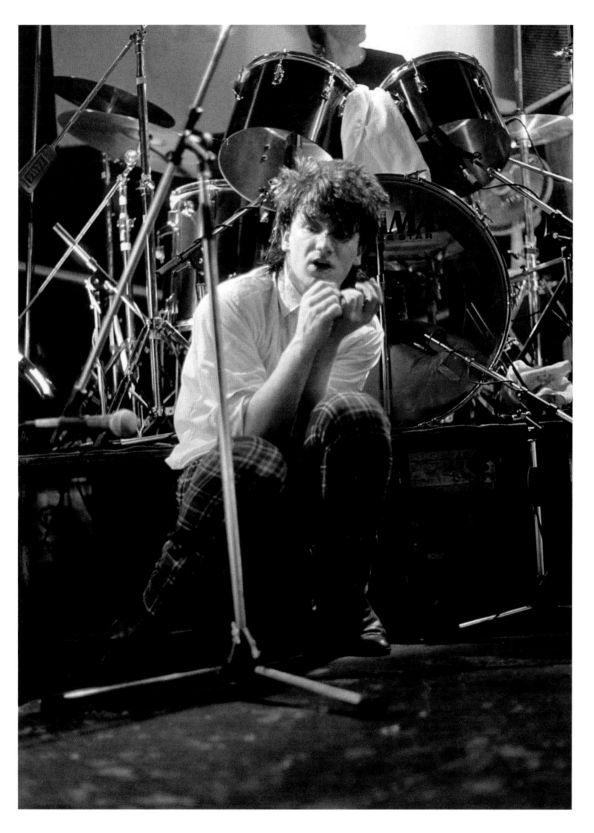

Tour to success

Left: Bono takes a break during the Palladium show on 29 May. The North American leg of the Boy tour finished on 31 May at Fast Lane, Asbury Park. The tour had gone as well as could be expected but it would be years rather than months before U2 would enjoy the peak of success, filling stadiums across the continent.

A shadow over the tour was the loss of Bono's briefcase in Foghorn, Portland. A farcical sequence of circumstances made Bono think it had been stolen by a couple of fans but in fact he simply left it behind and although retrieved by one of the crew, the case and Bono's songwriting-in-progress were not reunited with their owner until 2004.

Opposite: Photographed backstage, The Edge looks soulful during the Boy tour.

Paul McGuinness concluded that the only way to really break into North America would be intensive touring and the band set out to do this with a vengeance during the Boy tour and in the many North American tours to come. The strategy was repeated in virtually every continent and flying into the UK in June the band immediately was on stage again – at Salford University on 4 June.

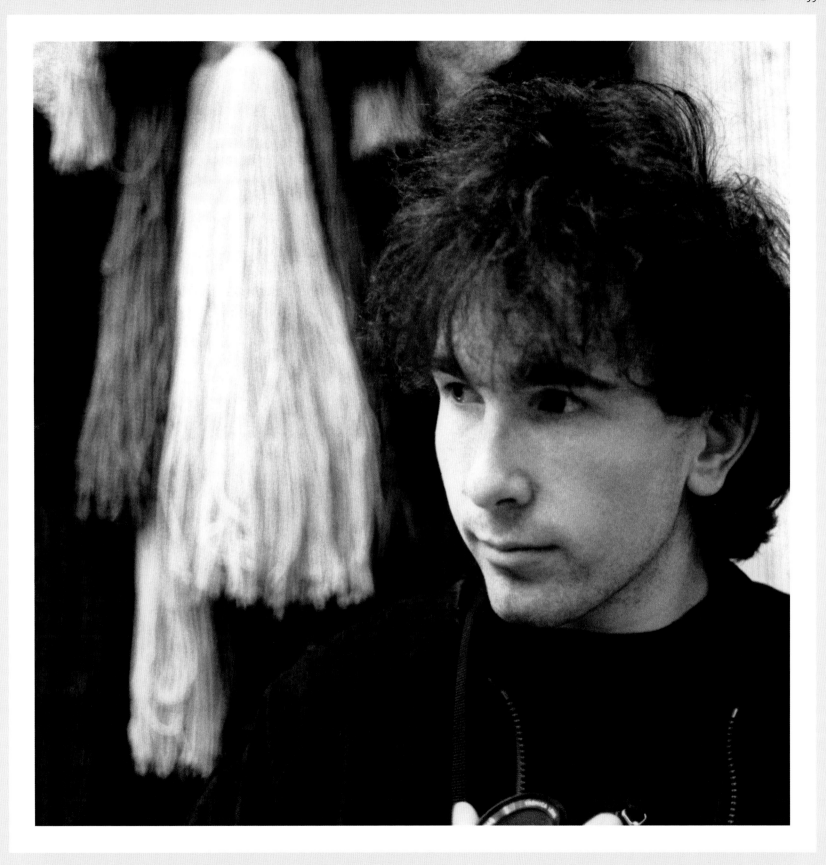

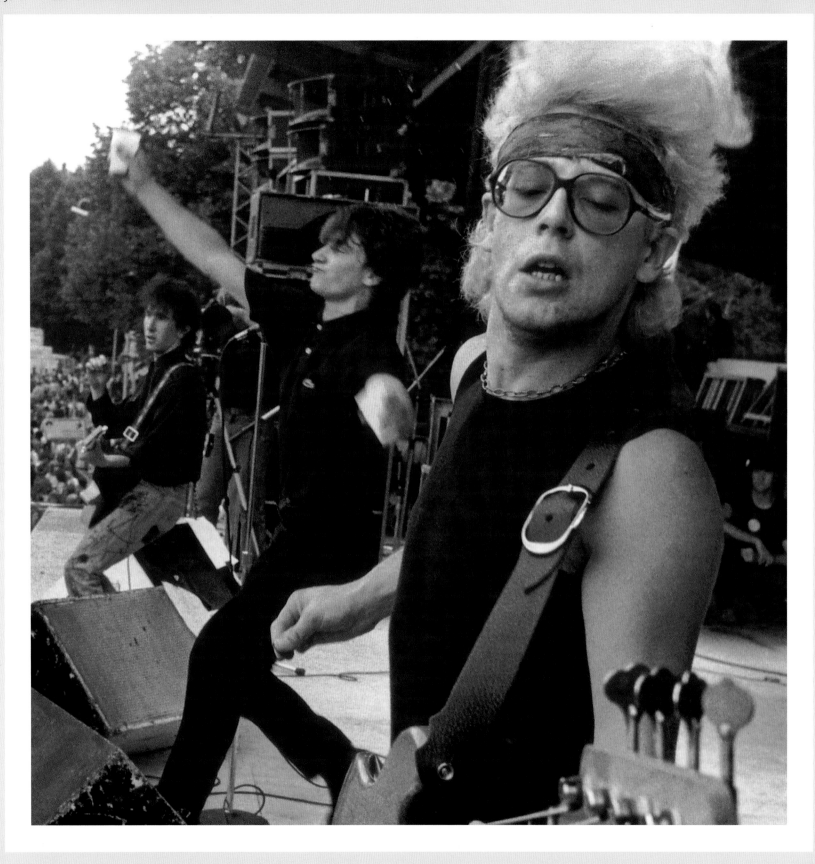

On fire

Opposite: Close to the on-stage action at the Netherlands Pinkpop Festival 8 June 1981. They are the second band to perform; a crowd of 50,000 is watching – U2's biggest to date. Their 9 June performance at Hammersmith Palais – the last of the Boy tour – was attended by Bruce Springsteen who went backstage after the show to greet the band; Pete Townshend was also a backstage visitor.

The next priority was the new album and in July they started work on *October*; things are not easy, the band are adjusting to their success and haven't too many clear ideas for the album. It's not helped by the loss of Bono's briefcase. Also in July their new single, "Fire", reached number 35 in the UK charts, bringing with it their debut on *Top of the Pops*.

Right: Bono climbs the stage rigging in San Bernardino, California during a U2 performance. Bono's stage energy became legendary early in the band's history; whether climbing the speaker stacks or throwing himself into the audience, his derring-do thrilled the crowds but gave his bandmates and their crew many scares. During a performance in Torhout, Belgium in July 1982 Bono developed what became a set piece when he carried a white flag as he climbed high into the lighting rig.

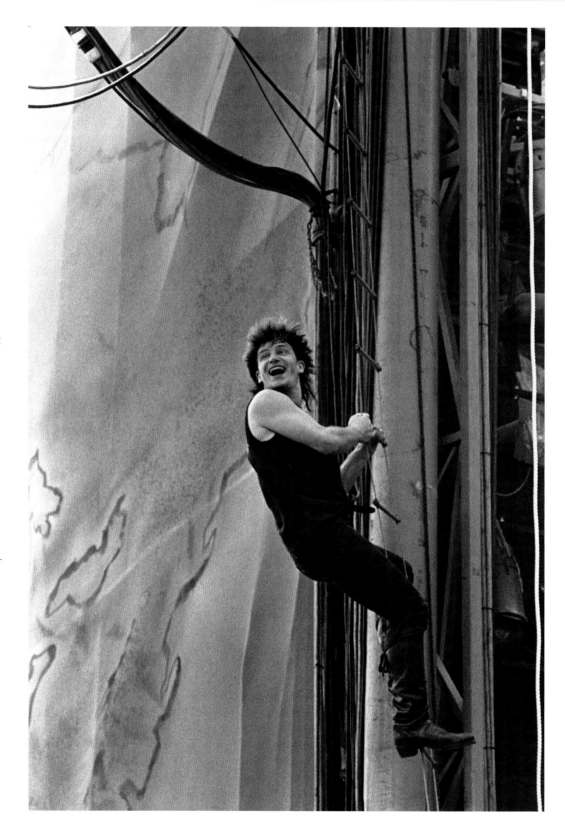

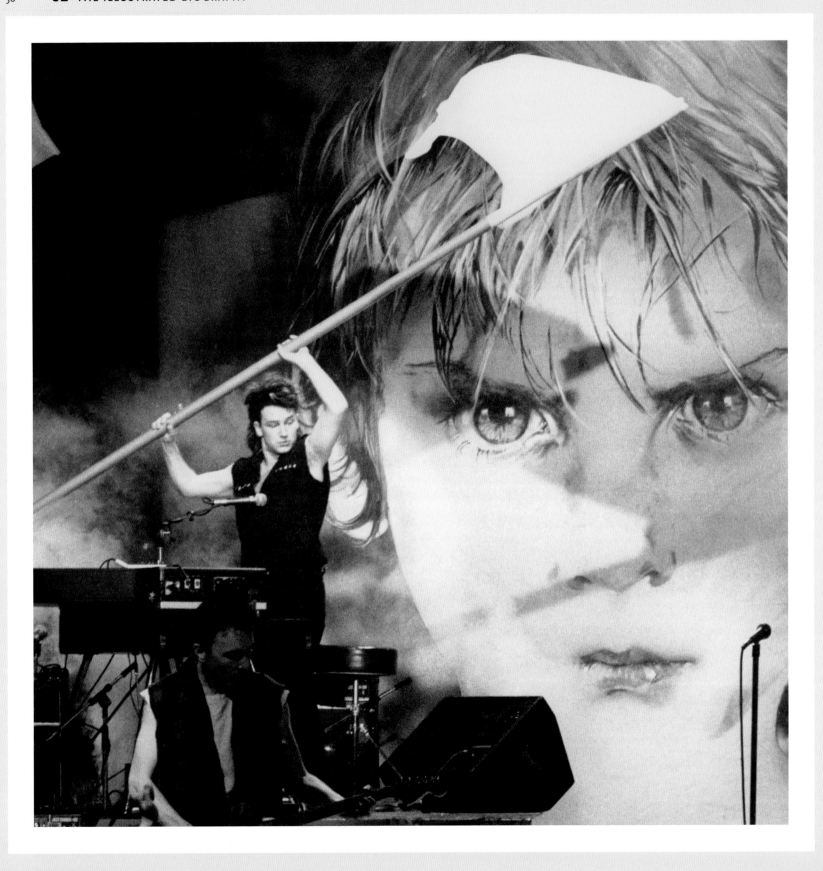

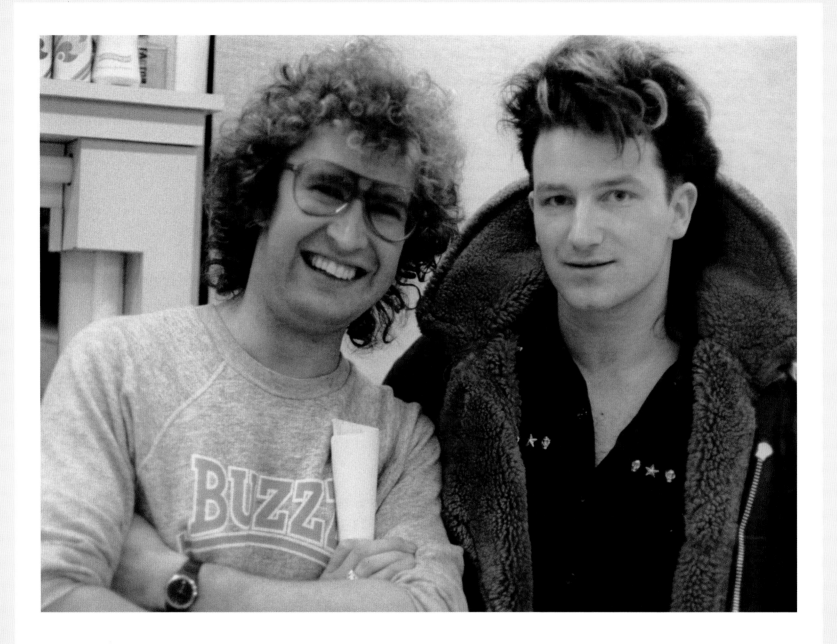

October crisis

Opposite: Bono brandishes a white flag during a live recording performance of cult TV programme *The Tube* in March 1983.

October was recorded in about 2 months to release in October 1981; in a year of much soul-searching that included an unscheduled performance at a christian festival, Greenbelt, the band was uncertain about the direction their lives were taking. After the last show of the European tour in early November they told Paul McGuinness they would not tour in North America and in fact were ready to break up. McGuinness reminded them of their contractual responsibilities to the record company and tour promoter as well as their moral responsibility to their fans, forcing Bono and The Edge to look at their situation in a more practical light. The crisis was averted, the North American tour went ahead but similar issues lurk for the future.

Above: Bono pictured with Malcolm Gerrie, producer of Tyne Tees TV's music show *The Tube*.

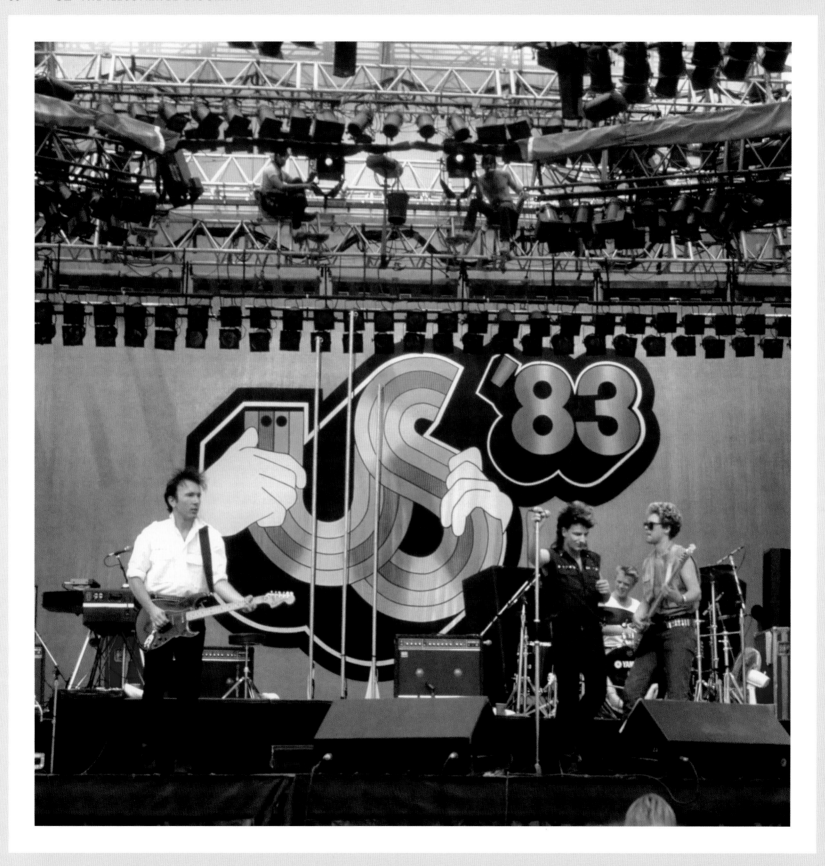

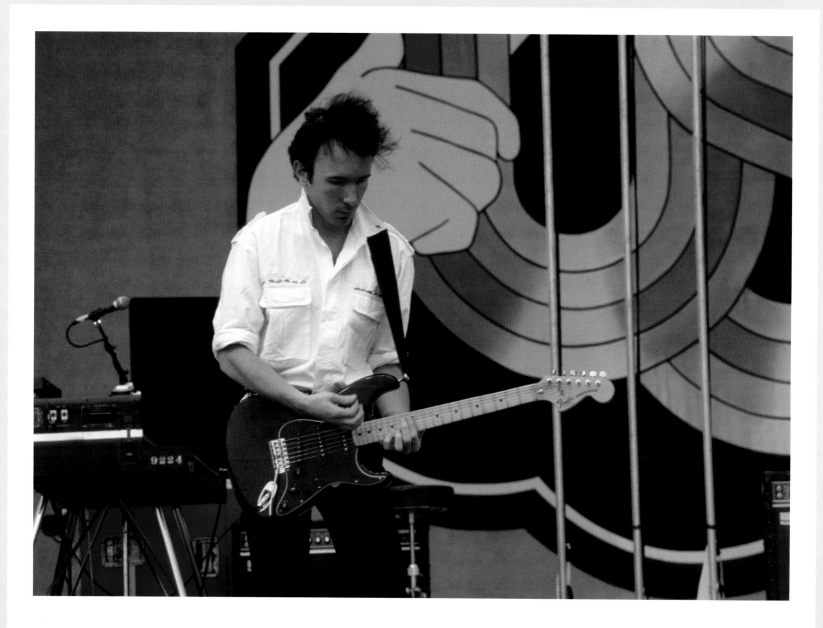

October gold

Opposite and above: U2 on stage at the giant US '83 Festival held in Glen Helen Regional Park, Devore, California, 30 May 1983.

During 1982 the band's artistic agenda had moved on from the confusion and self-analysis of the *October* era. Whilst still touring the album, in February 1982, U2 hooked up with Dutch photographer Anton Corbijn during a riverboat performance en route from New Orleans; he would become a major artistic and cultural influence on the band although he admitted that on first hearing he was not overly impressed by the music. Nonetheless on countless occasions he was called in to shoot stills, direct videos or simply hang out on tour.

October was certified Gold in the UK in December 1981 and in August 1982 a more prepared and determined U2 returned to Dublin's Windmill Lane Studios to start work on their next album, to be titled *War*. For the next three months the band's main activity would be recording. Except Bono married Alison on 20 August barely two weeks after they started in the studio. A two-week honeymoon followed – courtesy of Chris Blackwell – in his Jamaican Goldeneye estate, former home of James Bond creator Ian Fleming who wrote *Casino Royale*, amongst other Bond stories, while living there. While Bono and Ali honeymoon, Larry and Adam take a break; The Edge comes up with "Sunday, Bloody Sunday".

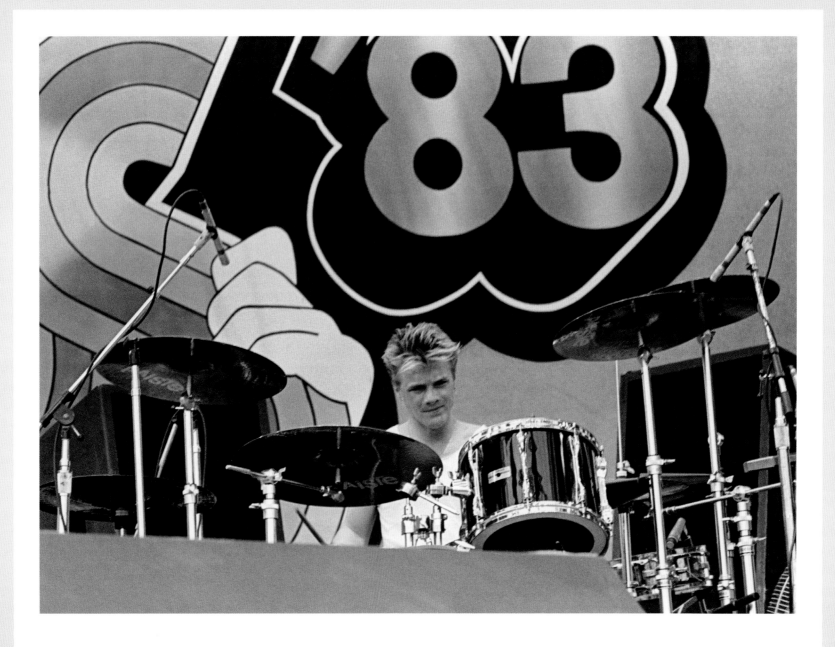

Making War

Opposite and above: Larry and Edge on stage at US '83, 30 May 1983. In their new album *War*, released on 28 February 1983, there is a new depth which arises from their increasing touring experience. The theme is out of kilter with the kitsch electronic sound of the early 1980s. Bob Geldof took exception to the exploration of conflict that comes across in the likes of "Sunday, Bloody Sunday" but the band had already applied a litmus test with that track, playing it for the first time to a Belfast audience on 20 December 1982 with the promise that if, after understanding what the song was about, the crowd didn't like it they would never perform

it again. At the end of the song the crowd roared their approval. Larry recalled later that it was a very emotional moment, "It's the first time we ever really made a statement."

Island Records watched the launch of the latest album with concern – particularly in the finance department as U2 were still deeply in the red as an act. Chris Blackwell's canny judgement held off the panicked accountants and the touring strategy to build North American sales continued. *War* debuted in the US charts at number 91 and climbed steadily eventually reaching number 12.

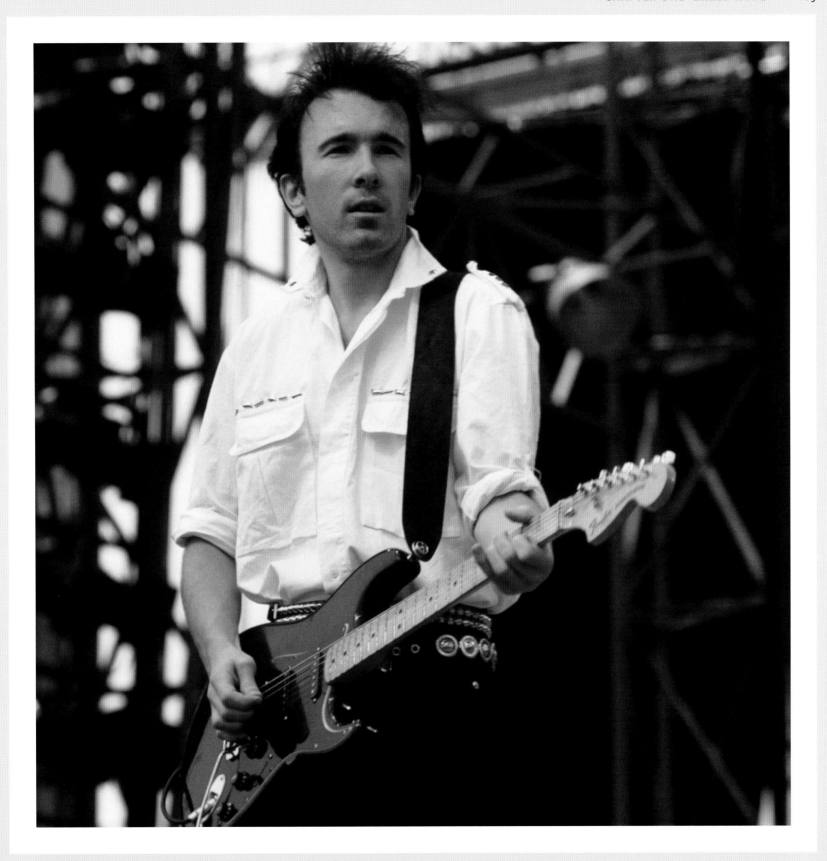

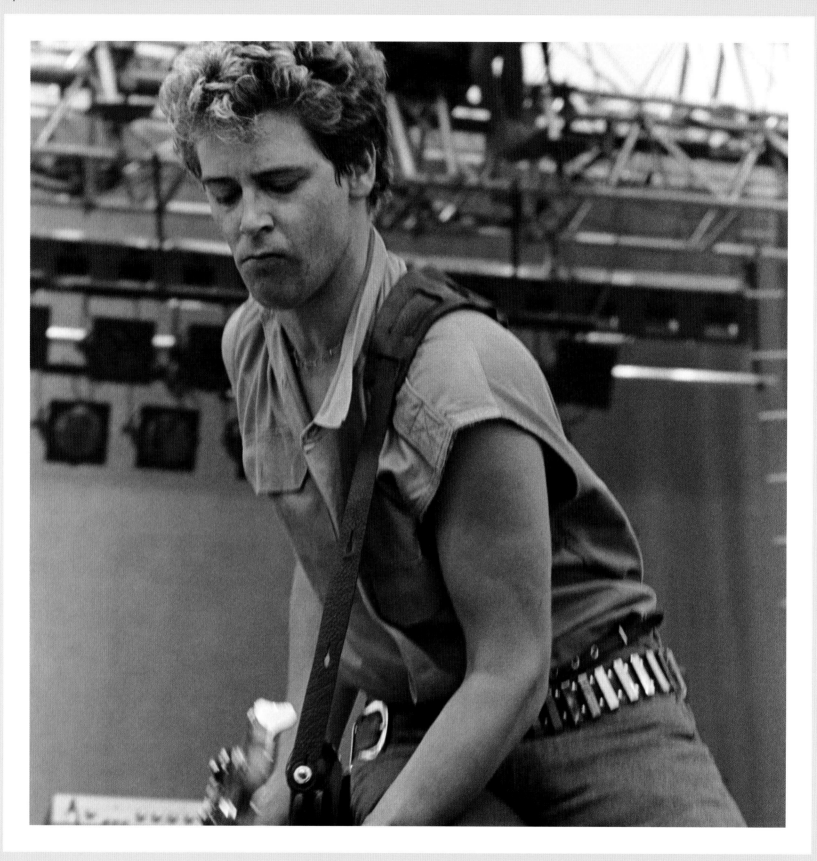

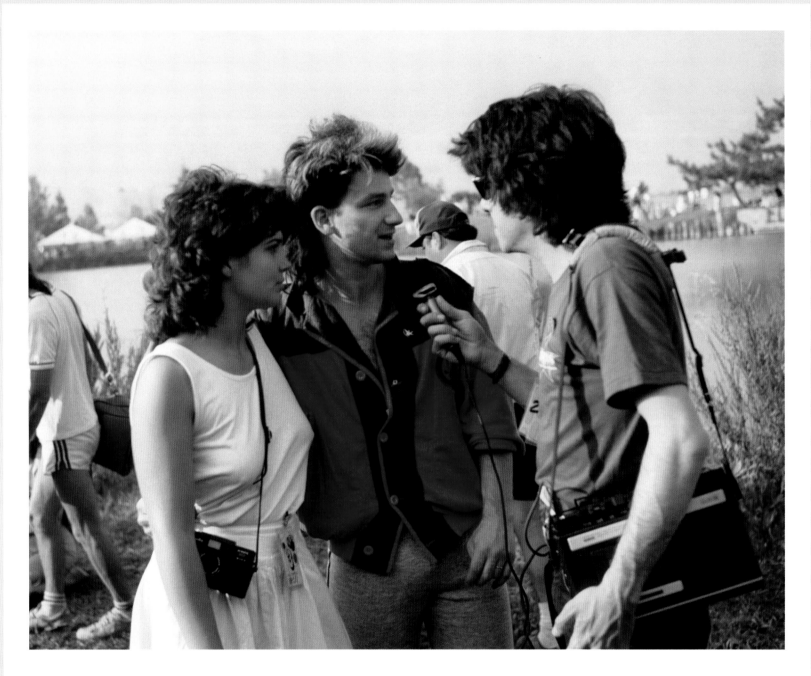

Flying the flag

Opposite: Adam in full concentration on his bass line onstage at US '83. Tense moments were not unusual in a U2 performance as the band pushed the limits of their show. Bono on adrenaline climbed the 100-foot-high lighting rig at US '83, and, waving a white flag, crossed the scaffolding over the stage during the performance – much to the consternation of his colleagues.

Above: Bono is interviewed with his wife Ali. Ali and Bono started dating in 1975 having met at school: Ali came into Bono's life soon after his mother's early death and has been a companion ever since, putting aside some of her career ambitions to fit in with Bono's busy public life. Travelling widely on tour with U2, she shared many life-changing experiences around the world and later pursued a humanitarian and spiritual agenda of her own.

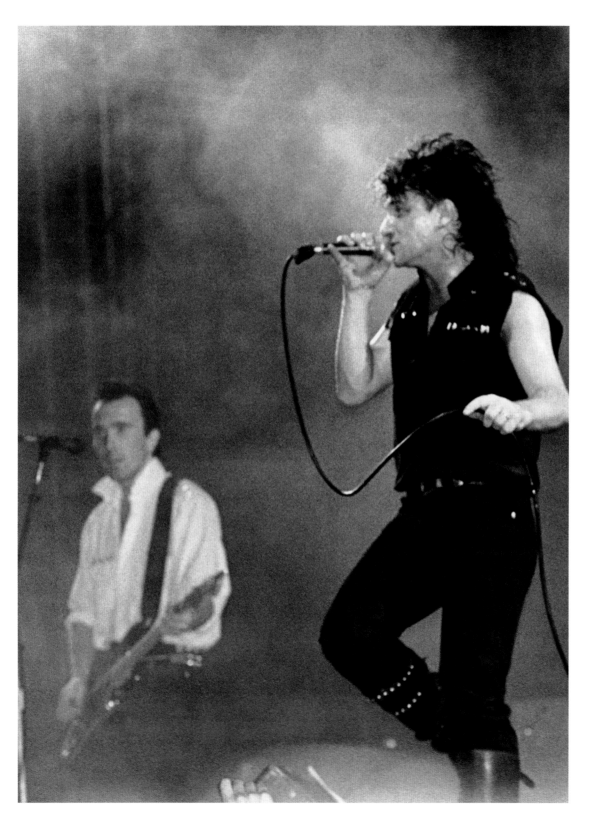

Red Rocks

Left: Dry ice clouds the stage at US '83. The huge scale of the May festival challenged the band to expand the scope of their act. They looked to the forthcoming 5 June gig at the remote Red Rocks Amphitheater outside Denver, Colorado, to be a dramatic show which would be videotaped and broadcast rights sold to the likes of NBC and MTV. McGuinness hired *The Tube* film crew from Newcastle upon Tyne in England and an audio crew from Boston. Terrible weather conditions made the show seem impossible but 5,000 devoted fans turned up at the amphitheatre to witness the performance of a lifetime from U2 as they all were soaked in a huge rainstorm.

Opposite: Bono sports the War tour insignia on his chest – a white flag – hardly a conventional medal of honour. The success of the various broadcasts of the Red Rocks show inspired the band to release a mini album: *U2 Live – Under a Blood Red Sky* which went on sale in late November, climbing to number 2 in the UK charts and 28 in the US. The proliferation of apocalyptic themes has begun, encouraged no doubt by U2's visit to the Chicago Peace Museum earlier in the year where the current exhibit of artworks made by survivors of Nagasaki's nuclear bomb was on show with the title of *The Unforgettable Fire*.

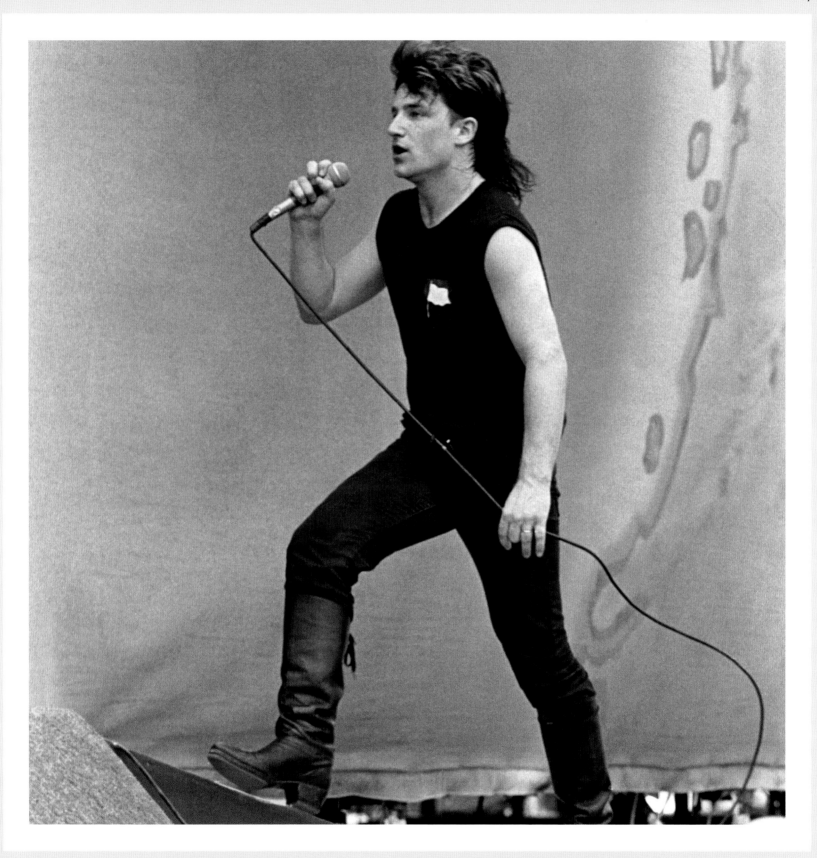

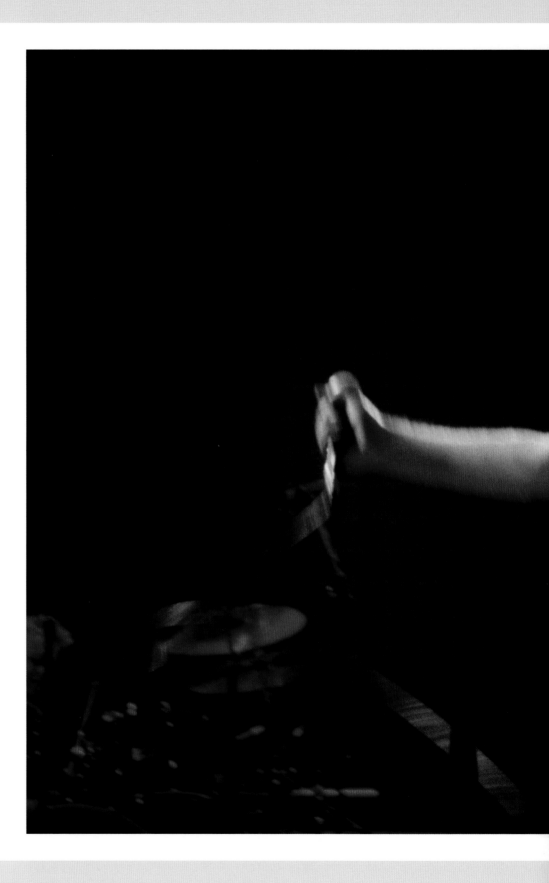

Down Under

Right: Bono feels the heat performing on stage at the Entertainment Centre, Sydney, during the Under Australian Skies tour in early September 1984.

The North America leg of the War tour wrapped up on 29 June 1983 in New York – it grossed $2m and was the first time the band had made profit from touring.

Back in Dublin on 12 July 1983, Edge married his long-term girlfriend Aislinn, with Bono as best man before the War tour started up again with the band flying out to Hawaii, performing a single gig in Honolulu on 16 November before travelling on to Japan to launch their first tour there in Osaka on 22 November. After six dates they returned to Dublin, meeting at Bono's place to get started on ideas for the next album. The recent experience of touring Japan will have significant influence on the making of the new album.

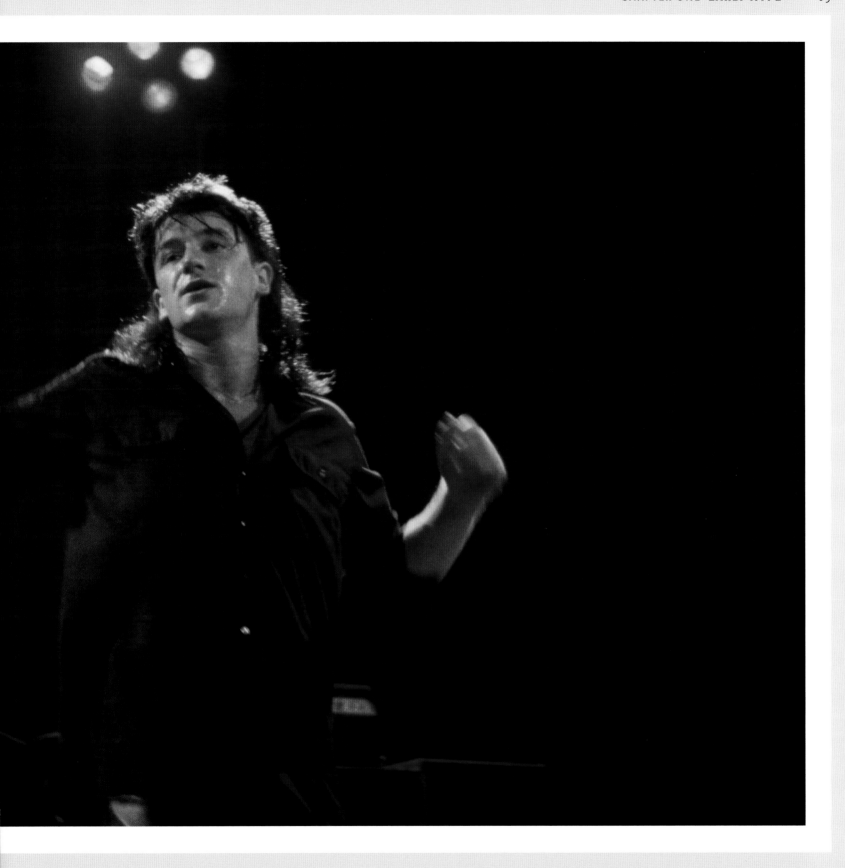

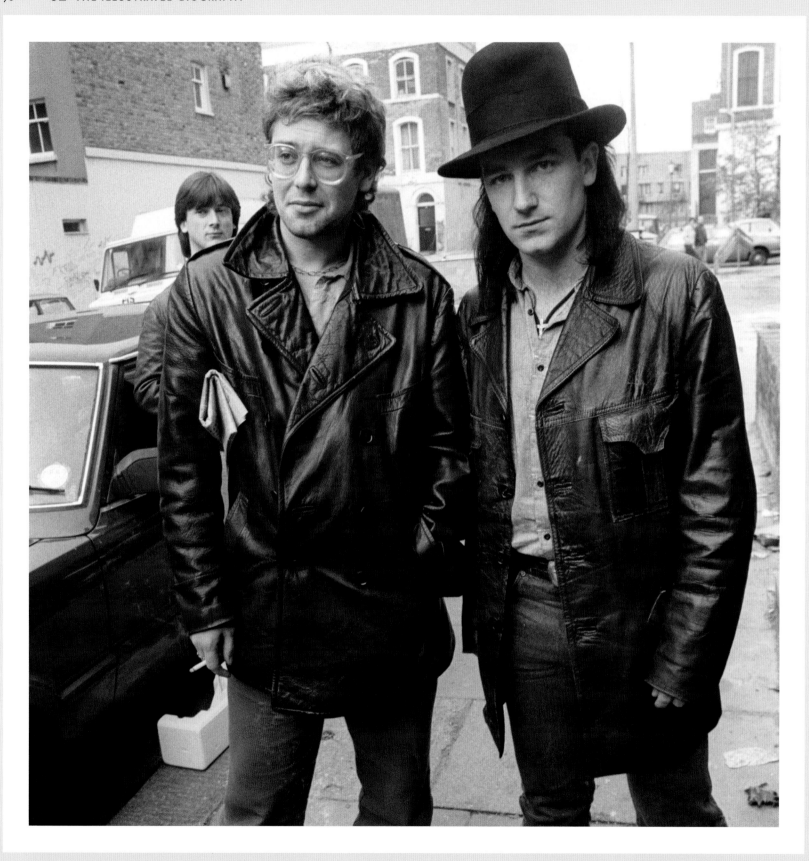

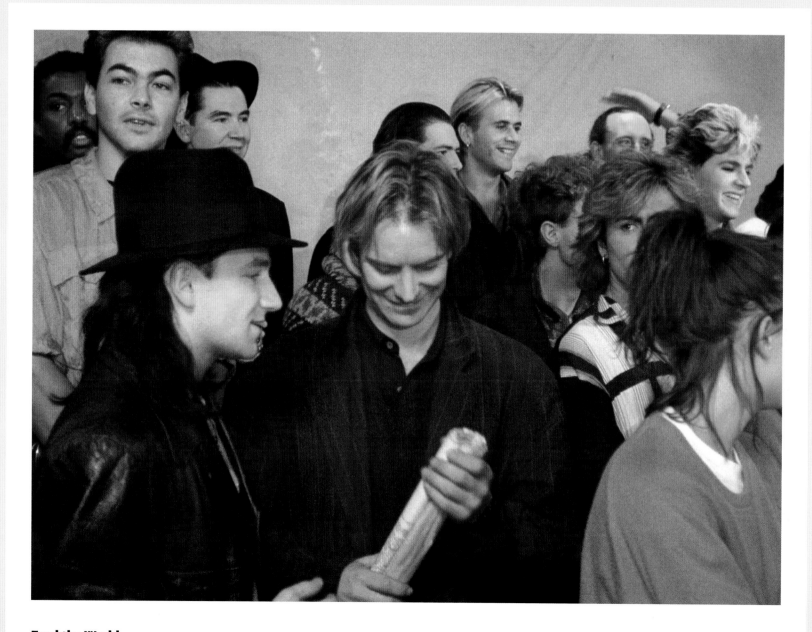

Feed the World

Opposite: Adam and Bono arrive at Island's Notting Hill Studios to record the Band Aid single, "Do They Know It's Christmas?", November 1984.

Above: Bono chats with Sting during the recording of the song which Bob Geldof hoped would help feed the world's hungry. The charity single was released on 3 December, going to number 1 in the UK and 12 other countries and raising £8m for famine relief in Africa.

1984 was an important year for U2: exerting their artistic freedom they announced in April that Brian Eno would produce their next album, taking their musical direction firmly out of the mainstream. Recording

The Unforgettable Fire began in Slane Castle north of Dublin on 7 May. After U2 moved back into Windmill Lane Studios in Dublin, Bob Dylan arrived to perform at Slane Castle on 8 July. Bono, Van Morrison and Dylan engaged in a broad discussion about the roots of rock. Bono found himself ignorant of his own country's traditional music and made a private vow to rectify this knowledge gap.

The Unforgettable Fire was released on 1 October reaching number 1 in the UK charts and 12 in the US. It was certified Gold in the USA on 3 December, the same day as the Band Aid single was released. The promotional tour set out from Lyon, France, on 18 October.

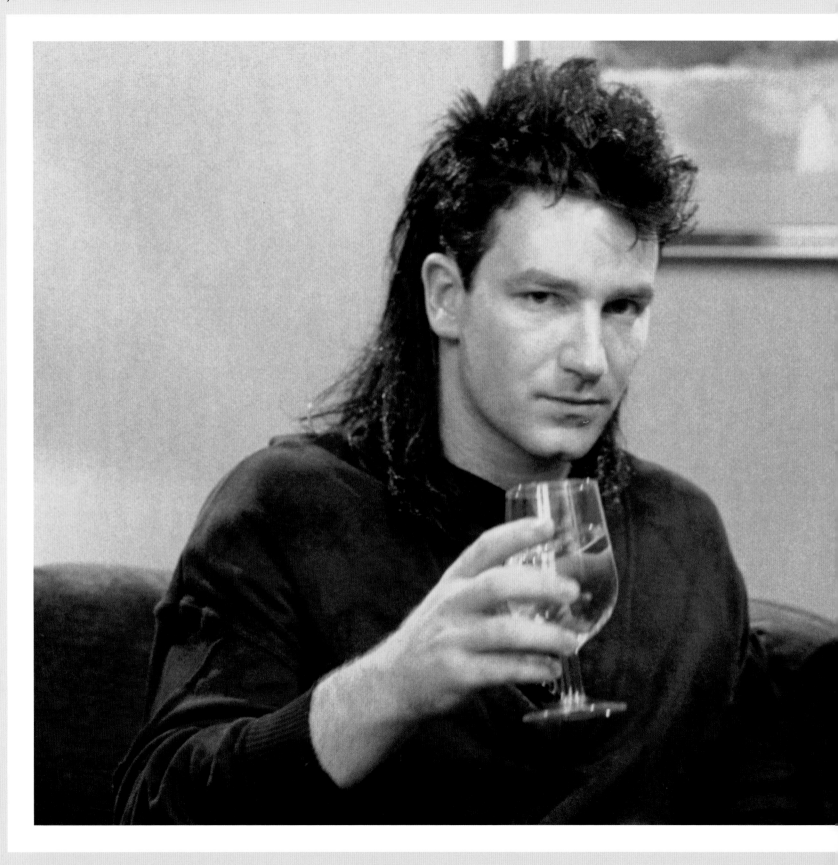

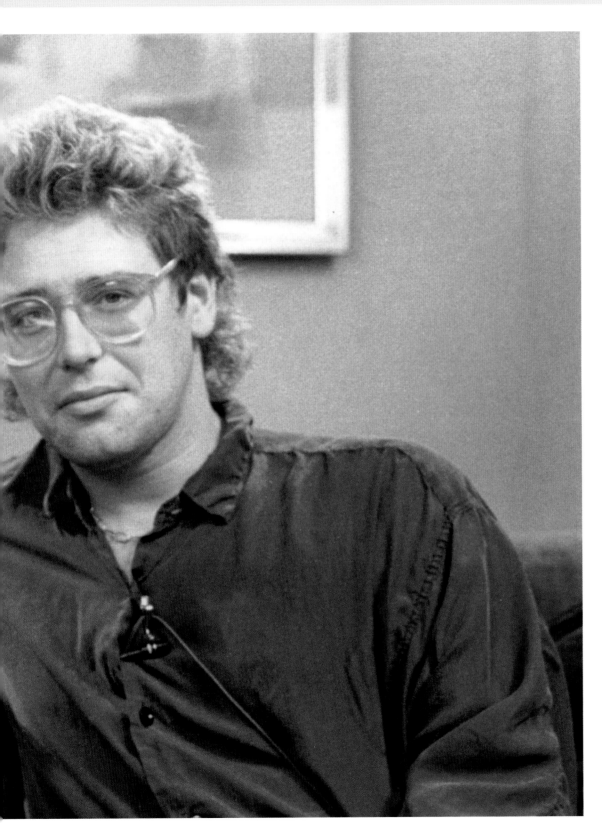

Back in the USA

Left: Bono and Adam photographed during a studio interview around the time of the Band Aid single.

On 29 November the U2 were on a plane to the USA for a quickfire tour, playing dates across the country and a single gig in Canada. The brief tour wound up in Long Beach on 16 December. In the year-end issue of *Rolling Stone* magazine, U2 albums featured three times in the chart of Top Albums of 1984.

Adam had entertained some demons in the past year and was arrested for drunken driving in March after failing to stop at a police checkpoint in Dublin. In a court hearing in January 1985 he lost his licence and received a fine of £225.

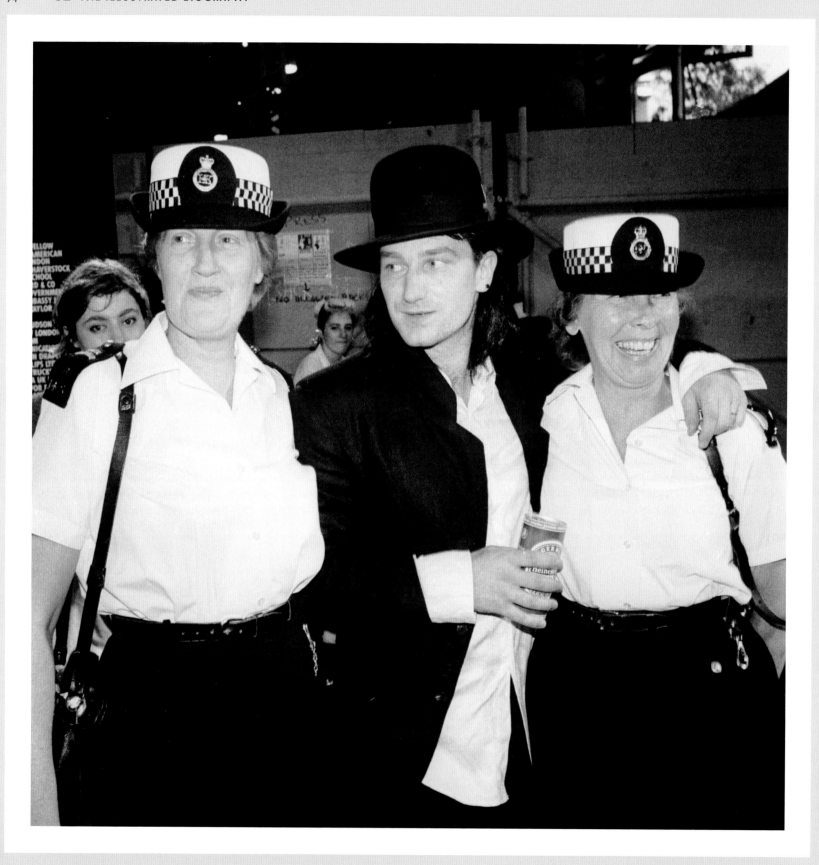

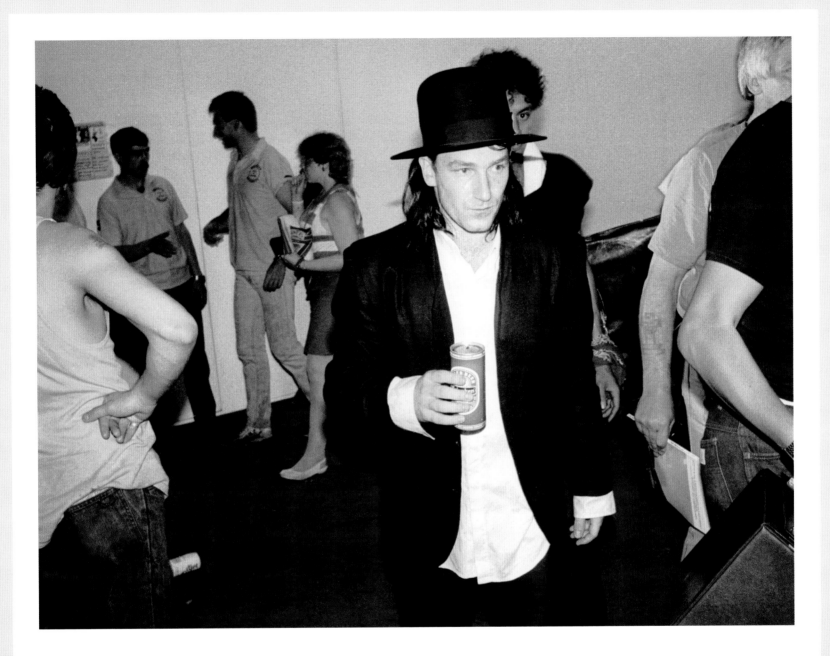

"The Band of the '80s"

Opposite: Bono enjoys a police escort backstage at Live Aid, 13 July 1985. 1985 turns into a year of ceaseless performing in Europe and North America but it was divided by the watershed experience of Live Aid which had a profound effect not just on Bono and U2 but on the global perception of the role and power of music and performing artists.

Above: Bono enjoys a cooling beer after the U2 Live Aid set, his expression pensive.

In the midst of touring the US in February, *The Unforgettable Fire* was certified Platinum in the USA – U2's first album to exceed one million sales there – but barely two weeks later it happened again with *War*. *Rolling Stone* magazine's 14 March edition shouts its choice of U2 as "Band of the '80s". U2 are on the crest of a wave and on 1 April they play Madison Square Garden for the first time, flying in family, friends and journalists from Ireland to share their big moment.

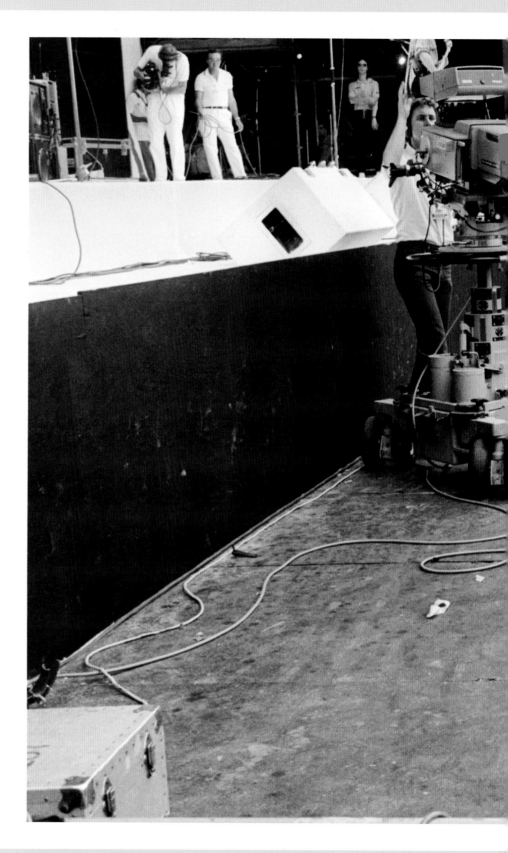

A problem for Larry

Right: Bono works the Live Aid audience at Wembley Stadium, London.

In San Francisco at their second gig at Cow Palace on 8 March, Larry developed a serious pain in his left hand and was rushed to hospital. This injury will require careful medical treatment after the first aid that allowed Larry to continue with the tour and will force him to be more careful with his hands and drumming technique in future.

The US tour ended on 4 May at Fort Lauderdale, Florida, and U2 immediately headed back to Dublin with expert medical treatment for Larry while the others took a two-week break. On 29 June the band performed at Croke Park, Dublin. Billed as their "Homecoming Concert" it attracted a capacity audience of 57,000, making this their first stadium show with U2 very much the conquering heroes!

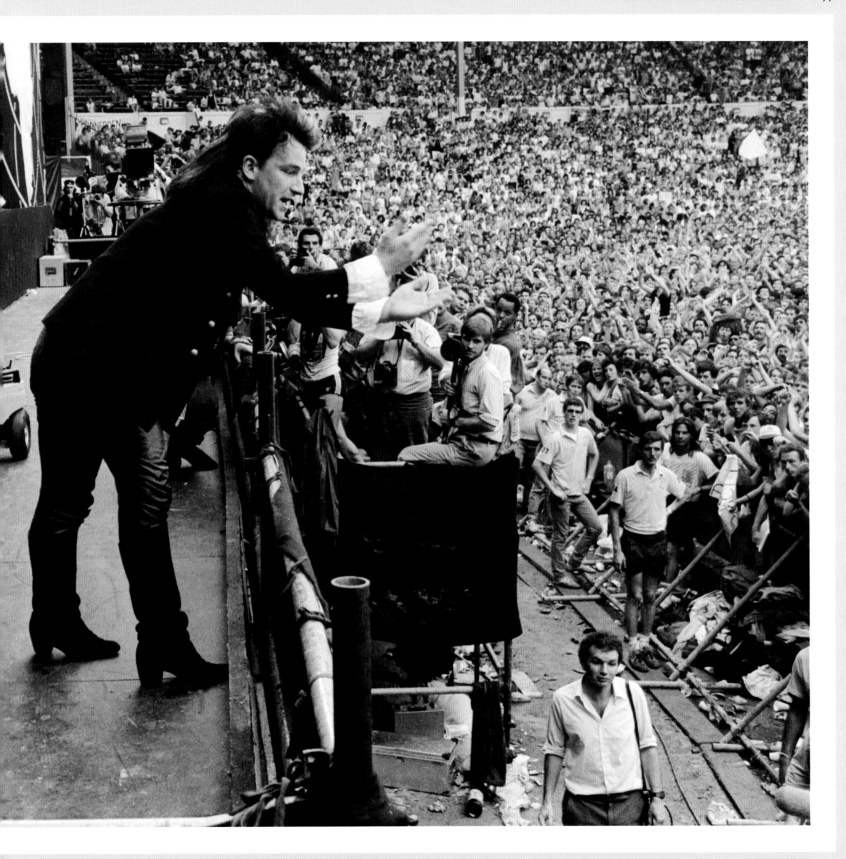

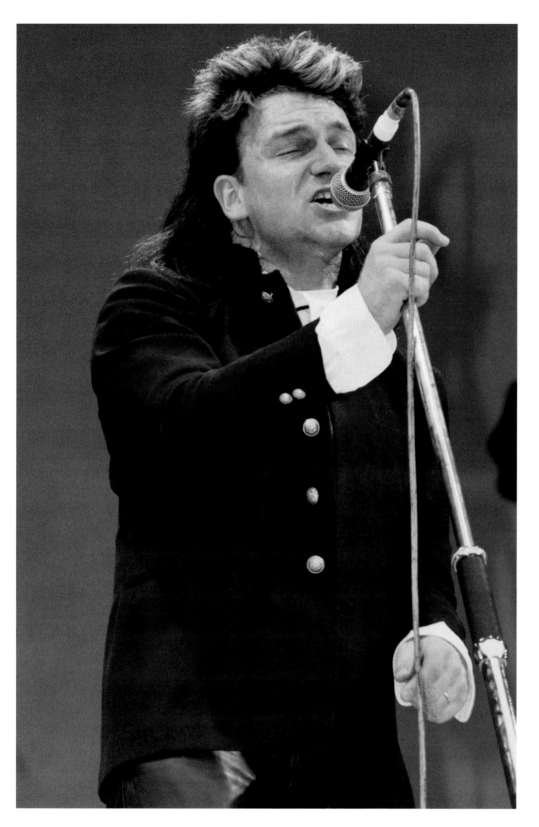

In with the crowd

Left and opposite: Bono performs at Live Aid. The task of introducing U2 fell to Jack Nicholson broadcasting from the JFK stadium in Philadelphia; his words induced a roar from the audiences both sides of the Atlantic and U2 burst into "Sunday, Bloody Sunday". Bono became irreversibly carried away while performing their second number, "Bad", jumping down from the stage into the crowd and dancing intimately with an unknown girl he picked out from the audience. Bono was invisible to the rest of the band who kept playing in some desperation as the song ran into its 14th minute. The careful allocation of U2's 20-minute set was thrown out by Bono, seemingly without thought by him or consultation with his bandmates. Despite the frustration and ire of the rest of the band, this impetuous and anarchic act of Bono's remained one of Live Aid's most memorable moments, reinforcing the connectedness of the performers with their audience. After a readers' poll *Rolling Stone* magazine announced that U2 have won the award for the Best Performance at Live Aid.

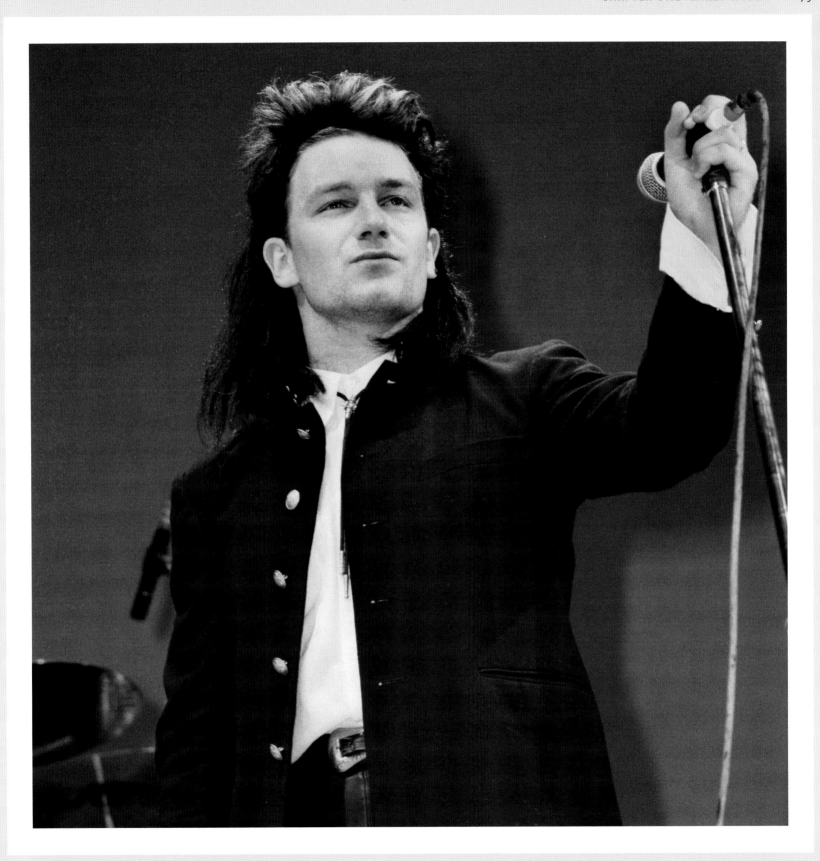

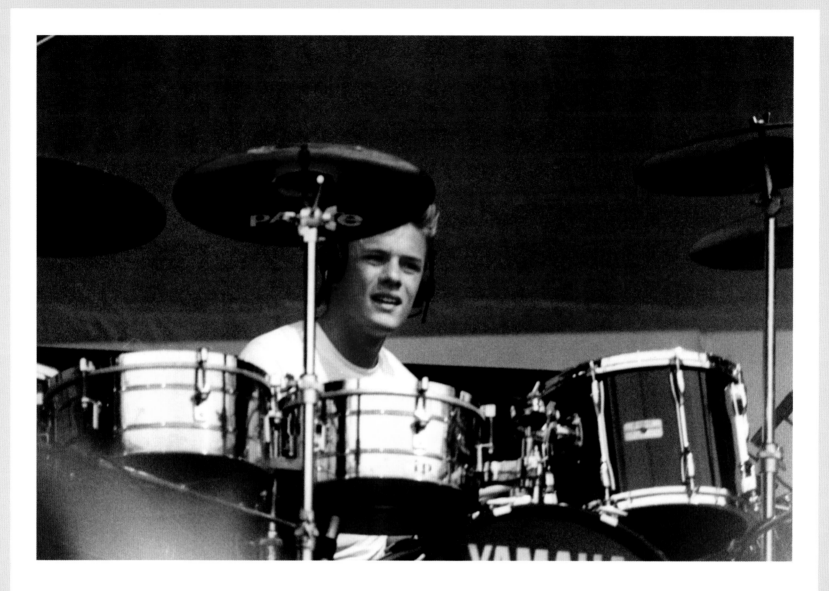

All's well that ends well

Above: During U2's Live Aid performance an anxious-looking Larry plugs away at the drums while Bono, out of sight, dances with a member of the audience.

Bono, coming down from his performance high, was overcome with embarrassment and guilt, which, soon after, took him into virtual hiding in the Irish countryside; he said afterwards that he fully expected to be fired from the band. However, it gradually dawned on everyone that his impulsive behaviour had actually added to the Live Aid show rather than detracted from its impact.

Opposite: George Michael, Bob Geldof, Bono and Freddie Mercury sing their hearts out during the finale of Live Aid.

Billions of people around the world were happily forced to change their understanding as a result of the Live Aid spectacle. Unbelievably, an anxious U2 had phoned Bob Geldof the night before trying to cancel because they wouldn't be able to carry out a sound check before their set; Bob would have none of it.

In September Bono returned to the challenge of exploring "roots music"; an acquaintance pointed him to Africa and, travelling to Cairo with Ali, a World Vision worker told them of the dire situation in Ethiopia. The couple then spent the rest of the month working alongside aid workers in the Ethiopian camps. The combination of Live Aid and the month in Ethiopia would have a lifelong influence on Bono.

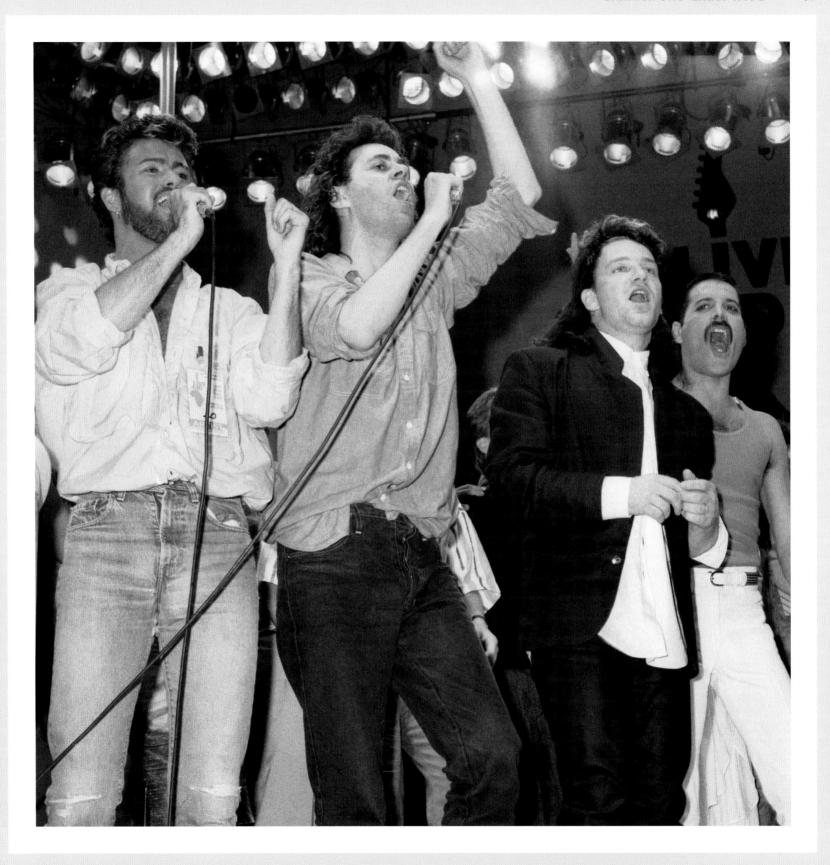

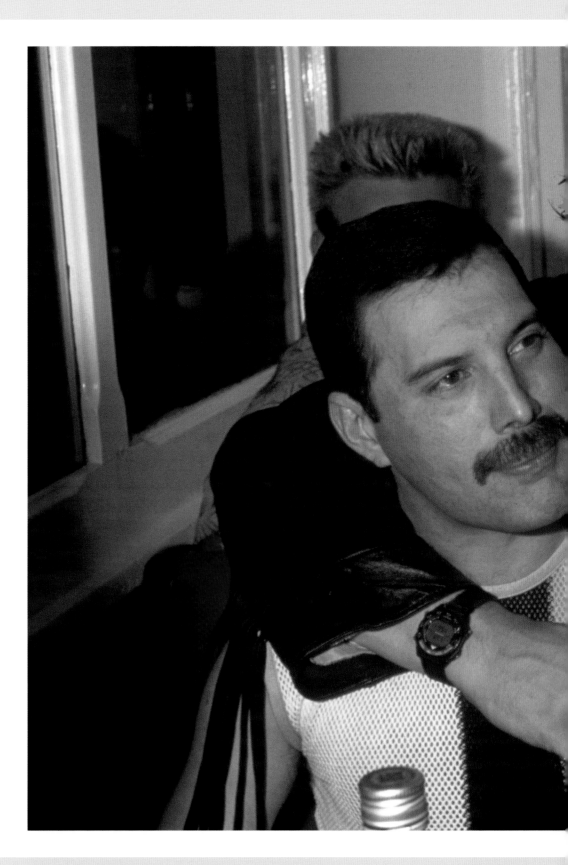

Expanding the repertoire

Right: A slightly demented-looking Bono larks with Freddie Mercury and friend.

Bono keenly felt the lack of "roots" in his musical repertoire in a jamming session in New York with Keith Richards of the Rolling Stones and Peter Wolf of the J Geils Band. As the others roll out blues classics they invite Bono to do the same but he can't: his punk orientation as a teenager meant that he even knew little of his own Irish music heritage. Unable to draw on such knowledge he decided to write his own blues number and the next day took it to the studio where the Stones were recording *Dirty Work*. Richards and Ronnie Wood agreed to record it with Bono.

Bono's main purpose in flying to New York in October 1985 was to help promote an Amnesty International initiative by its USA executive director, Jack Healey, who believed that targeting a college audience would be the best way to get Amnesty a bigger and better movement in the USA. Healey, having observed U2 live, was convinced that this band could play a key role.

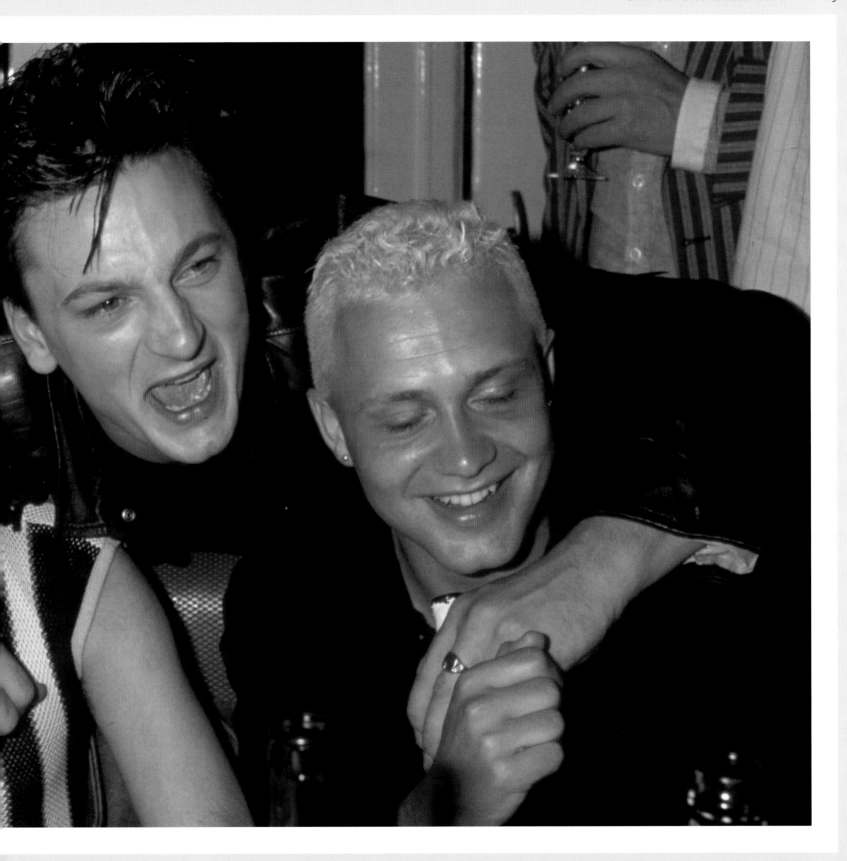

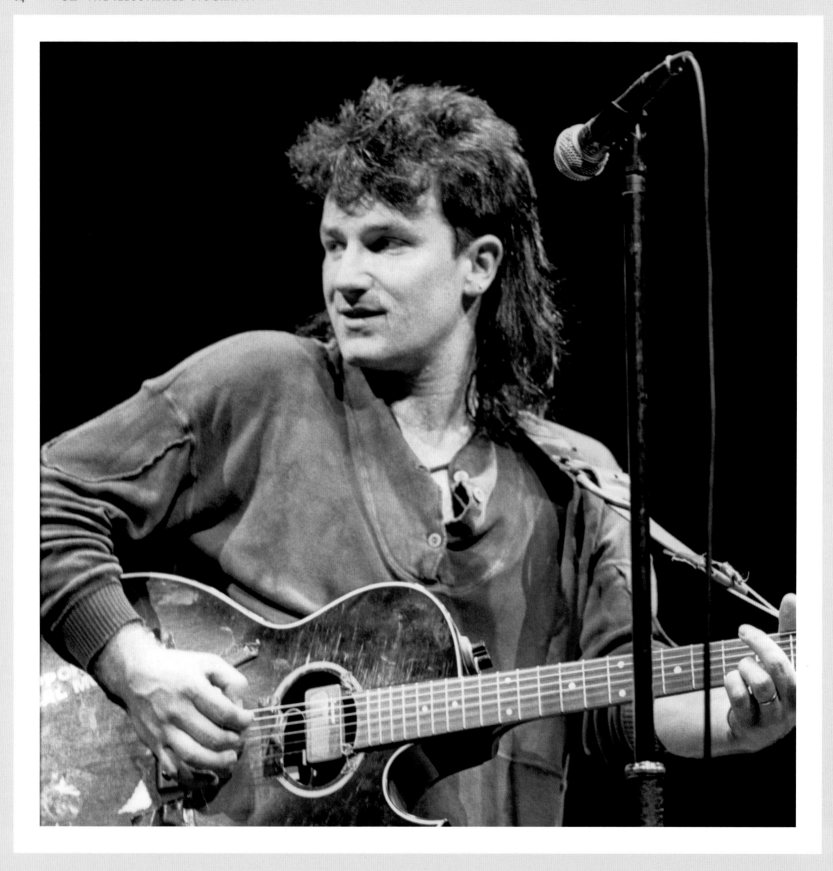

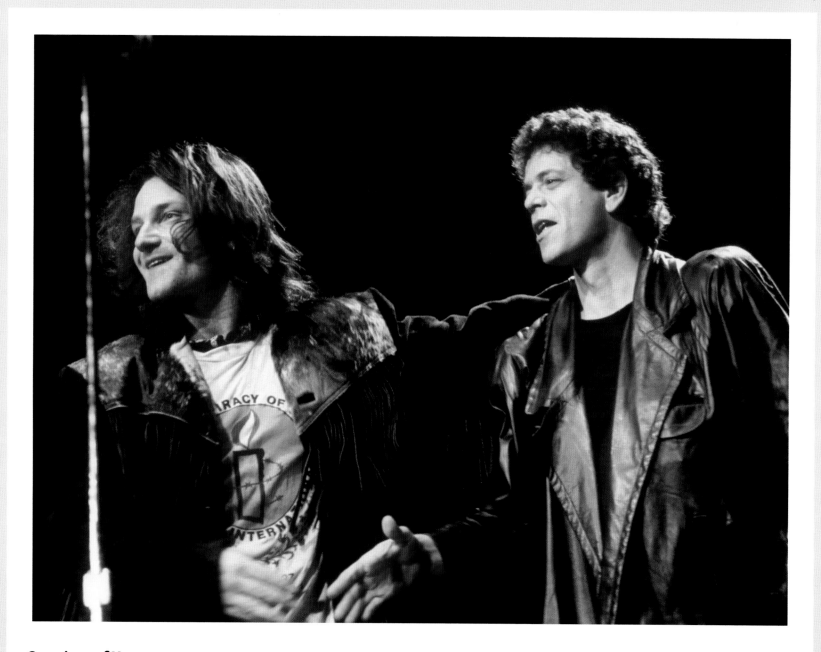

Conspiracy of Hope

Opposite: Bono plays acoustic guitar on stage during The Unforgettable Fire tour.

Bono called 1986 "an incredibly bad year" for him but, overall, it was not a bad year for the band: virtually the whole year in and out of the recording studio would give birth to their defining album *The Joshua Tree*. With good intentions the band supported Self Aid, giving a benefit performance at the end of May to help Irish unemployed in a much publicized initiative that backfired on the band, giving them widespread negative press in their home country.

Above: Bono and Lou Reed shake hands on stage during the Conspiracy of Hope tour in support of Amnesty International in June 1986. On 3 June U2 were at Cow Palace in San Francisco, where a press conference heralded the Conspiracy of Hope tour starting out there the next day. U2 were part of a high-profile line-up that would perform 6 shows across the USA over the next 11 days. Artists included Sting, Bryan Adams, Joan Baez, Lou Reed, Peter Gabriel and many other stars, some making guest appearances to introduce artists on stage. The whole event was managed by legendary rock impresario Bill Graham.

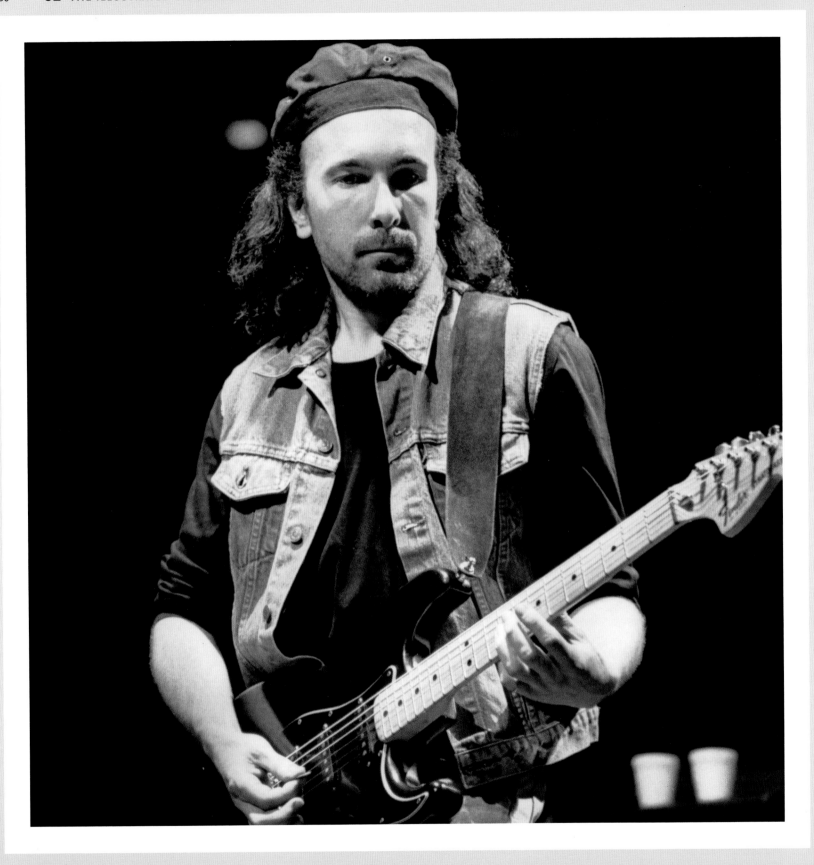

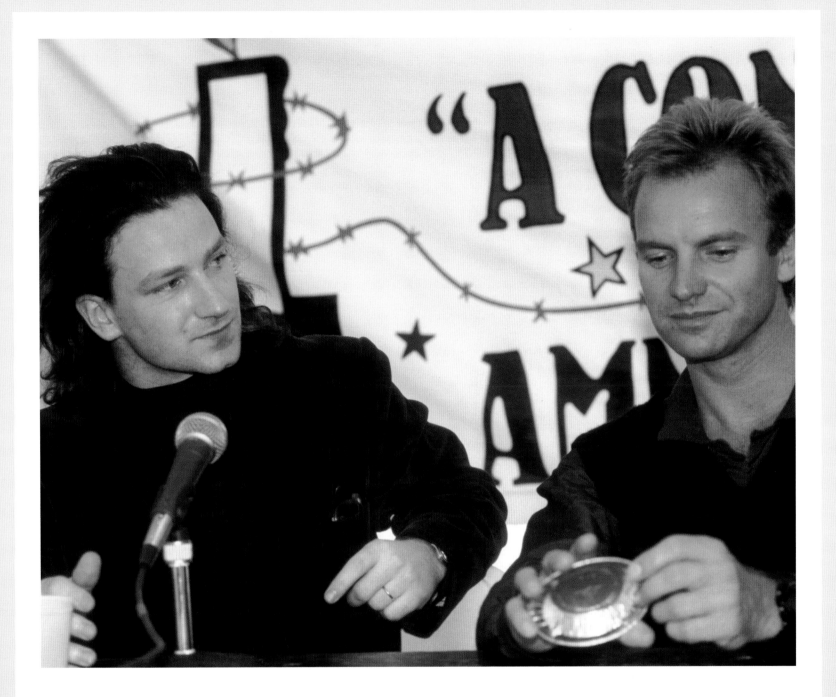

Conspiracy theory

Opposite: Edge works his Stratocaster on tour in 1986. The Amnesty tour moved on to Los Angeles on 6 June to be joined by a string of new guest artists including Bob Dylan, Tom Petty, Bob Geldof and Dave Stewart. But at Denver two days later the show performed to an arena that looked empty of crowds – the word "Conspiracy" had frightened the people away!

Above: Bono and Sting at the press conference in New York on 14 June preceding the final Conspiracy of Hope show on the 15th. Sting had been been a high-profile supporter of Amnesty since *The Secret Policeman's Ball* some years before, in which he had been involved. Completely unannounced, Sting reunited The Police for the last three shows to the delight and astonishment of the Atlanta crowd.

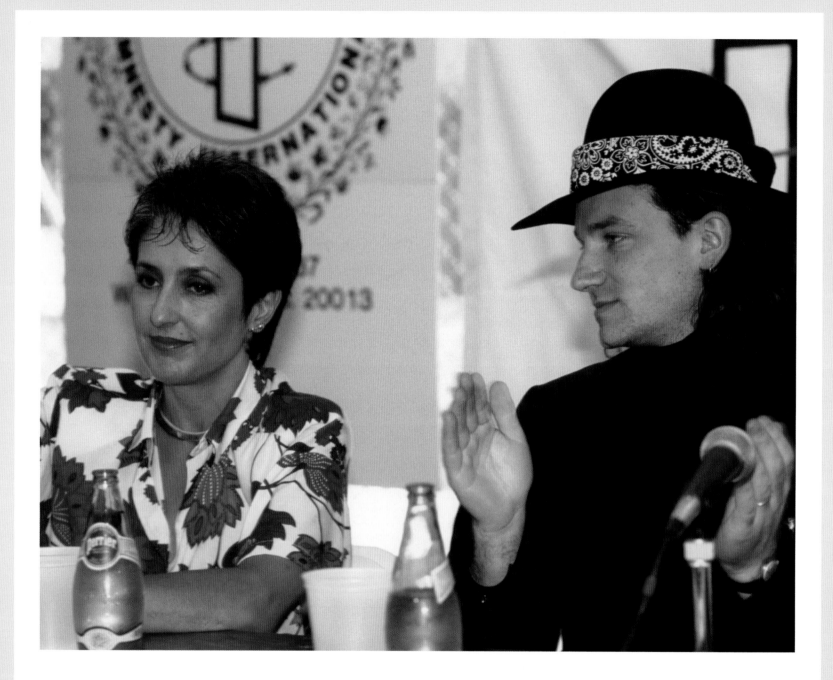

The old and the new

Above: Veteran campaigner Joan Baez sits next to Bono at the press conference before the last Conspiracy of Hope gig. The tour brought together the old guard and the new, with the likes of Peter, Paul and Mary returning to the stage; the rising stars of U2 and Peter Gabriel gained even more popularity from the tour. The spirit of collaboration for social and political ends also benefited the artists musically as they mixed their acts and sang along together on stage and jammed during the evenings. Bono sometimes joined The Police in "Invisible Sun", and Carlos Santana, Fela and the Neville Brothers would freely mix and match.

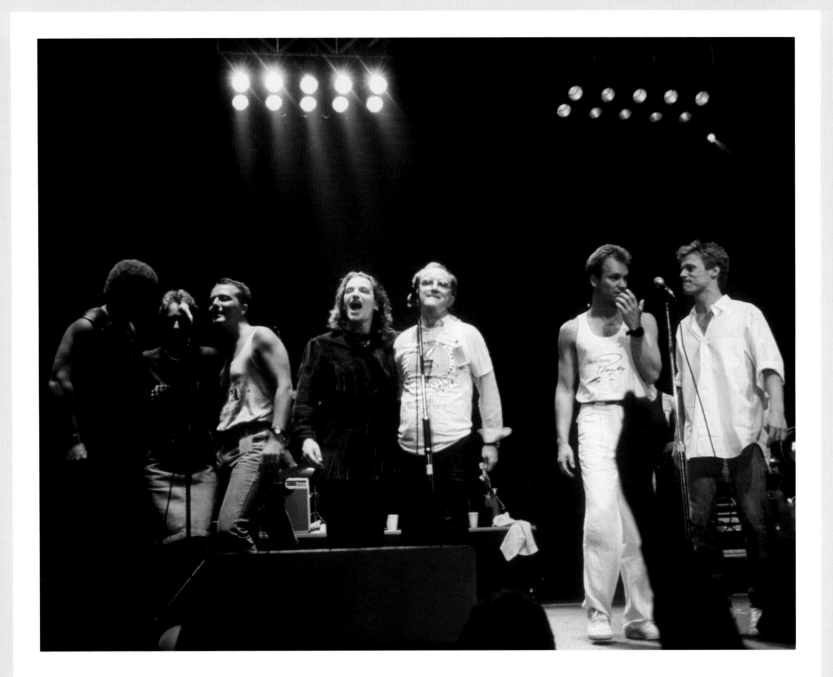

Best band in the world

Above: Stars of the Conspiracy of Hope tour line up for the finale at the Giants Stadium, East Rutherford, New Jersey, 15 June 1986. The finale was Dylan's aptly chosen "I Shall Be Released" where the artists gathered on stage and led the audience in a huge communal singalong. The Conspiracy of Hope tour was an enormous success: weeks after the tour ended Amnesty's USA membership had increased by 45,000 – all aged under 40; of the six prisoners of conscience "adopted" by the tour, two were released within months. In addition Amnesty International received $3m of proceeds from the tour: no wonder Jack Healey (next to Bono above) looks both dazed and ecstatic! However, his opinion of U2 was clear; "I think in Giants Stadium they were probably the best band in the world at that moment."

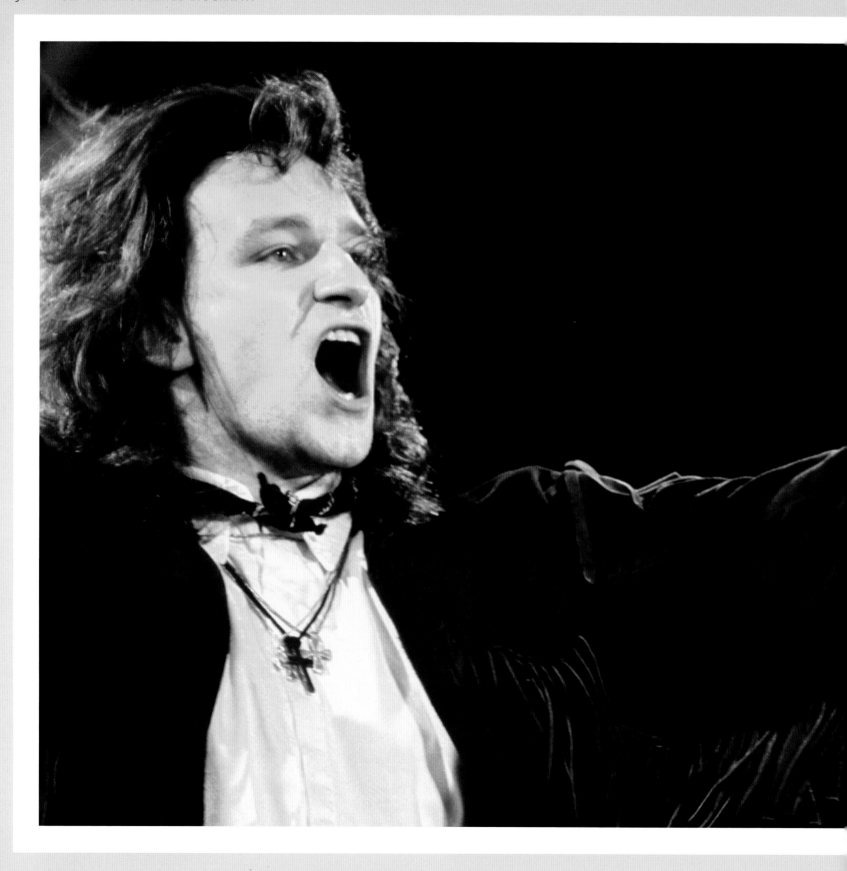

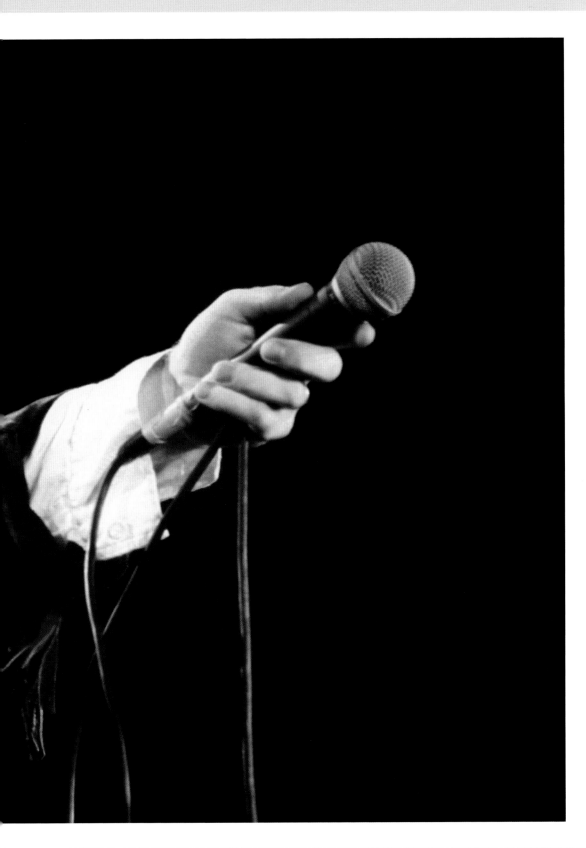

One Tree Hill

Left: 15 June 1986: Bono performs live onstage at Giants Stadium, Meadowlands, at the final performance of the Amnesty International benefit.

The euphoria of the Conspiracy tour continued briefly with other benefits planned but this was shattered by the death of Bono's personal assistant, Maori New Zealander Greg Carroll who died in a motorcycle accident in Dublin while Bono was on a plane to Texas; Bono simply went back on the next plane to join the band in mourning the loss of their highly-valued colleague. The force of Greg's personality led to his rising from a casually-hired hand during the New Zealand tour to a permanent member of the U2 organization. His life and early death would be enshrined in the song "One Tree Hill" for it was Greg who first took them to the place near Auckland that inspired the title. The new album would also be dedicated to him. Bono and Larry flew out to attend a traditional three-day Maori funeral for Carroll at Wanganui on 10 July; Ali and others from the U2 organization also attended.

From New Zealand Bono and Ali flew on to Nicaragua to take up the original plan of investigating the human rights situation in Central America; they went on to spend time in nearby El Salvador visiting farmers Bono had helped financially. Themes arising from this visit will appear in *The Joshua Tree*.

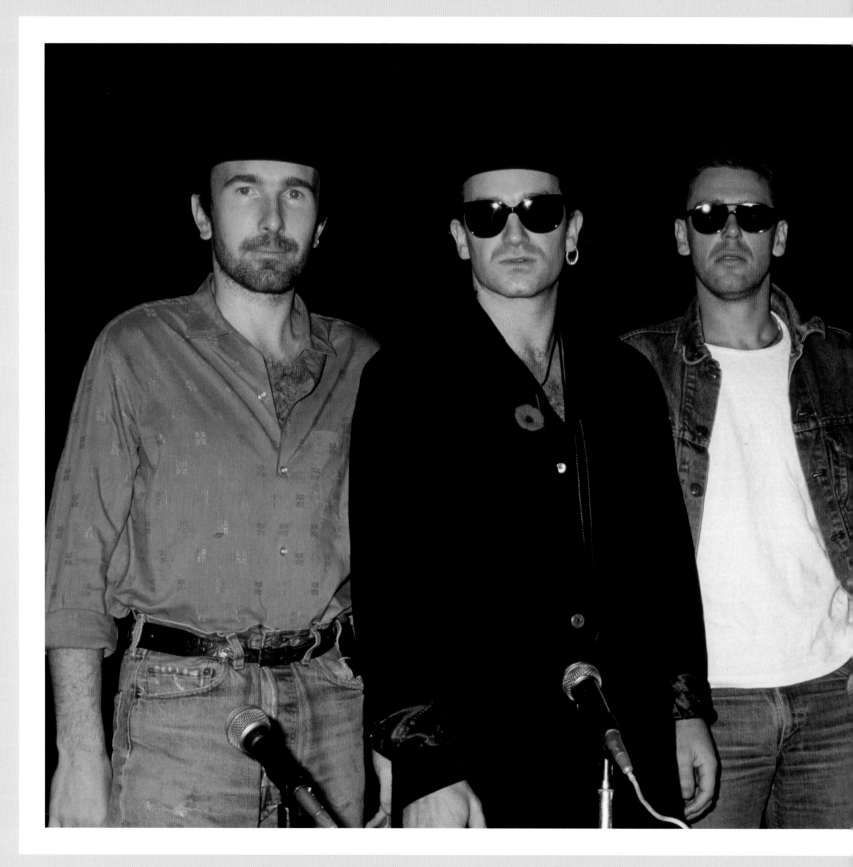

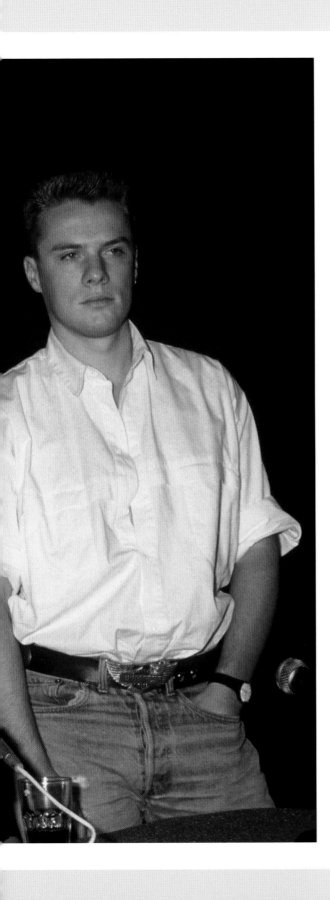

Chapter Two
The Joshua Tree

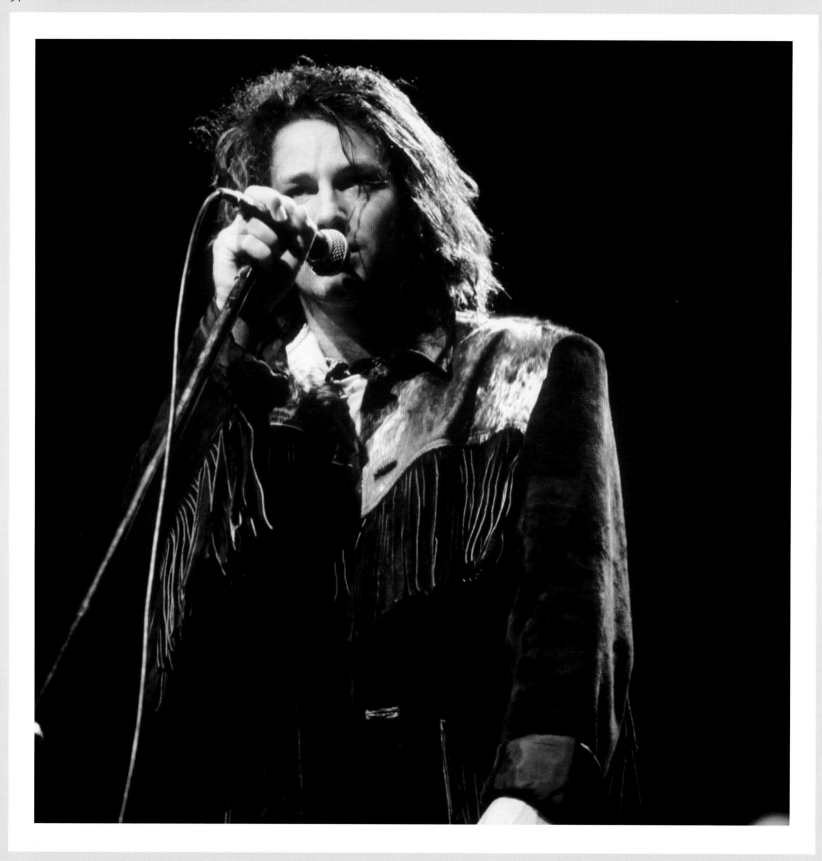

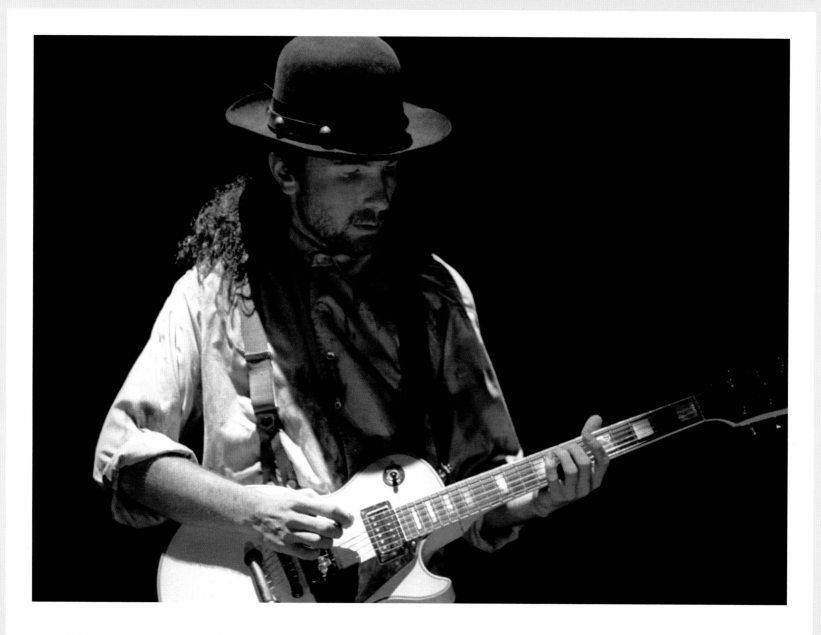

Finishing touches to *The Joshua Tree*

Opposite: Bono is pensive at the mic in Denver, Colorado.

Work on the new album was going well and a creative spurt introduced new material in October. Producers Eno and Lanois recommended they stick with the material in hand to avoid distraction or delay. In December with Anton Corbijn the band shot *The Joshua Tree* album cover at Zabriskie Point in Death Valley, California. Photographs of U2 and the real-life Joshua Tree were taken just outside of Death Valley National Park.

Above: The Edge caresses notes from one of his favourite guitars – a Gibson Les Paul Custom solid, finished in white with black tone and volume control knobs – during the 1987 Joshua Tree tour.

Looking like an early American pioneer seemed to fit the mood of the stark landscapes of *The Joshua Tree* album cover and the journey of discovery implicit in the new album which put the values of the modern-day USA under the magnifying glass. The album had been completed by the year's end but Brian Eno found final mixing of some of the new songs quite frustrating and Steve Lillywhite had to be brought in to Dublin, working over the New Year holidays to produce recording masters.

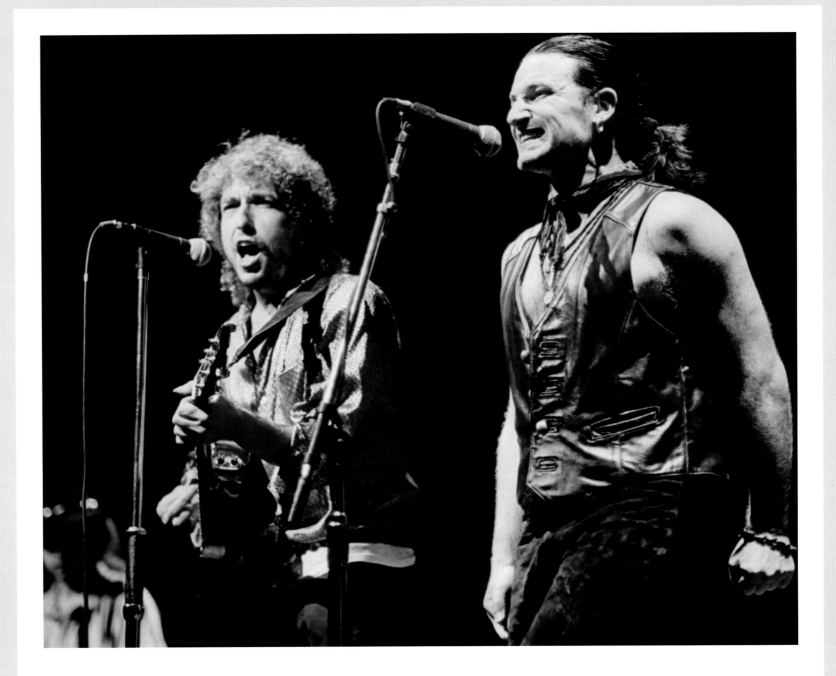

Joshua Tree — instant success

Above: Bob Dylan joins Bono on stage to sing "I Shall be Released" and "Knockin' On Heaven's Door" at Los Angeles Sports Arena on 20 April 1987 during The Joshua Tree tour.

The Joshua Tree was released on 9 March to become the fastest-selling album in British music history: 300,000 were sold in 48 hours taking it to number 1 in the album chart. The album debuted in the US album chart at number 7 rising to number 1 soon after.

Opposite: Adam plays guitar during the encore of their Joshua Tree show at Wembley Stadium, 12 June 1987. It was an established practice for Edge and Adam to swap instruments for their song "40" – a standard for the encore section of this tour.

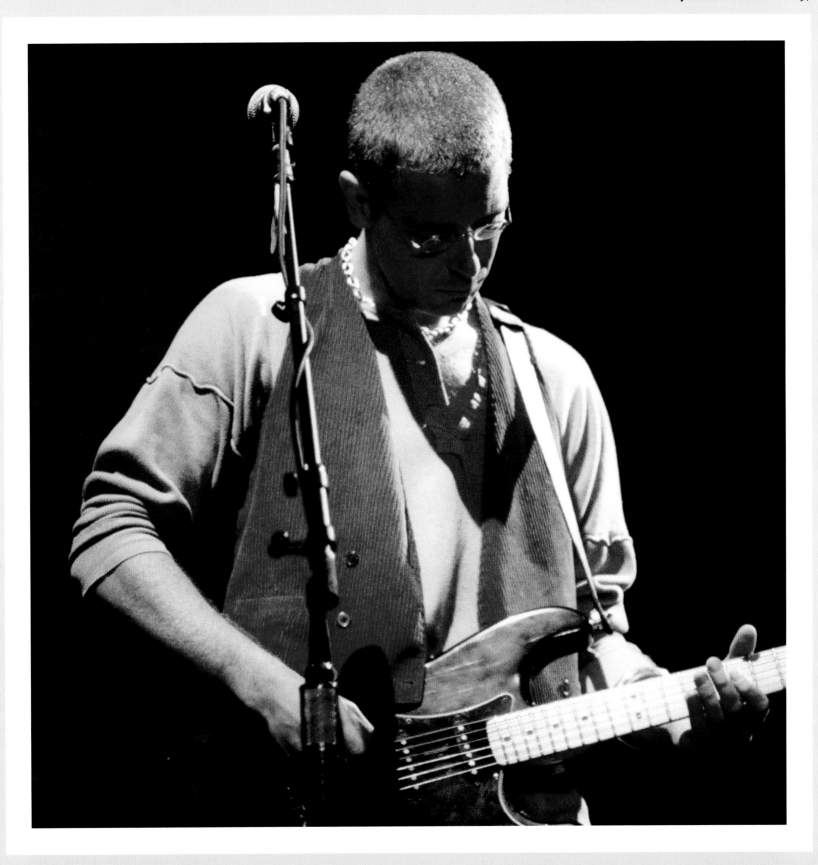

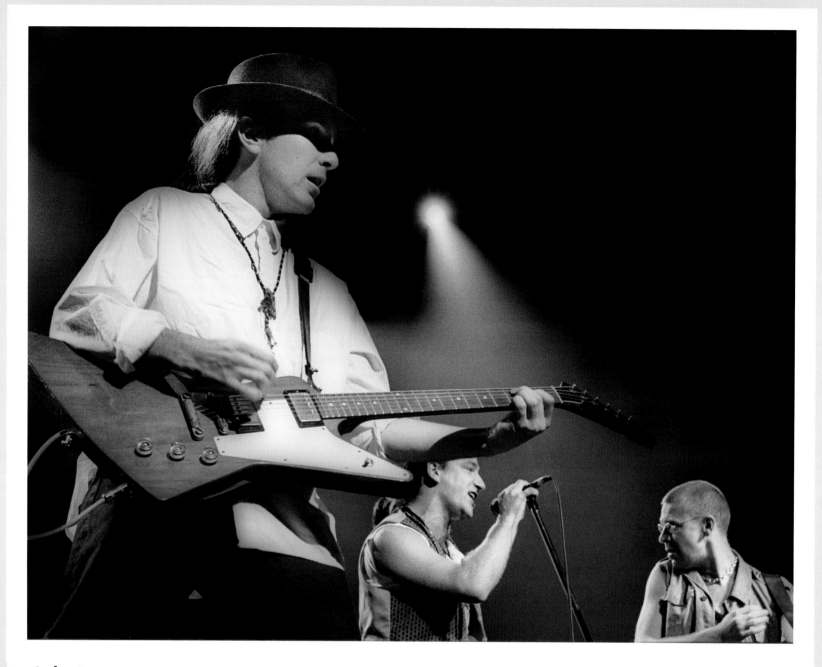

Joshua tour

Above: The Edge, Bono and Adam on stage at the Vorst Nationaal (National Forest arena) outside Brussels, Belgium, during the Joshua Tree tour, 8 July 1987.

  "With or Without You" was getting radio playtime in the US from 4 March. The success of album sales and the imminent tour encouraged Island Records to throw every bit of marketing budget into the fray – $100,000 was spent on store display alone. *The Joshua Tree* would be the first album to sell a million CDs in the USA.

Opposite: The crowd and dramatic stage set of the Joshua Tree tour at De Kuip, Rotterdam, The Netherlands on 10 July.

  The Joshua Tree tour set out from Arizona State University, Tempe, USA on 2 April amidst a storm of local publicity. The state governor had recently rescinded Martin Luther King Day. Numerous artists had refused to play in Arizona as a result but U2 used their performance as a protest platform, reading a formal statement condemning Governor Mecham and exhorting the electorate to recall him.

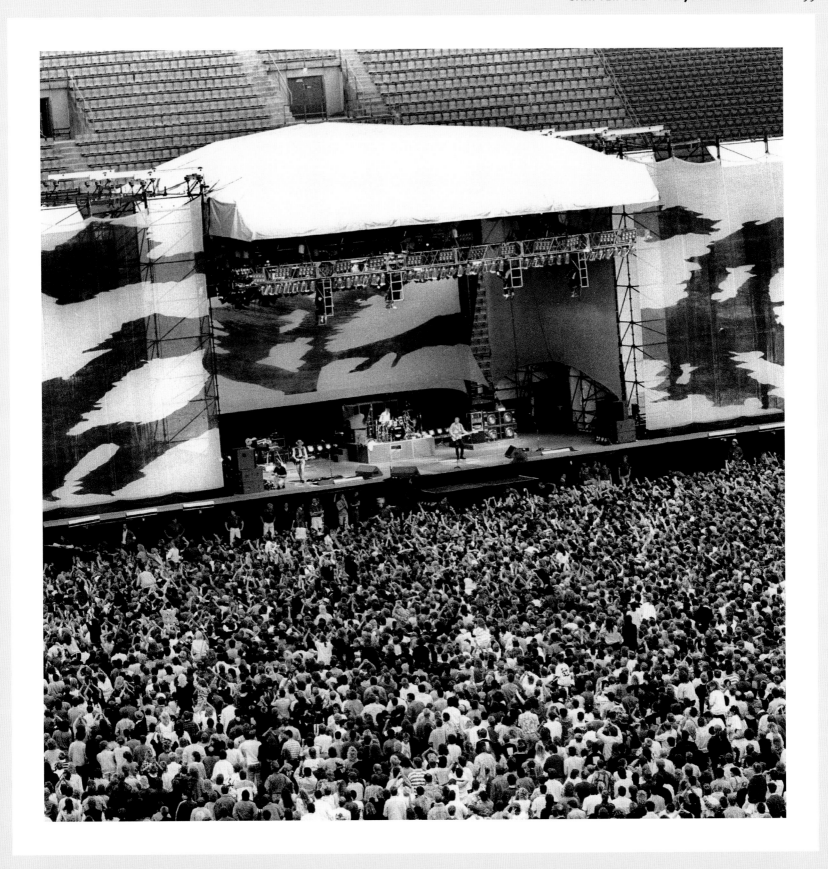

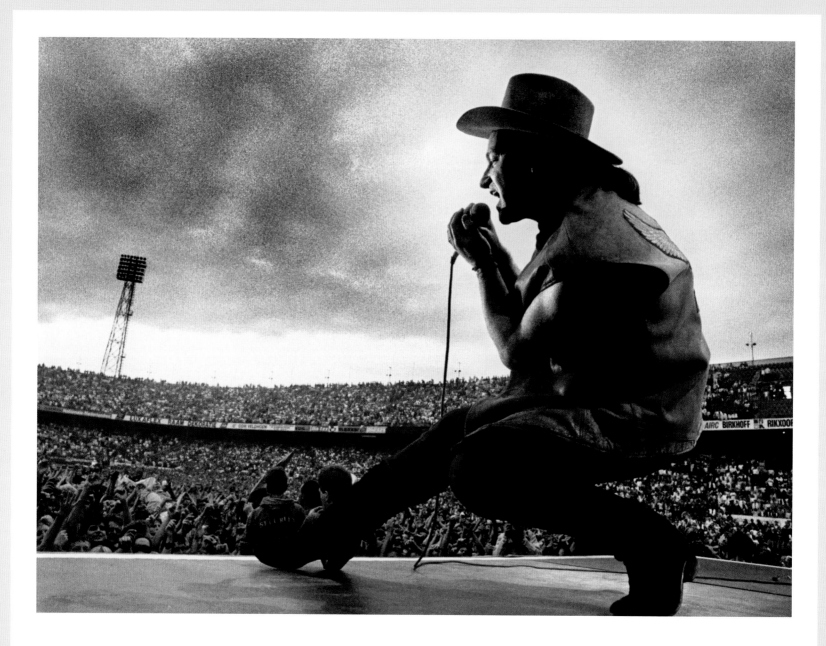

"Rock's Hottest Ticket"

Above: De Kuip Stadium 10 July 1987 – a Bono-eye view of the crowd! Ticket sales in the USA were rapid and they quickly became scarce – helped by *Time* magazine's cover story of U2 on 27 April proclaiming them "Rock's Hottest Ticket". On 30 April the band had their first sell-out US stadium audience but the full houses made it difficult for the whole crowd to see the stage act and the band began to consider video screens.

Opposite: Atmospheric picture of Larry Mullen playing at the Coliseum, New Haven, USA, in September 1987. The Joshua Tree tour fed a raging fire of enthusiasm worldwide for the current album and the band's back catalogue alike: barely two months after release, *The Joshua Tree* was certified multi-Platinum in the US with sales exceeding 2 million. Chris Blackwell's patience and Island's investment achieved their goals exceeding all expectations. Wrapping up the first leg of the tour on 16 May the band heads back to Dublin to prepare for the European leg and to discuss ideas for their next album.

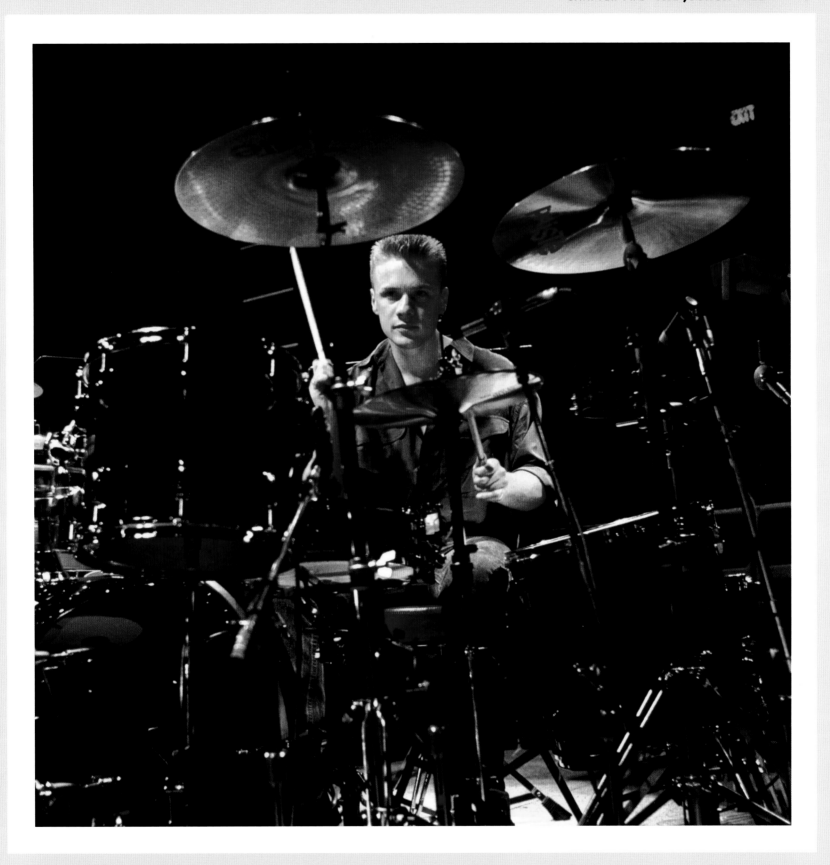

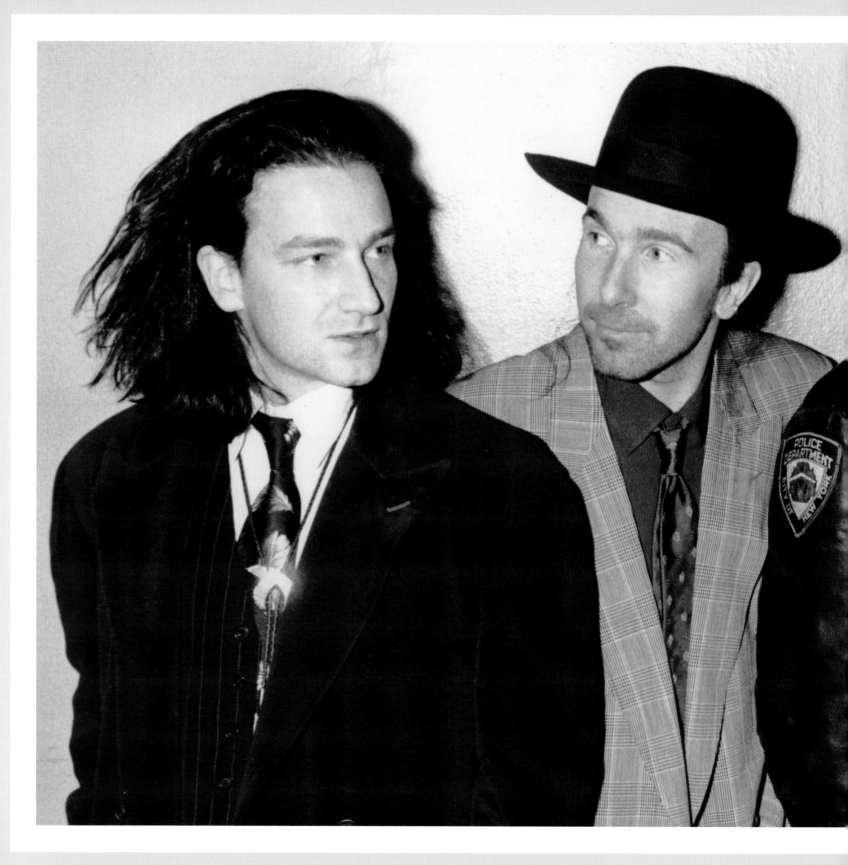

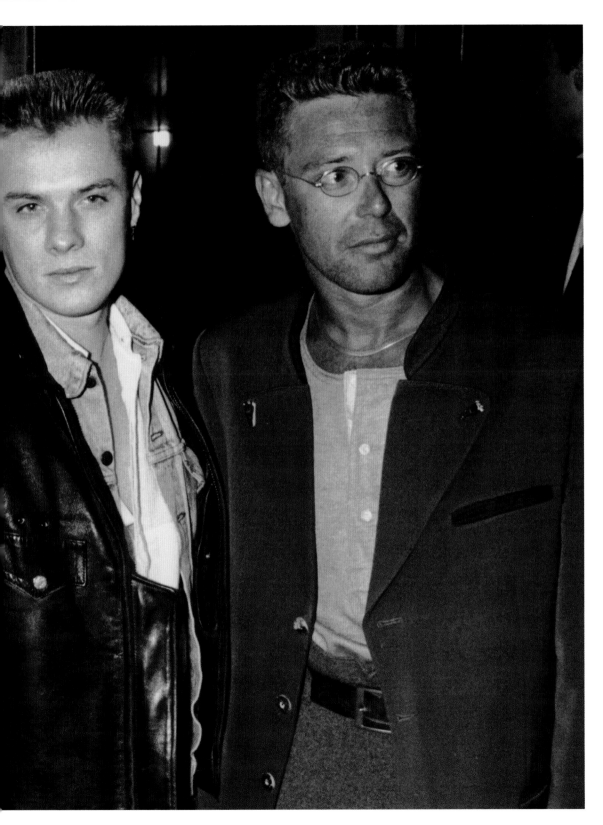

Brits

Opposite: U2 at the 1988 Brit Awards on 8 February where they won the award for Best International Band. Bono quipped that he's only there to see The Who pick up their award.

The Joshua Tree tour continued in Europe setting out from Rome at the end of May. It proved even more successful than the US leg in terms of audience numbers with the largest of the year attending on 15 July when 115,000 watched U2's Spanish debut.

Amidst this huge success came bad news that Island Records had financial difficulties brought on by investment in movie projects that, after initial success, had failed to make money; Island was unable to meet its royalty payments to U2 for the huge sales of *The Joshua Tree* and the massive increase in back catalogue sales. McGuinness negotiated a stake in Island Records against the $5m unpaid royalties: a move that would later pay off very handsomely!

In September the band was back in New York setting out on the second US leg of the tour; their next album was taking shape and earlier in the month, film-maker Phil Joanou had been commissioned to follow the band with a camera crew as part of their next artistic experiment.

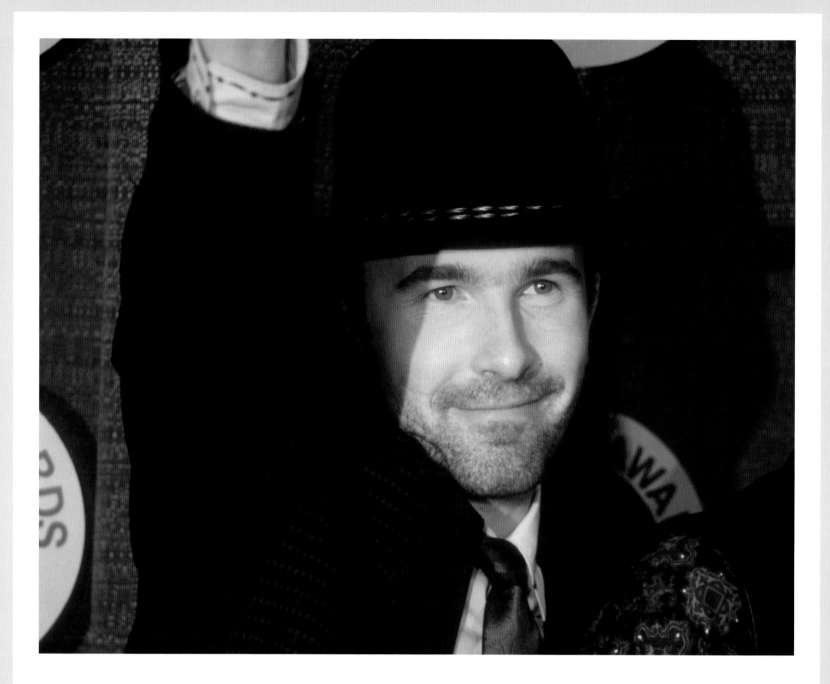

Double Grammy

Above and opposite: At the Grammys. On 2 March 1988 U2 collected their first two Grammy Awards – for Best Rock Performance by a Group or Duo for "I Still Haven't Found What I'm Looking For" and Album of the Year for *The Joshua Tree*.

On 28 September U2 performed the first of two dates at Madison Square Garden. Included in the line-up was the New Voices of Freedom gospel choir who had come up with a gospel version of "I Still Haven't

Found What I'm Looking For"; two days earlier U2 had visited the choir's home church in Harlem for rehearsals. Joanou and the film crew were in attendance and as well as the rehearsal they captured the band's experiences while moving around Harlem.

At the end of November U2 visited Elvis Presley's Graceland home and whilst in Memphis planned to record in the King's old outfit "Sun Studio" recently brought out of retirement after 20 years.

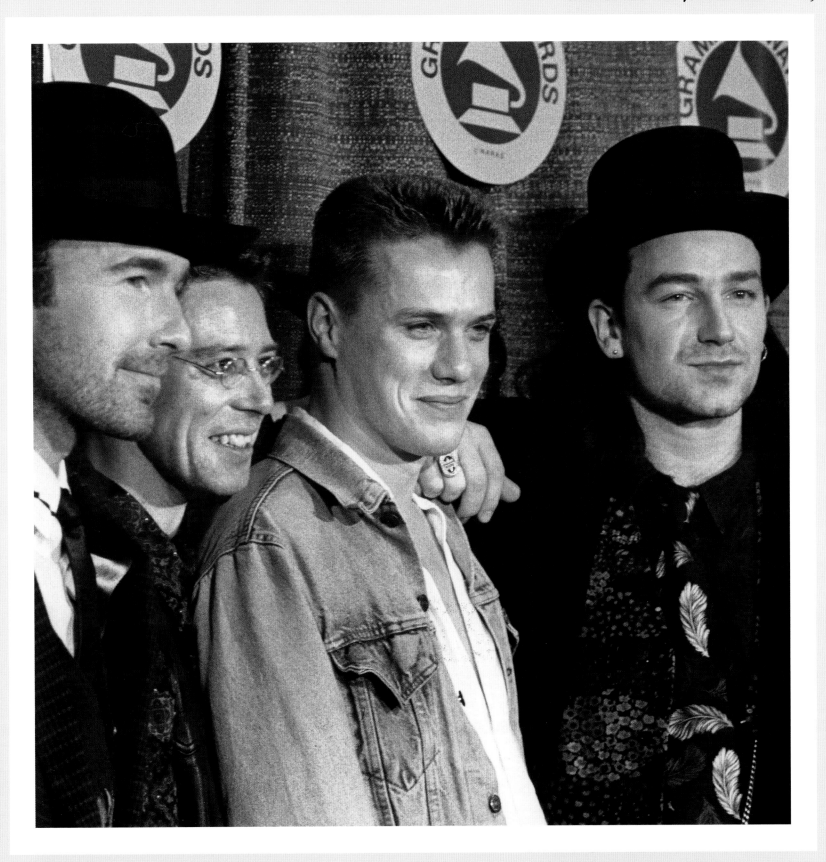

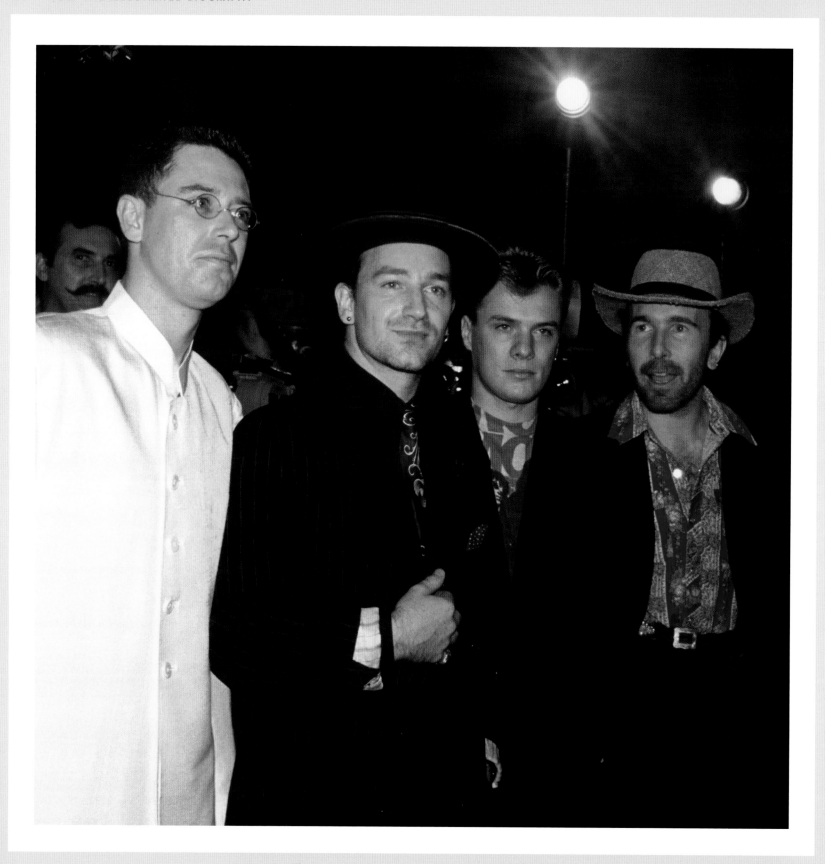

Boys on film

Opposite and right: U2 attend the Los Angeles premiere of their movie *Rattle and Hum* on 3 November 1988.

The filming of what will be *Rattle and Hum* – a full-length feature film as well as their next album – became a major driver in the planning of the rest of the Joshua Tree tour with the 19–20 December performances at Sun Devil Stadium, Tempe, a central event that involved meticulous planning. The first of the two gigs was something of a nightmare with rain falling and Bono distracted by the unusual set-up required for filming. Fortunately the fans only paid $5 each for a ticket and were warned about the disruption. The second gig went well, providing most of the colour footage for the movie. The great blues guitarist B.B. King was also on the bill for the Sun Devil Stadium shows.

Many high points of the tour were captured by Joanou, including the passionate performance given on 8 November when U2 heard of the IRA bombing in Enniskillen, Northern Ireland, which killed 11 people on Remembrance Sunday. Two central ambitions of the movie were to capture U2's live performances and to connect with the roots of folk and blues in America – essentially a response to Bob Dylan's challenge many months before.

The Joshua Tree tour ended on 21 December and the band returned to Dublin for a break. *The Joshua Tree* was certified multi-Platinum with US sales exceeding 4 million and was listed number three in *Rolling Stone*'s list of Top Albums of 1987.

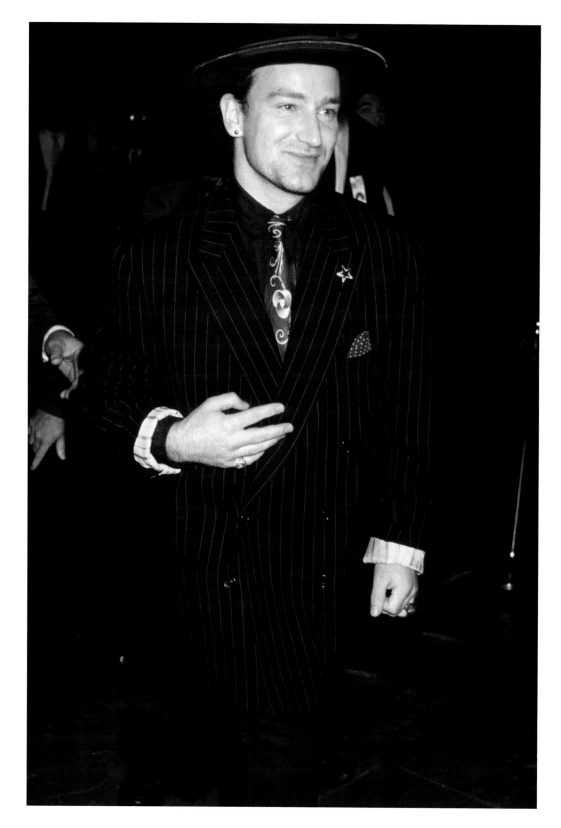

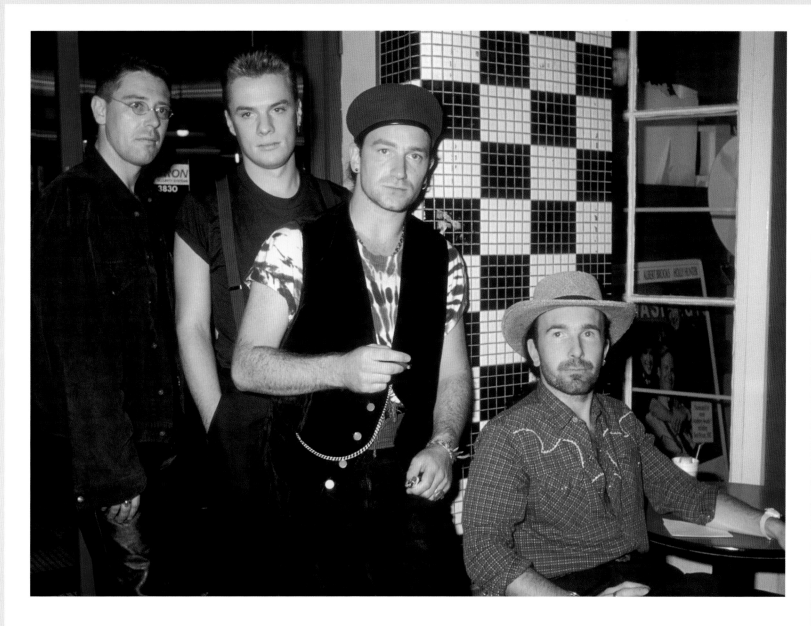

Rattle and Hum

Above: U2 photographed on the set during the filming of the music video for "Desire", Hollywood, California, August 1988.

In February 1988 the band re-located to Los Angeles to work on the *Rattle and Hum* movie and album; to do this they had to postpone a planned Australia and New Zealand Tour. However, in March they went ahead with the release of the single "One Tree Hill" in that market, where it quickly went to number one locally. At the *Rolling Stone* 1987 Music Awards in February U2 swept the board with each band member winning best musician as well as the group winning many other categories.

Opposite: Bono and Ali at Langan's Brasserie in Mayfair, London, 2 February 1989. A closer look reveals that Ali is pregnant; she will give birth to their first child, daughter Jordan, on 10 May (sharing Bono's birthday) and just in time for Ali to take her finals for a bachelor's degree in Sociology and Political Science.

The life of the band was not easy on relationships: moving to LA involved The Edge in transporting Aislinn and his two young daughters to a family house in the Hollywood Hills, while the rest of the band rented a large house in Bel Air. With the weight of work and another daughter on the way, Edge felt guilty that his family were not getting enough attention.

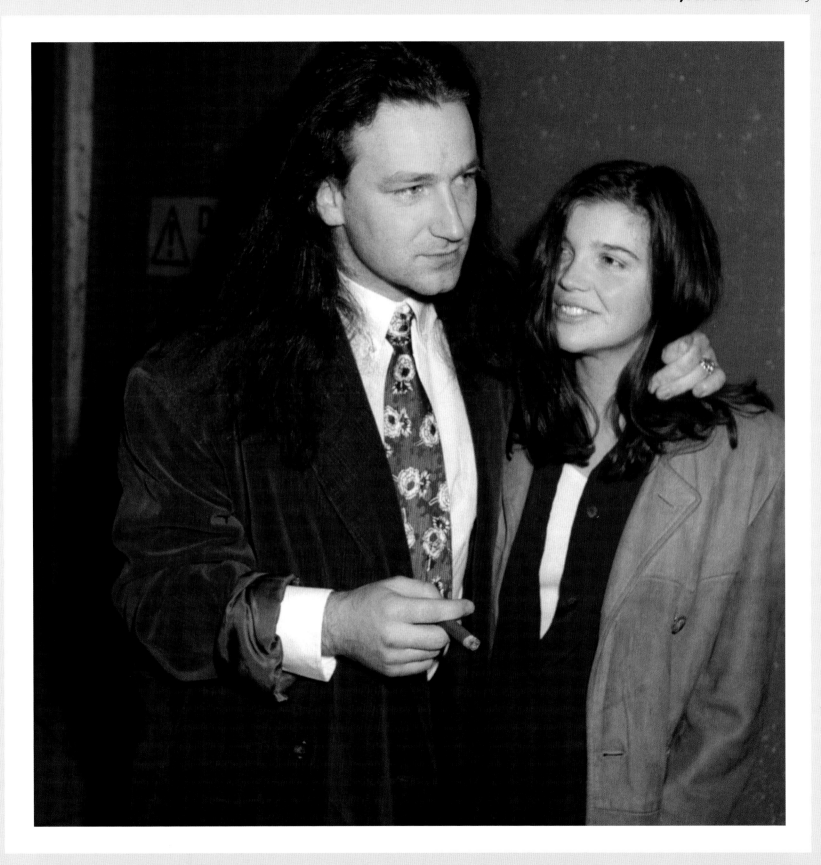

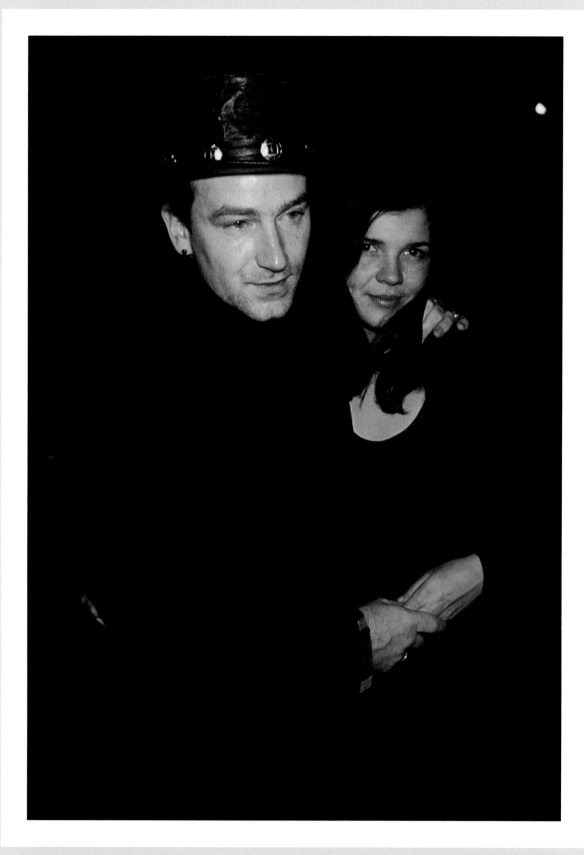

First UK No. 1 single

Left: Bono and Ali photographed at the Mayfair Hotel in London, 9 August 1989. During this visit to London, Edge and Bono agreed to write new music for an updated version of *A Clockwork Orange*, commissioned by the Royal Shakespeare Company.

Opposite: The Edge on stage during the Lovetown Tour which set out from Perth, Australia, on 21 September 1989.

Much of 1988 was given up to the many commitments of completing the *Rattle and Hum* album and movie. The album was released on 10 October, its 17 tracks intended to be a homage to musical greats of the past. Some of the press interpreted this as hubris but the fans didn't see it that way, buying three million copies in the first month, taking it to number one in US, Canada, UK, Australia and numerous other countries. The album had been successfully trailed by the single "Desire" released three weeks earlier which gave U2 their first number 1 in the UK singles chart.

A couple of weeks after the album release the movie premiered in Dublin on 27 October followed swiftly by the US premiere in New York on 1 November. The band attended the LA premiere on 3 November. *Rattle and Hum* grossed $3.8 million in box offices across the US in the first weekend: despite mixed reviews the movie was a success – good news for U2 who had run out of production budget halfway through filming, obliging them to make a deal with Paramount Pictures.

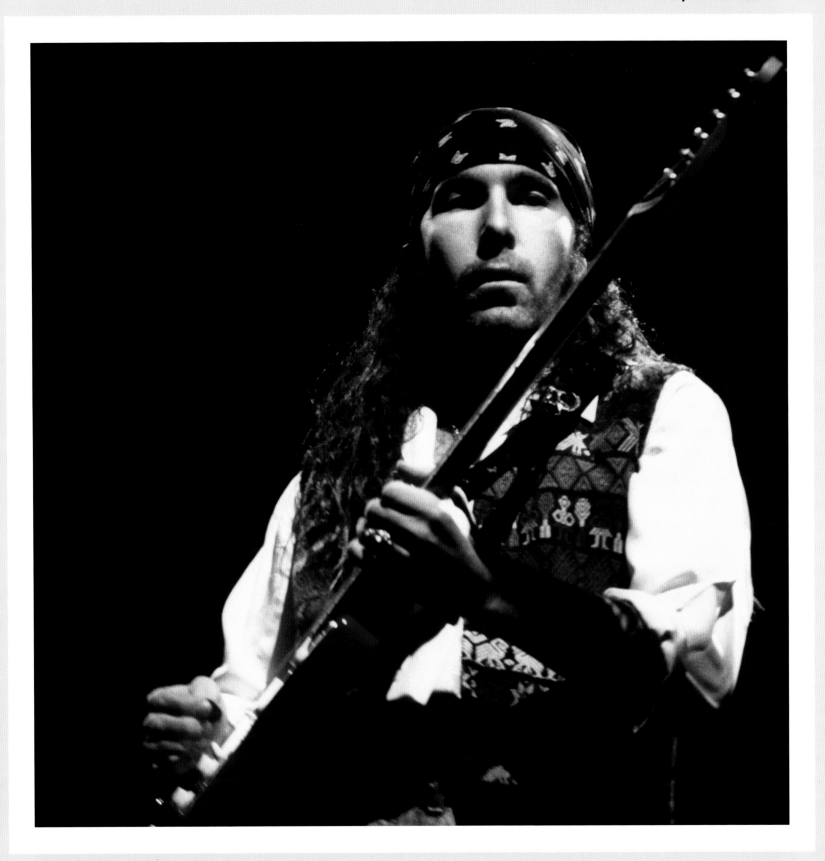

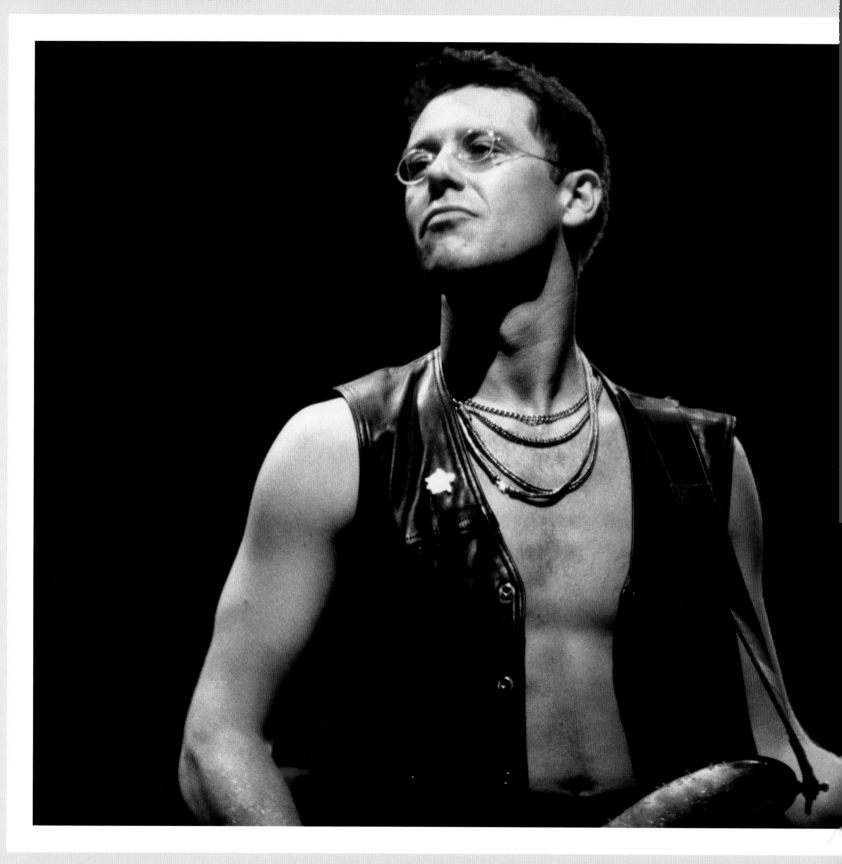

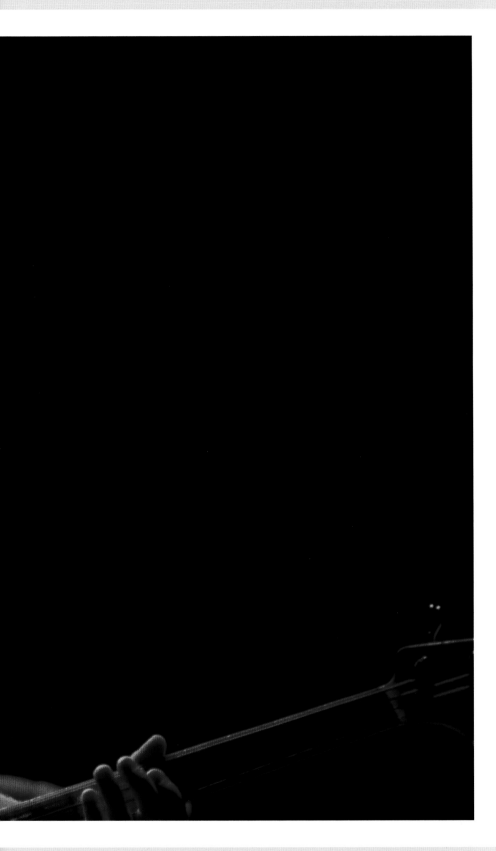

Lovetown tour

Left: Adam photographed during the the Australian leg of the Lovetown tour, September 1989.

The year began well for the band with two more Grammys in February for Best Rock Performance by Duo or Group with Vocal for their single "Desire" and Best Performance Music Video for "Where the Streets Have No Name". Edge gave active support to Greenpeace in promoting the fundraiser album, *Rainbow Warriors* which, in addition to U2, brought together a number of artists including Annie Lennox and Peter Gabriel.

However, in June and then again in August, Adam found himself on the wrong side of the law, arrested once again for drunken driving and then for possession of marijuana with intent to supply. In September a sympathetic judge let him off the intent to supply charge in exchange for a plea of guilty and a substantial donation to charity. A different result could have made it impossible for Adam to tour America in future.

The Lovetown tour drew near and U2 travelled to Sydney, Australia, to begin their preparation for the first leg. B.B. King toured with U2 during the Lovetown tour, performing the keynote song with the band "When Love Comes to Town". While in Sydney on 16 September, King turned 64 and the band threw him a surprise birthday party on board a luxury yacht in Sydney Harbour. B.B. King recollects, "..Bono sang a song he wrote for me, 'Happy birthday B.B. King,' and it was so good, I cried. I couldn't hold back the tears. We came back at sunset, and I thought it was all over. We'd had such a wonderful time. Then I saw one of the greatest fireworks displays I've ever seen, and it was in my honour, so I cried some more."

The tour set off around Australia and New Zealand from Perth on 21 September, wrapping up on 19 November in Sydney after performing three gigs that had been re-scheduled because of Bono's laryngitis. Flying on to Japan they continued the tour on 20 November with six shows in Japan over 10 days.

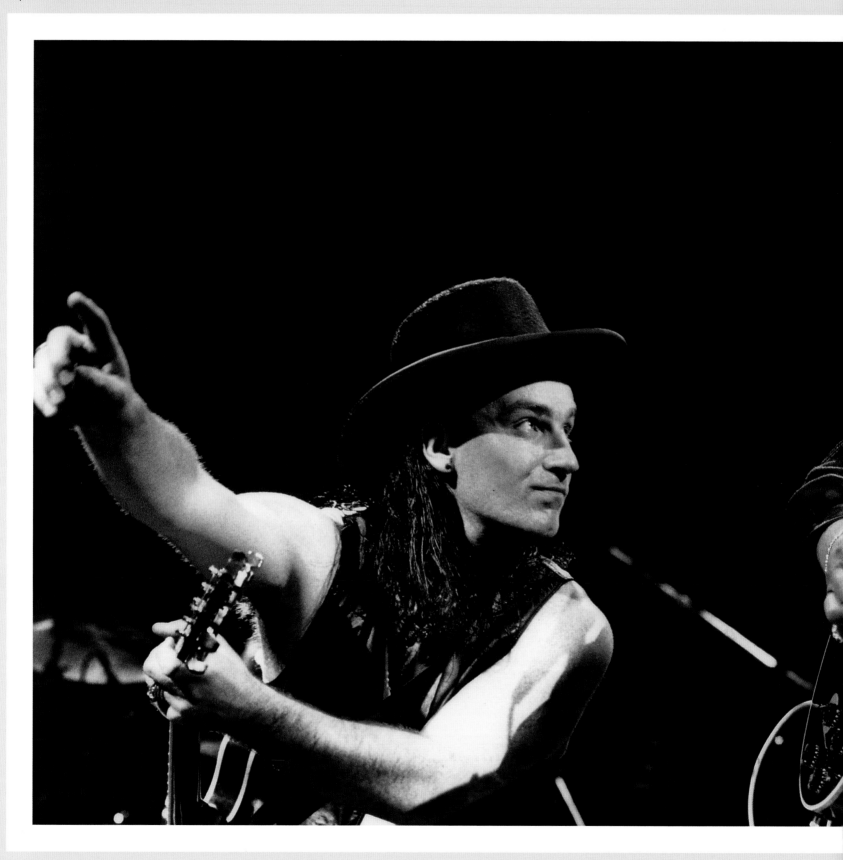

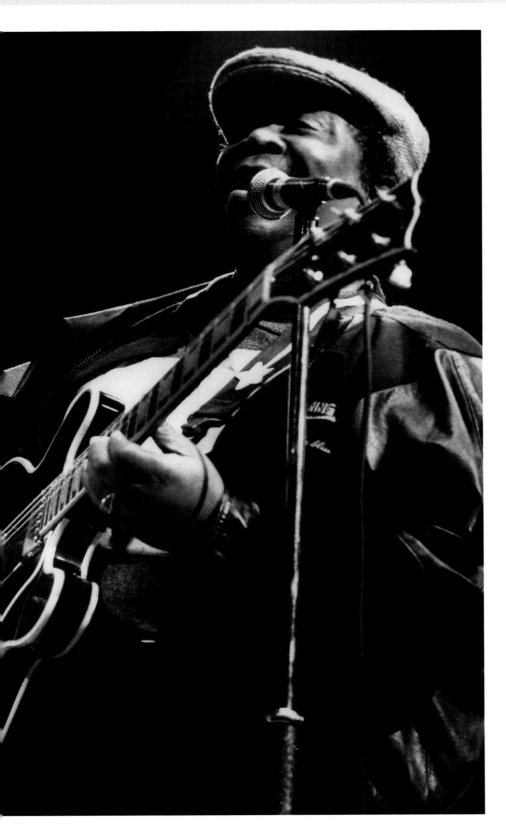

End of the Eighties

Left: B.B. King and Bono duet at Rotterdam's Ahoy centre on 5 January 1990 during the Lovetown tour. The Lovetown tour continued in Europe during December 1989 with two dates in Paris, Bono's voice steadily deteriorated through subsequent German and Dutch shows; this culminated in two cancelled shows in Amsterdam after the singer was told to rest his voice or risk permanent damage.

Four long-awaited shows took place on 26, 27, 30 and 31 December at The Point, Dublin – the band's first indoor shows in their home city since 1982. The venue held only 5,000 – for which they received much criticism – and so even four nights were insufficient to meet the demand from local fans. The fourth concert featured a midnight countdown to 1990 and was broadcast across Europe live on BBC Radio. Paul McGuinness wanted the concert to be heard particularly in the Eastern European countries that were gradually shrugging off the yoke of Communism.

At the Dublin concert on 30 December, Bono intimated that the band was looking for change and needed to go away to "dream it all up again". Bono's voice was weak and the band were weary from touring; the impetus of *The Joshua Tree* and *Rattle and Hum* had now ground to a halt and U2 would turn 1990 into something of a sabbatical. Nonetheless Bono and Edge's commitment to the Royal Shakespeare Company required them to finish the sound track for *Clockwork Orange*, disrupted by the rescheduled Amsterdam dates in January.

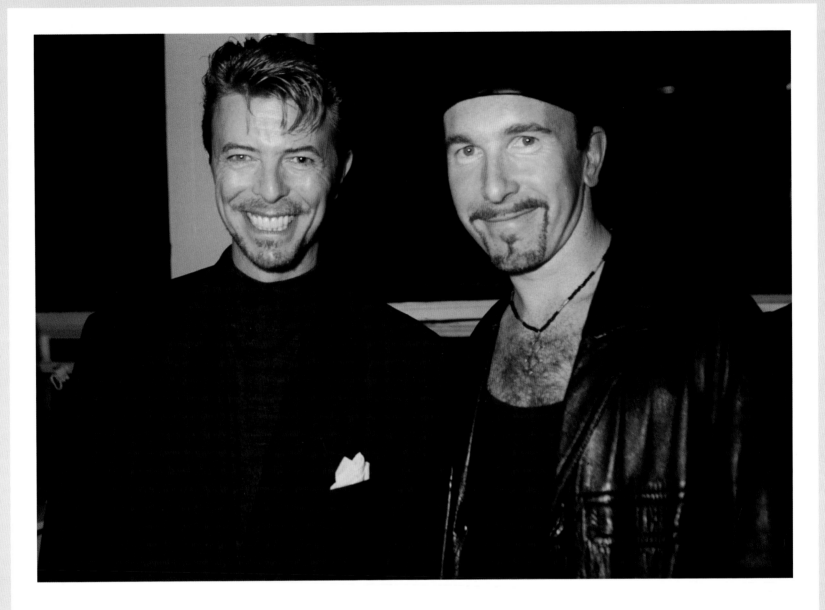

Cutting down the Joshua Tree

Above: The Edge with David Bowie in London 1990.

As U2 set about "dreaming it all up again" they looked towards the experimental music and performance icon, David Bowie. In June 1990 Bono and Adam attended a Bowie show in Cleveland, Ohio, during the legendary Sound and Vision tour; Bono joined Bowie on stage to sing Them's anthemic "Gloria". Bowie's stage show used new technology and video screens and U2 were considering using both as part of their re-invention. The interaction with Bowie continued when he performed in Dublin in August: Bono hosted a dinner with other music industry people in attendance. Around this time, the band were piloting early material for the next album in Dublin's STS Studio.

Opposite: An unusually impassive Bono.

In early October U2 assembled at the Hansa Tonstudio in Berlin where Bowie had found the inspiration for his *Low* and *Heroes* albums during the seventies. Brian Eno and Daniel Lanois were in the producers' chairs once more but quickly found themselves at sea as Bono and Edge pushed the creative envelope in new directions driven by their exploration of electronic and heavy metal music over the preceding months; the band was near to breaking point. In December Edge led a jam session that led to the song "One" – finally a breakthrough that enabled the band to resume as a functional unit. Putting Berlin behind them they returned to Ireland to talk things through.

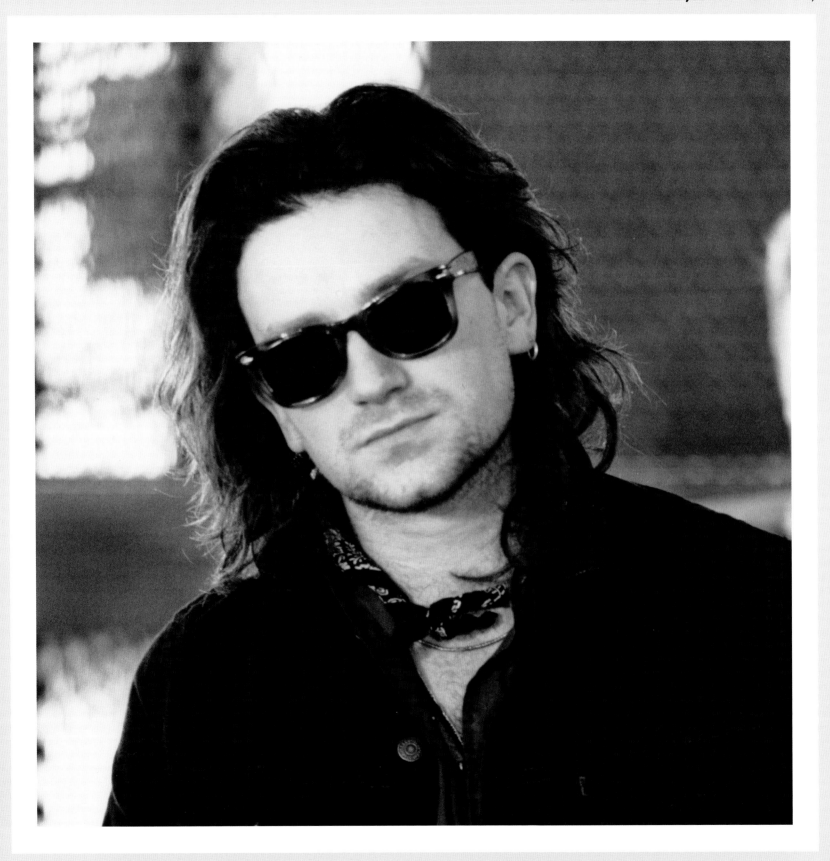

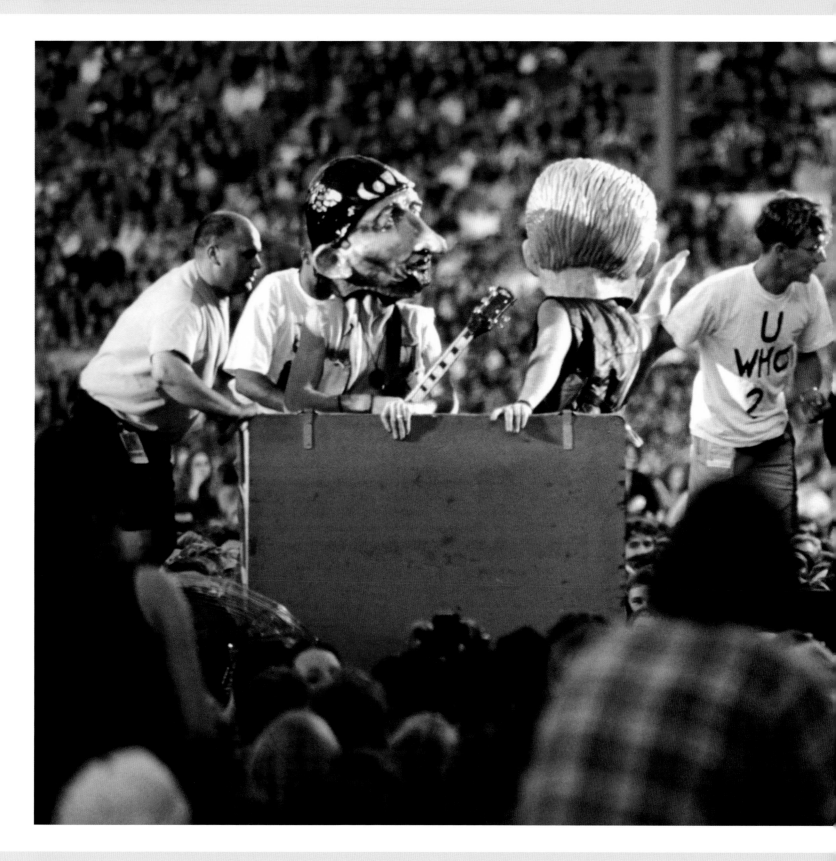

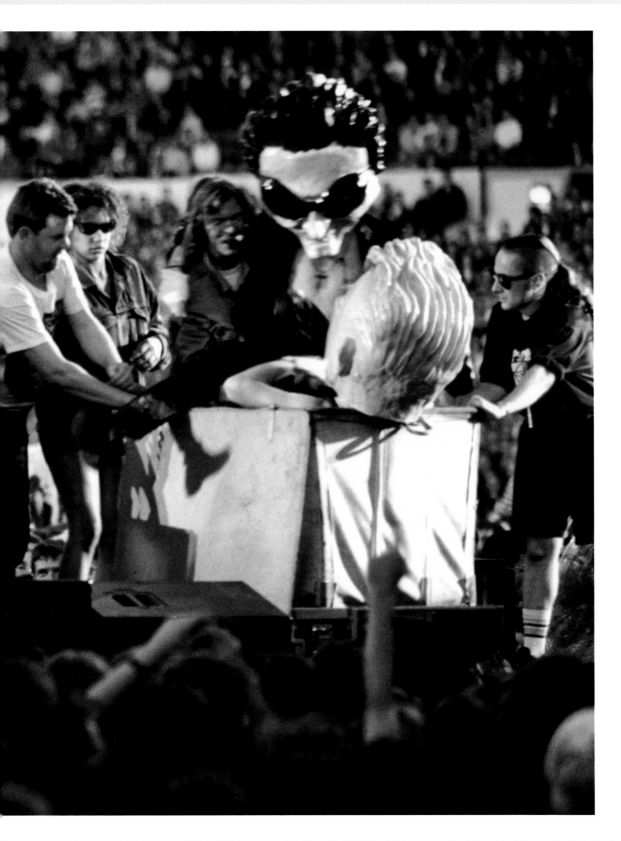

Thinking out of the box

Left: Puppets of the band are unpacked from transit cases as the audience watches at London's Earls Court on 31 May 1992 during the ZooTV tour During their stay in Berlin U2 lived through some turbulence: arriving in the city in 1990 they found the city celebrating Liberation Day with crowds moving to and from the areas previously separated by the Wall. With their equipment still in Hansa Tonstudio they returned to Berlin in January 1991 to continue recording. They witnessed daily reporting of the Gulf War, which broke out on 16 January: Bono found it hard to believe he could be watching the intense conflict unfold from the safety and comfort of his own armchair.

In February 1991 the band sought inspiration for their new image in the Canary Islands. Anton Corbijn accompanied them everywhere. It was carnival time in Santa Cruz and the opportunity to wear masks and dress in costume encouraged a theatrical vibe. Willie Williams was invited out to share the spectacle and help develop the concept of ZooTV which would be the theme of the next tour in support of the new album *Achtung Baby*. Williams recognized strange things were afoot when a Trabant, the archetypal East German car, was shipped in; after witnessing the drama of Bowie's Sound and Vision tour, U2 expected Williams to help them create the greatest live show ever.

Back in Dublin in March the album was making progress but not all was good in the band's personal life: at Easter time Edge and Aislinn separated.

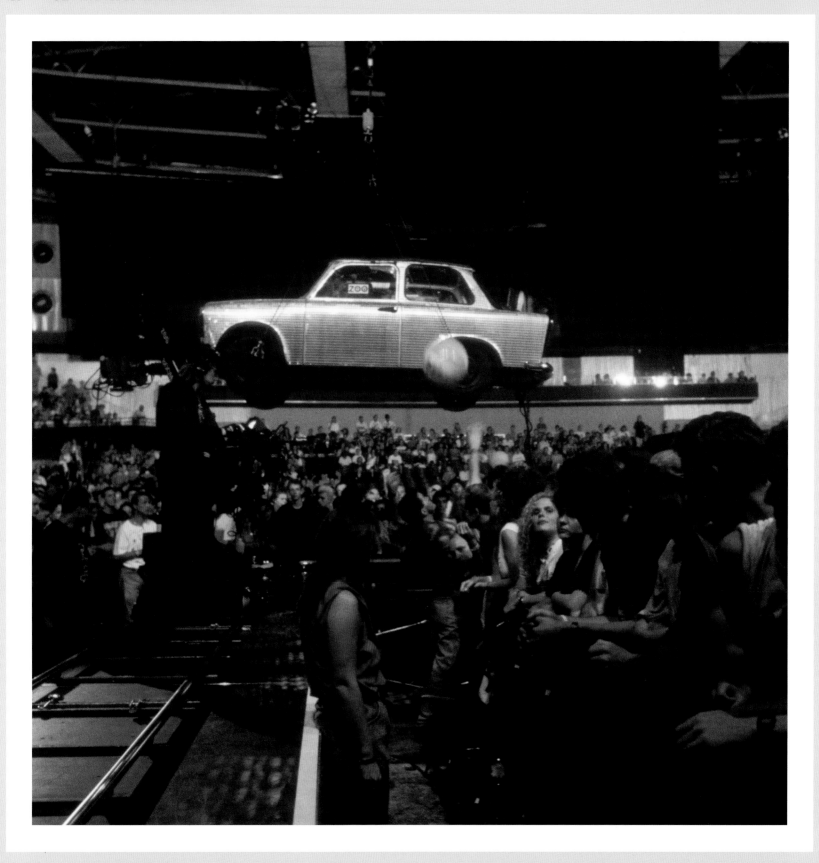

ZooTV

Opposite: Ahoy, Rotterdam, 15 June 1992; a
Trabant hangs above the audience, part of the
light show of the ZooTV tour. A video camera
is mounted on a rig with rails for interactive
filming.

The album *Achtung Baby* was completed right
up against the wire as the band worked through
the night for The Edge to take the masters to
New York in person on 22 September. A month
later the first single release from the album, "The
Fly", was in stores with the news that it would
only be on sale for three weeks in order for the
band to get two singles and their new album
released before Christmas.

The album came out worldwide on 18/19
November and spent 30 weeks on *Billboard's*
Top 20 Albums Chart. There was general
agreement that Bono's promise to "dream it
up all over again" had been fulfilled. Strong
sales were important since this was the
first album under Island's new ownership
by Polygram who bought the label for $300
million the previous year, instantly turning U2's
investment into $30m.

Right: Adam and Naomi Campbell during
London Fashion Week 18 October 1993. After
extensive rehearsals the ZooTV tour set out
from Lakeland Civic Center, Florida, on
29 February 1992. It was on the third leg of the
tour in August that Adam met the supermodel
for the first time. Although they didn't hit it off
at this time, a later encounter just before the
Grammys in February 1993 sparked their on-off
romance.

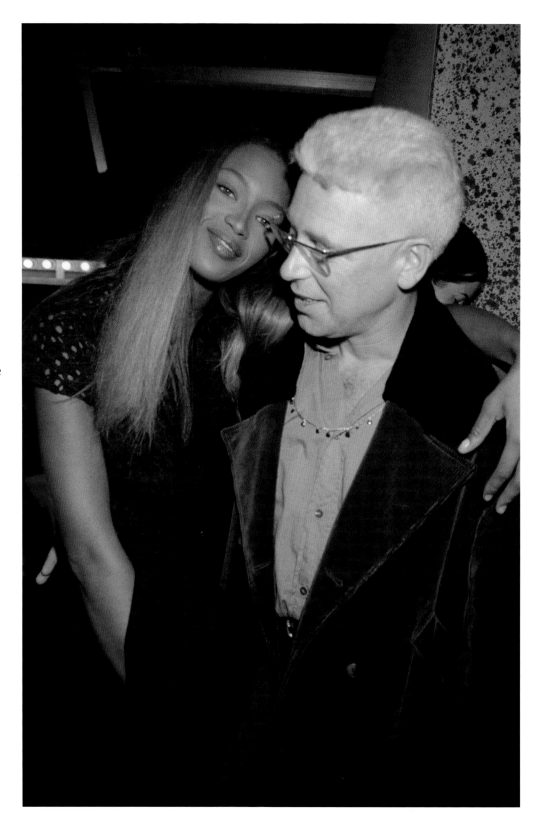

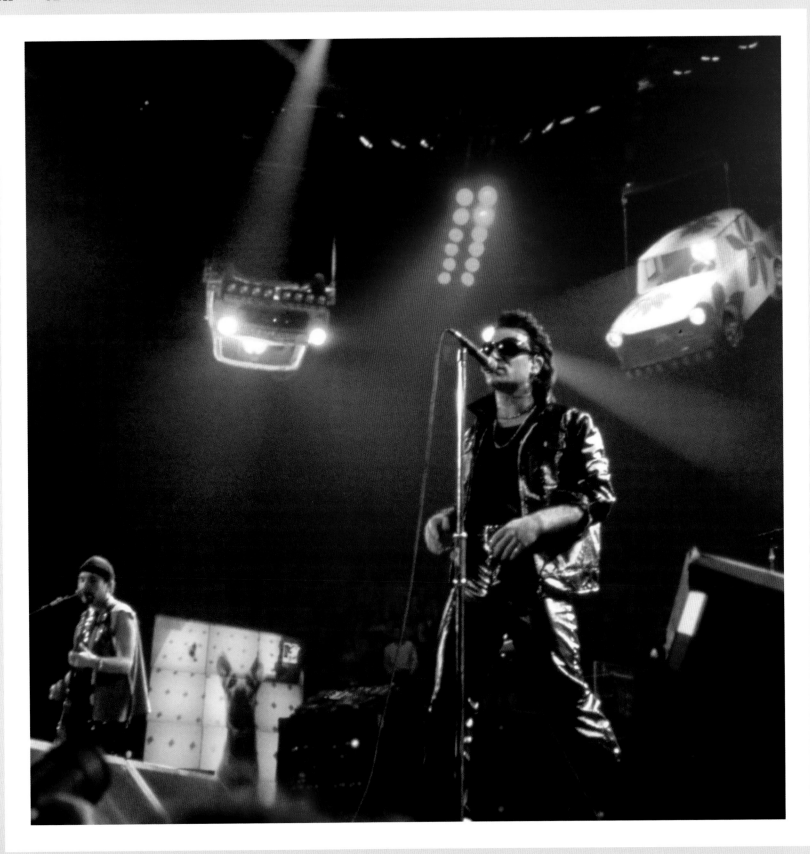

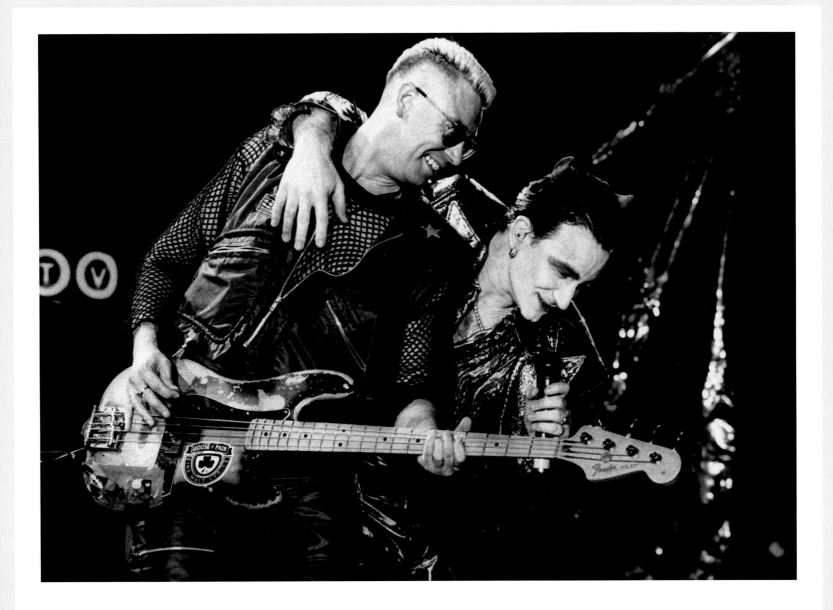

Sensory overload

Opposite: U2 on stage are surrounded by the audience and the different elements of their set during the ZooTV tour in 1992. Trabants hang in the air and a large screen mixes live video transmission with recorded footage. Ticket sales for the ZooTV were brisk with US venues selling out quickly – the first gig sold out in 4 minutes. The band insisted that the tickets for this US tour should be sold by phone to avoid ticket touts purchasing to re-sell at heavily inflated prices; this caused chaos to some local phone networks.

Above: Adam and Bono on stage at Feyenoord Stadium, Rotterdam, 10 May 1993. Bono is in his stage guise of Mr MacPhisto – a reincarnation of Mirrorball Man who had sported a silver suit and is interested in nothing except ratings. The new character is in gold lamé and horns sprout from his head.

The multimedia circus that greeted the fans at the concerts blew them away but left many confused as they had to process total media overload in what Bono described as a touring TV station: breaking news was piped in live from the war-torn Balkans, Bono made live phone calls on stage and pre-recorded confessions by members of the audience were screened while slogans and catchwords flashed on. This was an all-out bid to capture the MTV generation.

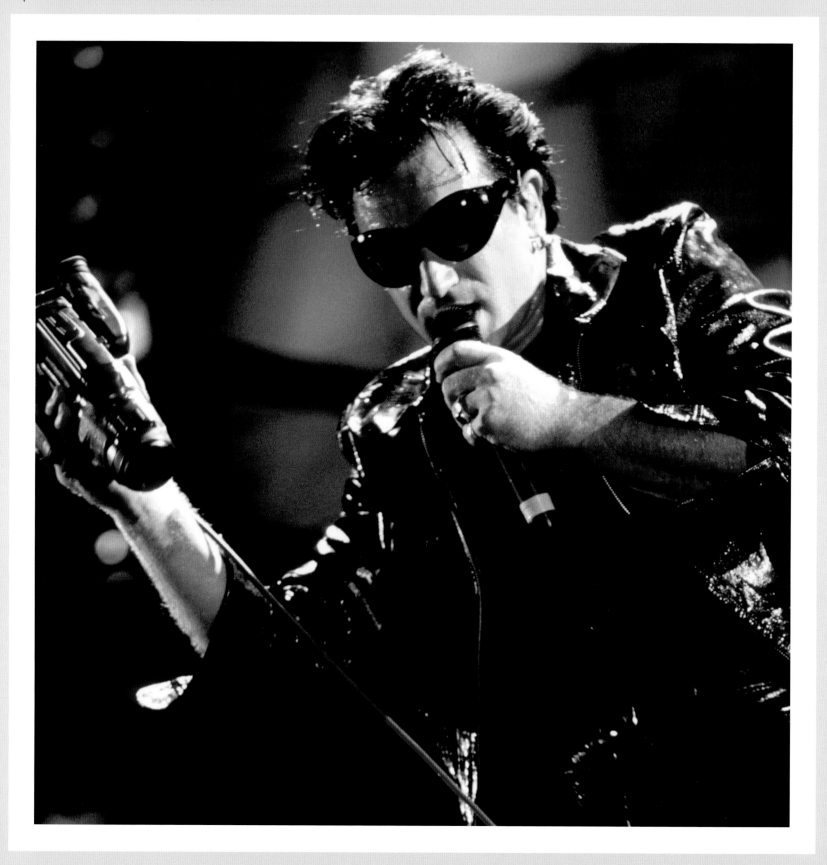

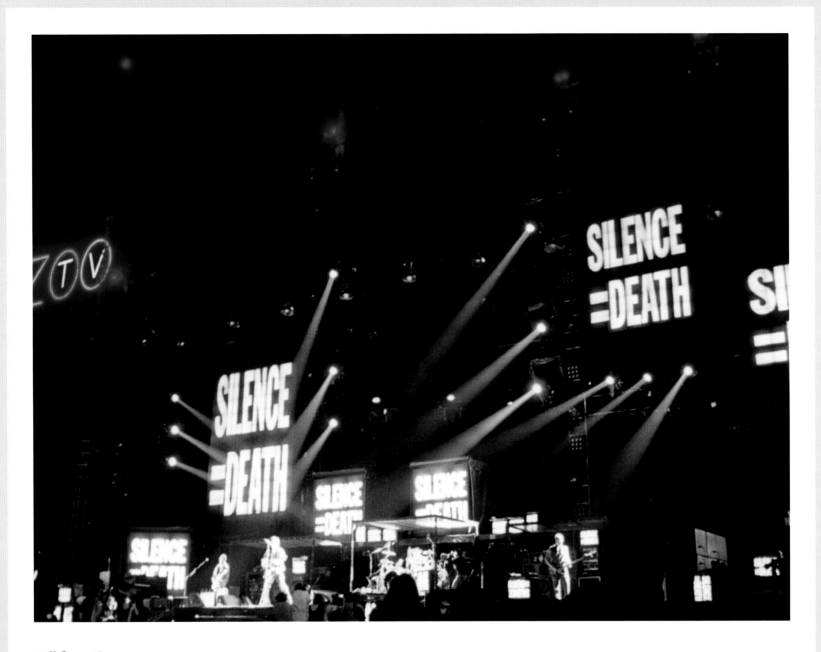

Call for action

Opposite: Bono sings on stage at Wembley Arena, 11 August 1993, during the Zooropa tour. He holds a video camera connected to the main console to project different views of the stage onto video screens.

The European leg of the ZooTV began in early May 1992 and at the end of the month at Earls Court, London, the onstage screens called for protest action against a second nuclear installation at Sellafield in north-west England. U2 joined in with the Greenpeace personnel on 20 June arriving at the nuclear power station by inflatable dinghy and clad in radiation protection clothing.

Above: The stage at Wembley Arena. In August 1992 U2 launched the Outside Broadcast version of the ZooTV show in New Jersey. A young belly dancer called Morleigh Steinberg entered the picture to perform during "Mysterious Ways" and before long caught the eye of The Edge. It was election year in the USA and during September the band crossed the path of presidential candidate Bill Clinton and got on well with him in a personal meeting in their Chicago hotel. A confident Clinton invited them to play at his inauguration the following January.

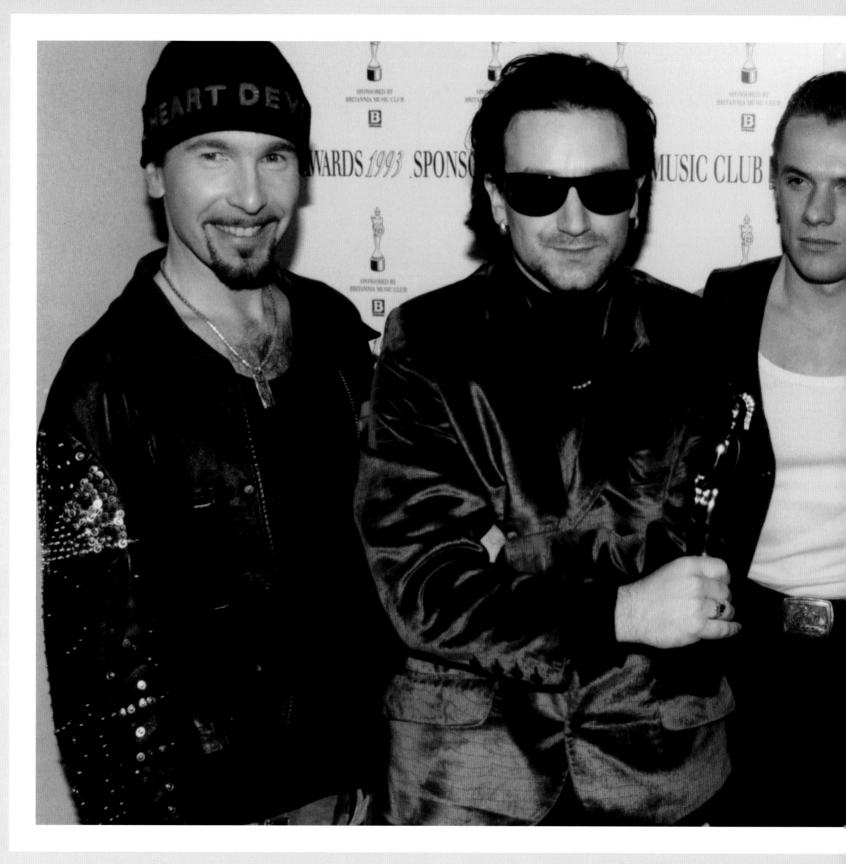

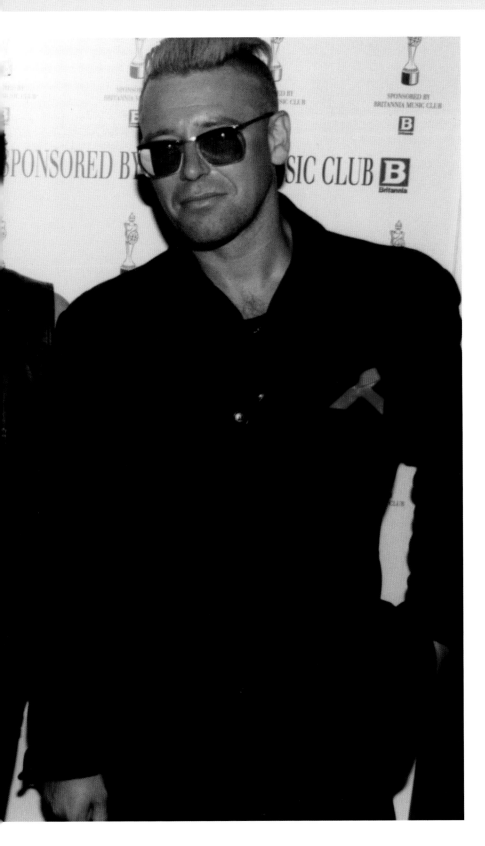

Left: U2 pose for photographers at the Brit Awards on 17 February 1993; Bono holds their award figurine – for Most Successful Live Band.

During February 1993 the band used their break from touring to discuss plans for a new album. Their idea was that they should make an EP to be called *Zooropa* but with time this progressed into a full-length album, a lot of which they recorded in commuter trips to Dublin from wherever they happened to be performing in Europe. The album was released worldwide on 5/6 July 1993. Like the Zooropa and ZooTV tours, the new album appeared to many as not much more than a segue extending the themes of *Achtung Baby* overlaid with some socio-political comment about the European Union. For U2 this was not an issue as they were now positioning themselves as performance artists rather than conventional rock musicians. It wouldn't be fair to say this was hubris: the band's outspoken ideas on things going on in the world drew attention to the awful conflict in the Balkans and in July they arranged a live hookup on stage with film-maker Bill Carter broadcasting from Sarajevo.

Sometimes the band's engagement with social issues was highly effective – as at Wembley when Bono tried to telephone the author Salman Rushdie, in hiding because of a *fatwah* against him. Not only did Rushdie answer the call he actually strode on to the stage appearing in front of a delighted crowd of 70,000. The band filled Wembley three more times in August before heading back to Ireland for the two final gigs of the Zooropa tour, at Royal Dublin Showgrounds in front of 35,000 people; they donated the proceeds of the Dublin shows to local charities.

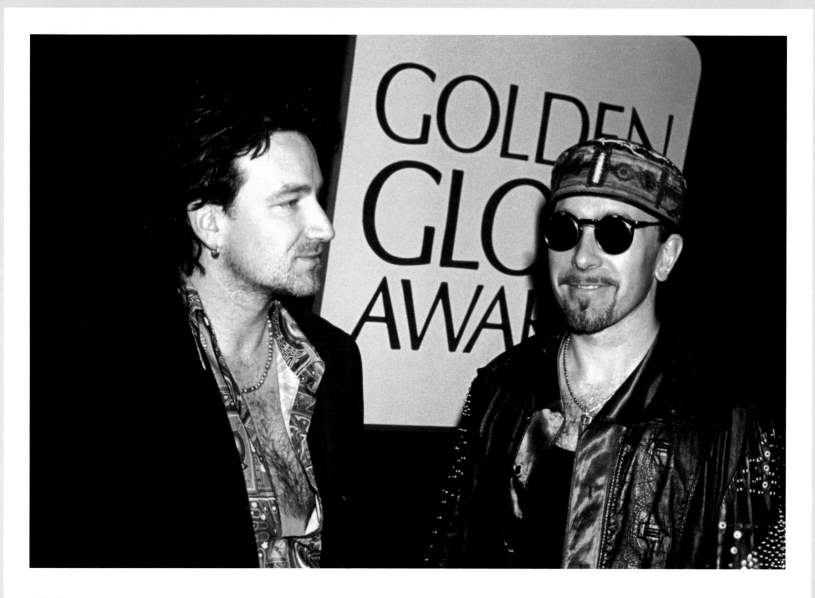

Ol' Blue Eyes

Above: Bono and The Edge at the 51st Golden Globe Awards in Los Angeles, 22 January 1994, where Bono has two nominations for Best Song; but Bruce Springsteen is the winner.

With nearly two years of ZooTV completed, the band is in need of a lengthy break. The intense touring seemed to have a particularly bad effect on Adam whose relationship with Naomi Campbell fizzled out, despite a general understanding that they would marry. Adam also had a notorious alchohol binge during the Australian tour (nicknamed Zoomerang) when on 26 November 1993 he simply didn't show up for the gig in Sydney and his guitar tech Stuart Morgan had to fill in for him.

Opposite: Bono with Frank Sinatra at the Grammys on 1 March 1994. Bono delivered a very elegant introduction to the veteran star who was there to collect a Living Legend award. U2 were recipients of their fifth Grammy, for Best Alternative Album –*Zooropa*. The previous year Bono had recorded a version of "I've Got You Under My Skin" with Sinatra to go out on his album *Duets*; the two got on well together and Bono and The Edge even composed a song for the legendary crooner.

U2 had now achieved the status of rock royalty and were hot news at any awards ceremony; in January Bono had inaugurated Bob Marley posthumously into the Rock and Roll Hall of Fame with his widow, Rita Marley accepting the honour on behalf of her dead husband.

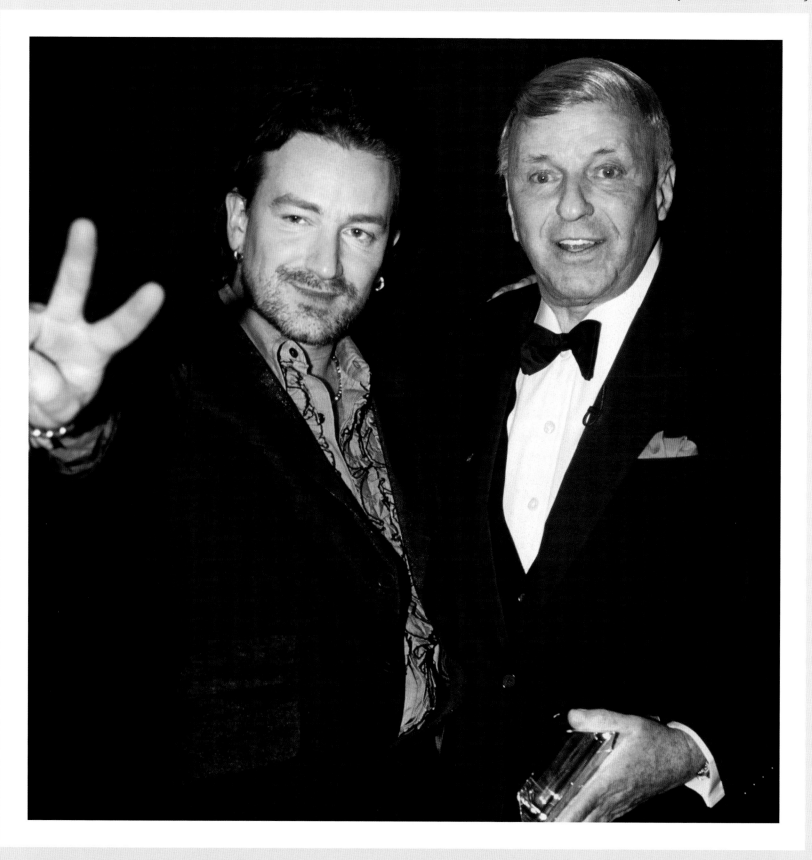

Passengers

Right: U2 photographed at the 1995 MTV Europe Music Awards in Paris, France, 23 November where they took the award for Best Group. At the event they and other artists openly criticized French President Jacques Chirac for recently commissioning undersea nuclear tests in the Pacific Ocean.

1994 was a year of recuperation for the band with individual members doing their own thing but joining up with Brian Eno in November to record an experimental album which the record company decided should be released by a differently named band – Passengers – that included Brian Eno. The album, *Original Soundtracks I*, was released worldwide on 6/7 November 1995. At the other end of the scale, Bono and Edge's title song for the Bond movie, *Goldeneye*, performed by Tina Turner, was released the same day as the Passengers album. One of the reasons Island/Polygram encouraged U2 to release their collaboration album with Eno under another name was the record-breaking renewal of the U2 recording contract in 1993 which paid the band $60m advance against six albums with a 25 per cent royalty. They had to live on those earnings as the tours barely broke even, they were so expensive to mount. ZooTV made no money and had it not been for the $30m of merchandise sold during the tour the band would have been in the red.

In September 1995 Bono, Edge and Eno performed with Luciano Pavarotti at his annual charity show in Modena, singing "Ms Sarajevo" together. Princess Diana was in the audience and attended a formal dinner with the artists after the show.

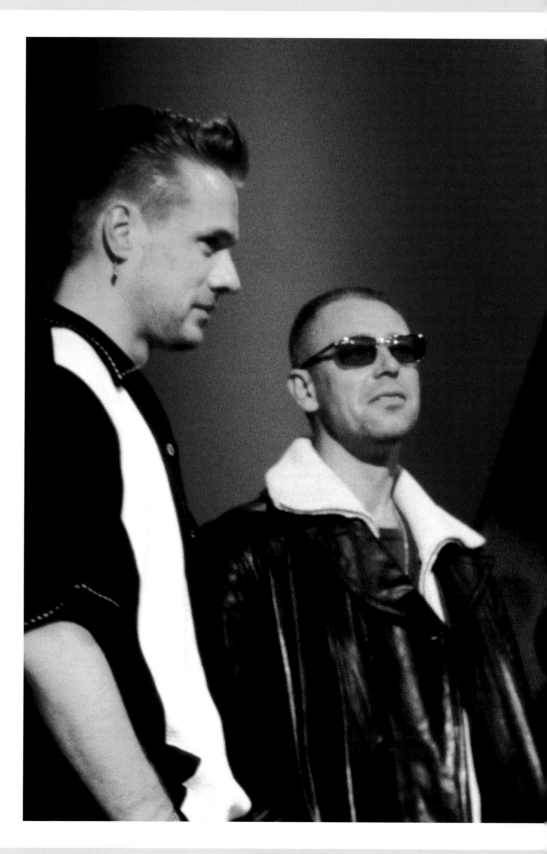

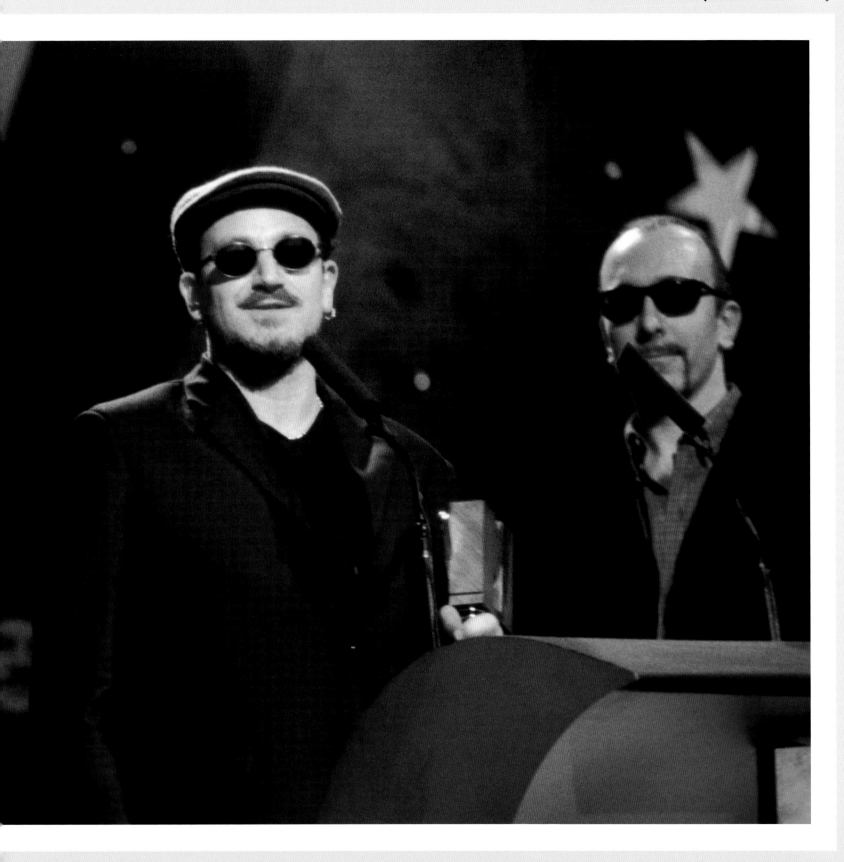

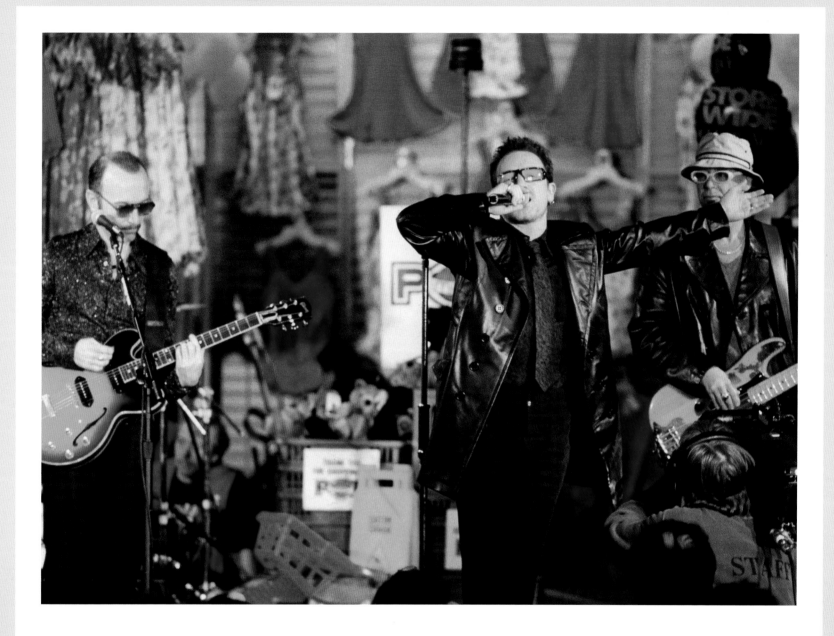

Popmart

Above: U2 launch their PopMart world tour at a Manhattan K-Mart store on 12 February 1997; they announce that the tour will take in 62 cities in 20 countries, playing on a giant stage that combines elements of the supermarket, science fiction and discotheque.

Putting together the next album proved just as difficult as *Achtung Baby* and the band struggled during 1996 to meet Polygram's schedule for the release. Every deadline was missed but eventually, on 20 November 1996, *Pop* went to final mixing and was released worldwide on 3/4 March 1997.

Opposite: The Edge and Adam walk through the audience to the stage at the first date of the PopMart tour at the Sam Boyd Stadium, Las Vegas, on 25 April 1997. Bono is dressed like a boxer in a silk dressing gown, the others look more like Village People!

Pop was well received, going straight to number 1 in the UK album charts but it seemed to lack staying power as the Spice Girls knocked them off the top spot a week later. A degree of uncertainty descended on the band as the tour kicked off, accentuated by the relatively weak sales of the latest single "Staring at the Sun" and voice problems for Bono on the opening night.

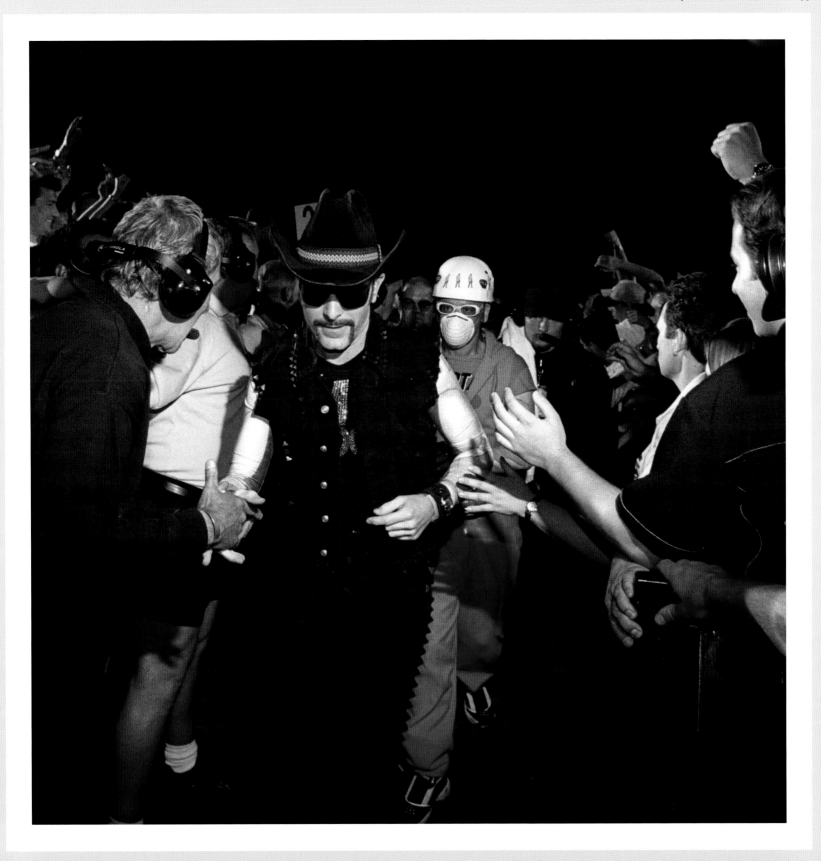

Glitzfest

Right: The jaw-dropping set of PopMart on opening night at the Sam Boyd Stadium, Las Vegas.

It's hardly surprising that the band was nervous: the whole show was a mix of parody and kitsch and heavily dependent on cutting-edge technology; the video screen alone was the largest known to man at the time. Even the means of the band's return to stage for their encore was over the top as they were transported in a giant 40-foot mirrorball lemon. Playing under the golden arch was a clear nod to McDonald's. But if U2 were holding up a mirror to their modern society they also were participating in its overblown symbols; the tour and its massive entourage (over 50 stagehands and riggers alone) was costing a reported $250,000 a day. Las Vegas had provided the band with a symbol on previous occasions; Bono was taken by the idea of Americans working hard all year round just to have money to lose at the machines and tables of Vegas.

For the opening night many celebrities were in the audience including Sigourney Weaver, Robert de Niro, Dennis Hopper and Michael Stipe of R.E.M.

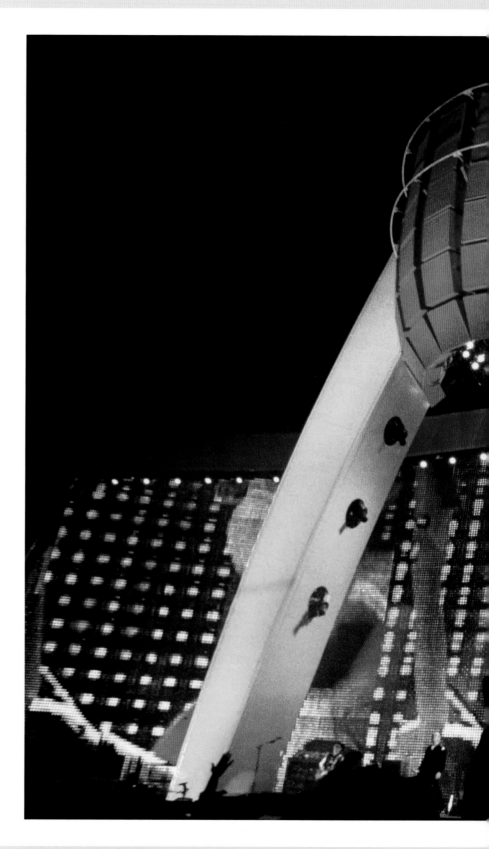

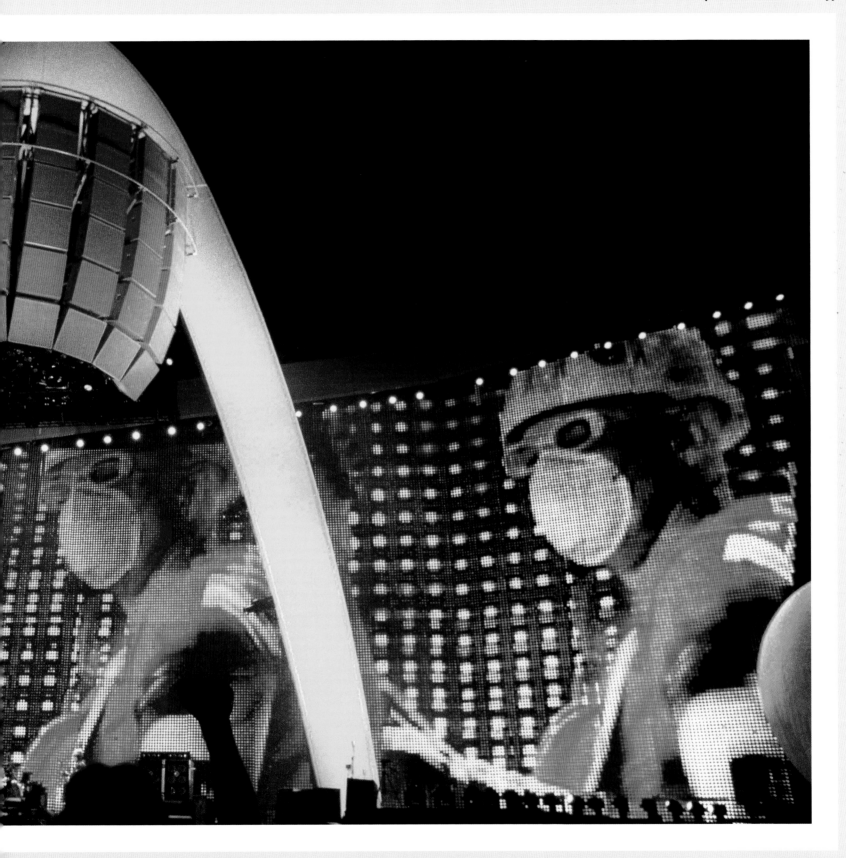

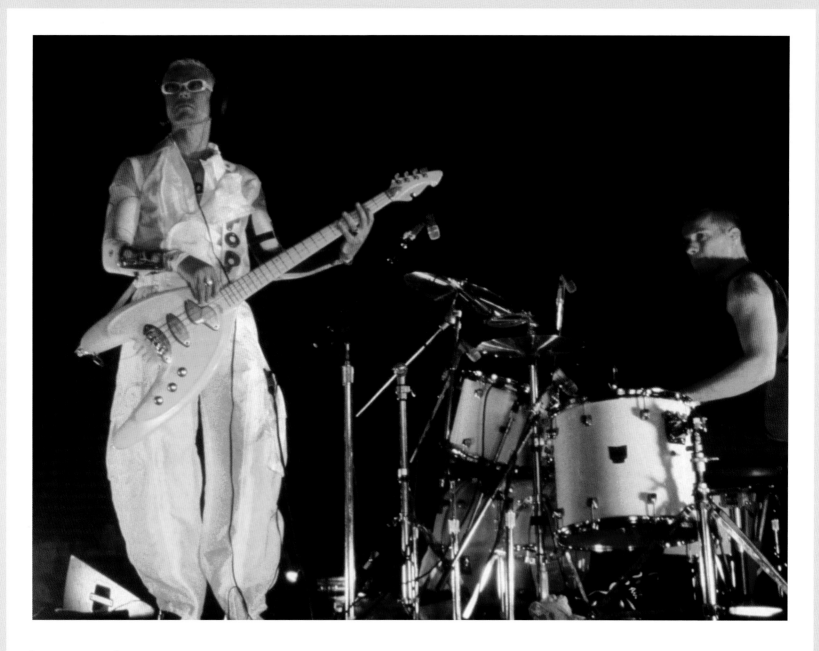

Larry goes techno

Above: Adam and Larry onstage in Las Vegas at the opening night of the PopMart tour. The tour moved on playing stadia from San Diego to Foxboro where the US leg ended on 2 July. Minor problems occurred during the tour which gave the appearance of poor planning and rehearsal or just nervous discomfort. Bono repeatedly had problems with starting "Staring at the Sun" in the right key, even having to restart the song on 14 May.

Opposite: Bono in a superhero t-shirt leans over the stage towards the sell-out crowd at the Giants Stadium, New Jersey, on 31 May. Amid rumours of poor ticket sales, the cancellation of concerts and uneven performances, the tour was finding its pace. Ever ready to reference iconic names, the band used the graphic art of Roy Liechtenstein and Run Wrake in the PopMart show; both were in the audience in New Jersey. On the second show at the venue Bono sang a brief version of "Hallelujah" marking the recent death by drowning of Jeff Buckley for whom it had been a huge hit.

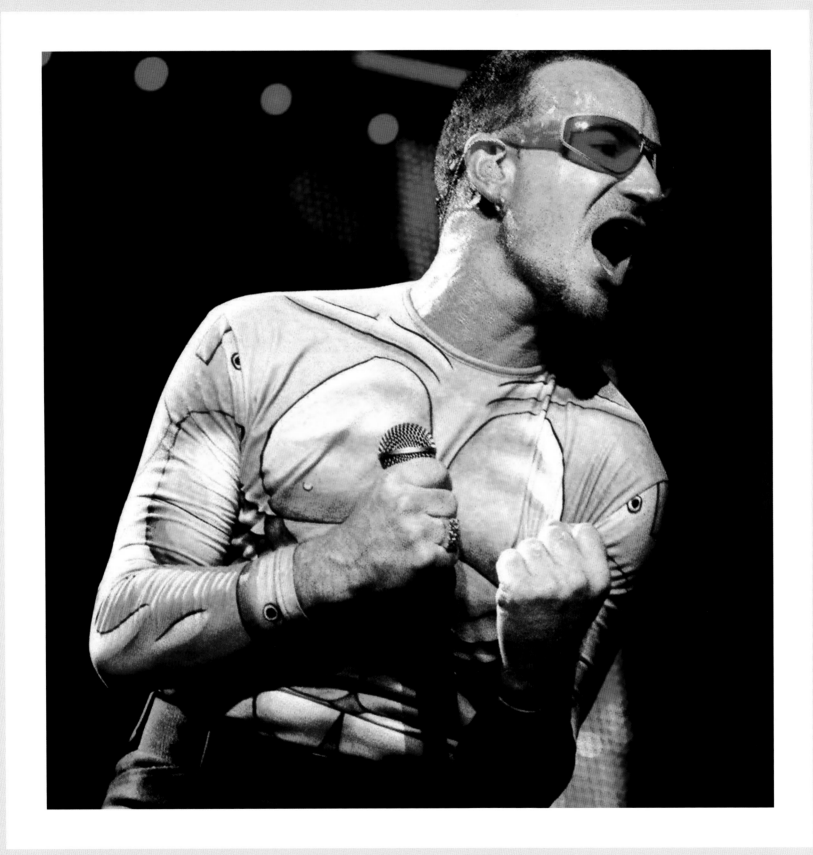

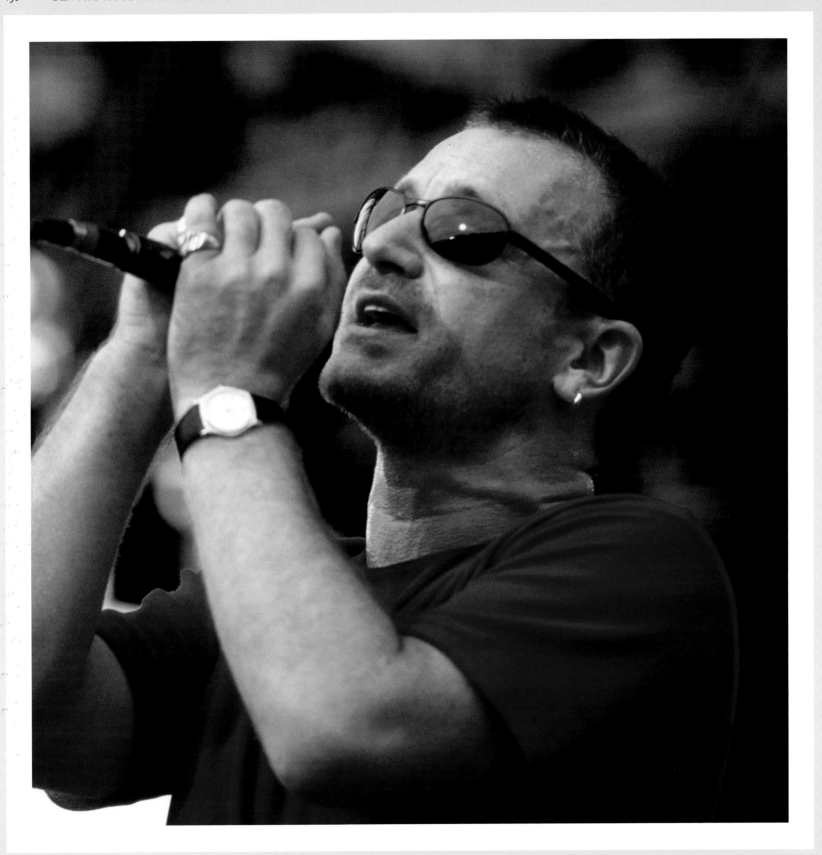

Tibetan Freedom

Opposite: Bono performs at the Tibetan Freedom Festival at Randall's Island, New York City on 8 June 1997. The two-day festival attracted 50,000 people and raised $250,000; artists included Noel Gallagher of Oasis, Alanis Morissette and Blur among many others. U2 played a five-song set.

Right: Adam plays his yellow custom bass at Oakland Alameda Coliseum on 18 June. After discussing Adam's technical needs, the bass was hand-built in Germany by Auerswald Instruments, with collaboration between Jerry Auerswald and Adam Clayton's bass tech, Stuart Morgan. Adam wanted a futuristic "Flash Gordon" styled instrument but with improved weight distribution over a typical Flying V. Auerswald made three of the A Clayton Customs in fretted and fretless versions. Solid in construction and made from 100+ year-old cherrywood, the guitar is set up to give characteristics similar to both Precision and Jazz basses. Other than Adam and Jerry Auerswald no one knows the cost of this instrument but guesstimates put each at over $10,000.

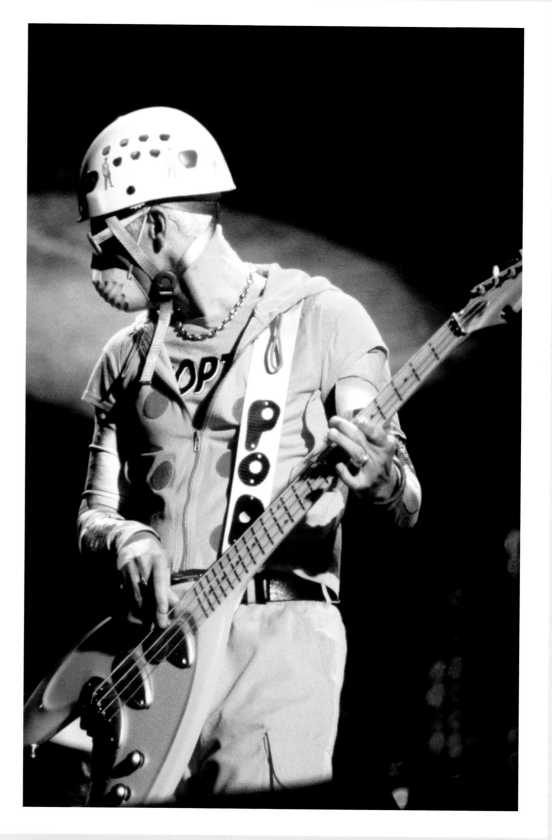

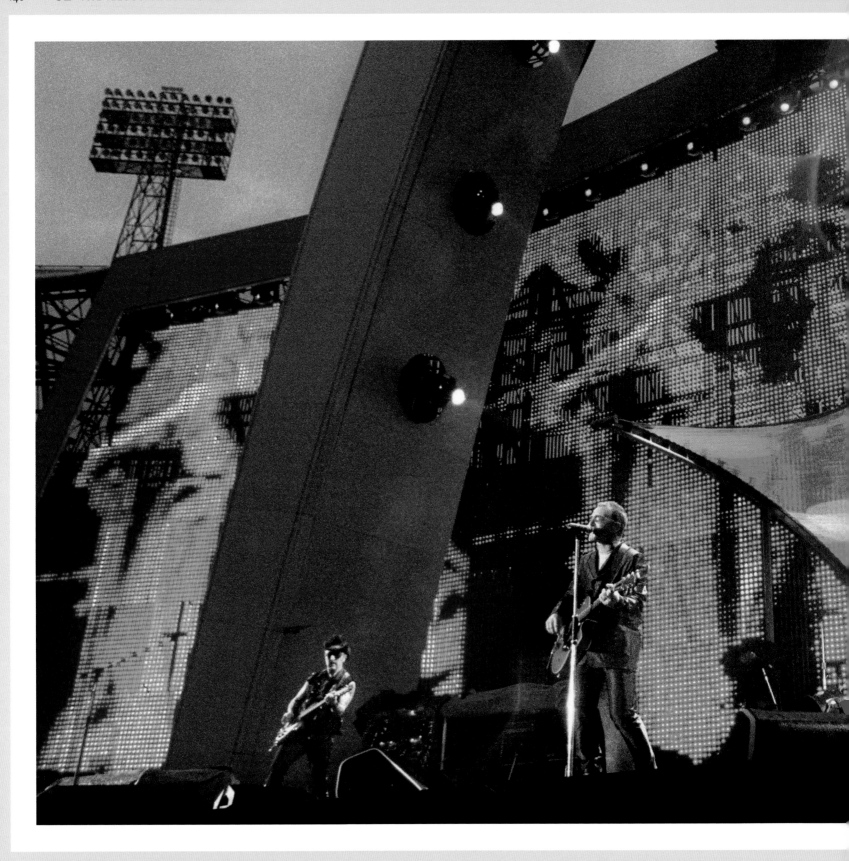

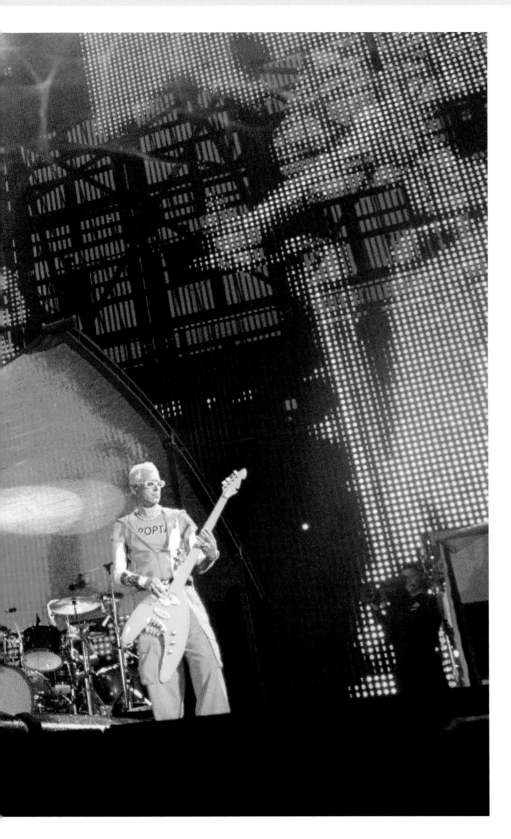

PopMart Europe

Left: After wrapping the US leg of the PopMart tour on
2 July U2 opened at Rotterdam's Feyenoord Stadium.
The first half-hour of the first-night show was broadcast
on the internet.

With most of the teething problems of the US behind them
PopMart moved at full stride, taking U2 into former Eastern
Bloc countries of Poland and Czech Republic for the first
time and attracting record-breaking audiences such as the
estimated 150-175,000 that turned up for the festival in
Reggio Emilia, Italy, on 20 September.

The next gig on 23 September fulfilled a long-held dream
of Bono's when U2 performed at the Kosevo Stadium,
Sarajevo, Bosnia-Herzegovina. The city recognized this
landmark event and resurrected the rail system that had been
inoperative since the war of the 80s to help the audience
travel into the city. There was still plenty of devastation to be
seen and the next day the band saw in person some of the
ruins in places where the fighting had been intense.

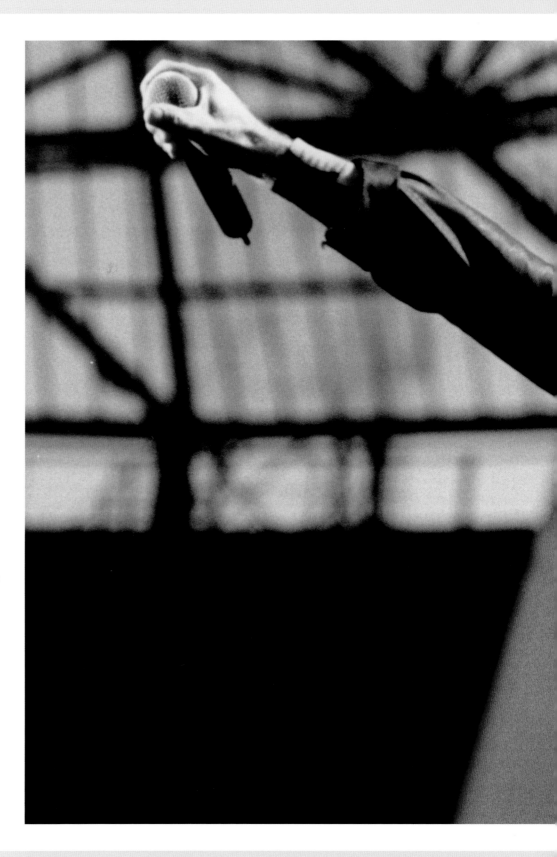

Lows and highs

Right: Bono gets the audience to sing along; on
stage at Feyenoord Stadium, Rotterdam, on 19 July.
The European tour had some dark moments:
amidst jubilation at the band playing two dates in
their home city at Lansdowne Road Stadium on
30 and 31 August, news broke of Princess Diana's
fatal car crash on the night before the second date.
U2's response was a passionate performance which
incorporated both their own personal responses
to the death of an icon whilst building a formal
element into the performance, with a large image of
Diana projected at one point onto the giant screen
while singing "MLK".

   Another epic moment happened earlier in the
tour at the Zeppelinfeld, Nuremberg, site of the
Nazi rallies where Hitler whipped the crowd into
a nationalistic frenzy. Their warm-up DJ Howie B
who had been in the production team of *Pop* found
the emotion too much. He was Jewish and as he
opened his set with the Three Degrees' "When Will
I See You Again" Bono recollects seeing the tears
streaming down Howie's cheeks.

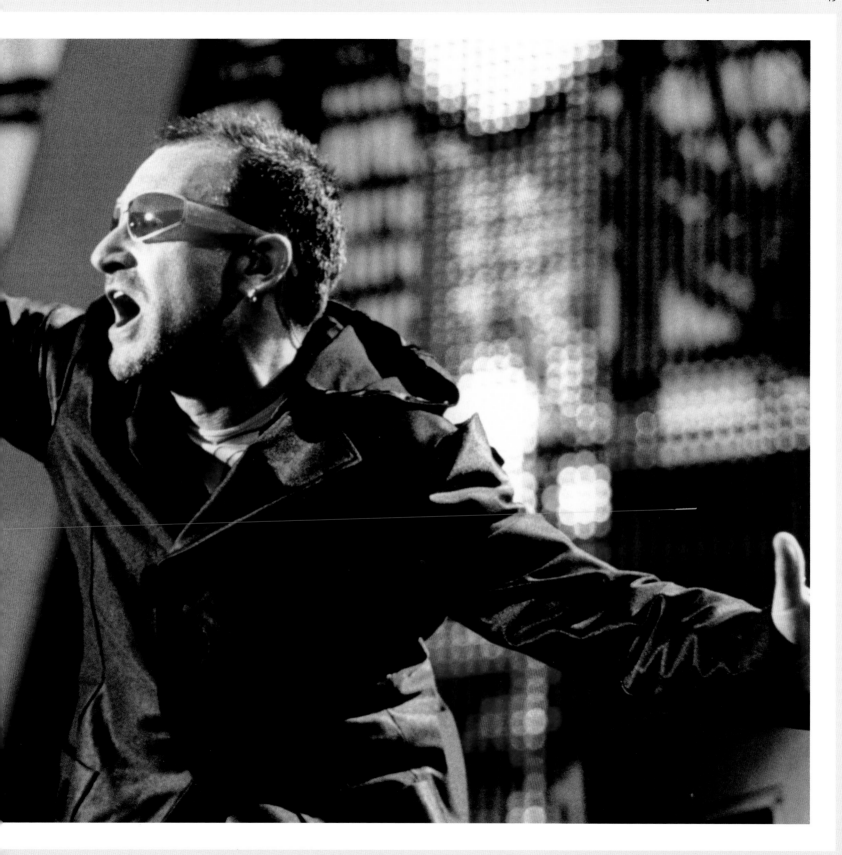

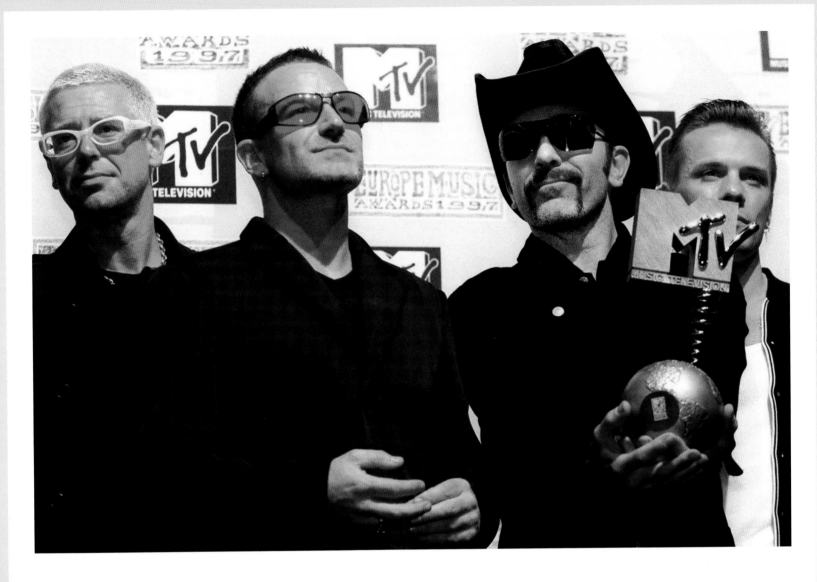

NetAid

Above: U2 pictured with the MTV Europe Music Award for Best Live Performance during the awards ceremony at Ahoy, Rotterdam, The Netherlands, 6 November 1997.

After the European tour's last gig in Tel Aviv on 30 September The Edge rushed back to California where girlfriend Morleigh was about to give birth; Edge was still on the plane when their daughter, Sian, was born. The third leg of PopMart started back in North and Central America at the end of October; the band had to take a flying break to attend the MTV Europe Awards in Rotterdam. After a spell in Australia followed by Japan and South Africa the PopMart tour finally ended on 21 March 1998. Despite the huge running costs of the tour it was a financial success; however, U2 were fully aware of some mistakes they had made and spoke of their determination not to repeat them.

Opposite: Giants Stadium, New Jersey, 9 October 1999 – Bono performs at the US segment of the NetAid Concert which also had shows running in London and Geneva.

At the close of the PopMart tour, there were no big promises about "dreaming it all up again", partly because Polygram cut them some slack with a three-compilation-album deal that gave them breathing space and kept them high in the album charts; however, in mid-September 1998, U2 met Brian Eno and Daniel Lanois to discuss the next album which took shape slowly over the next year or so.

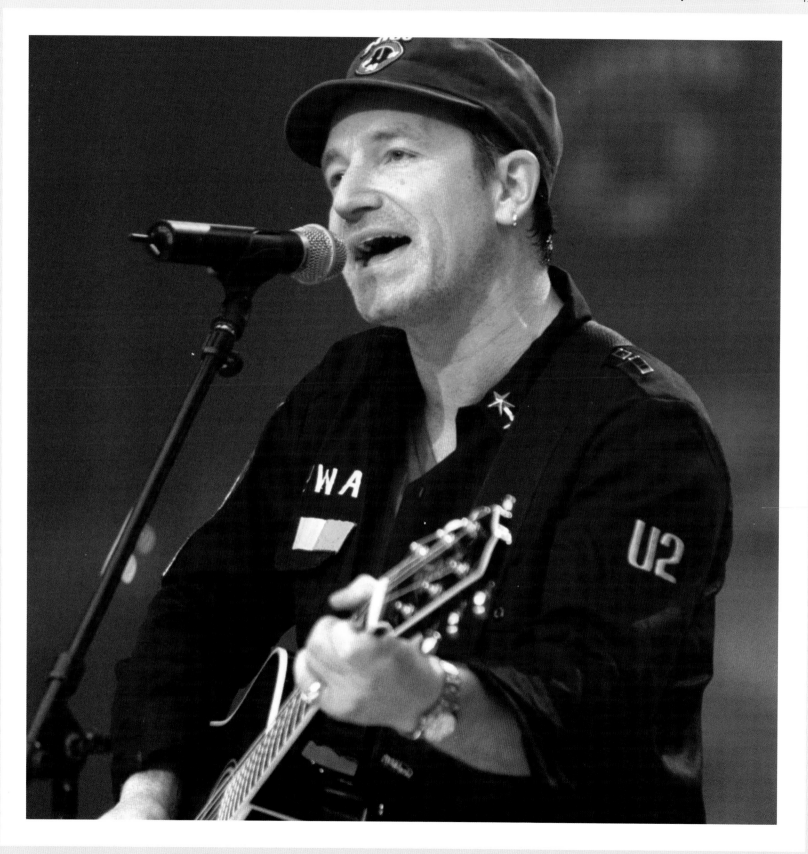

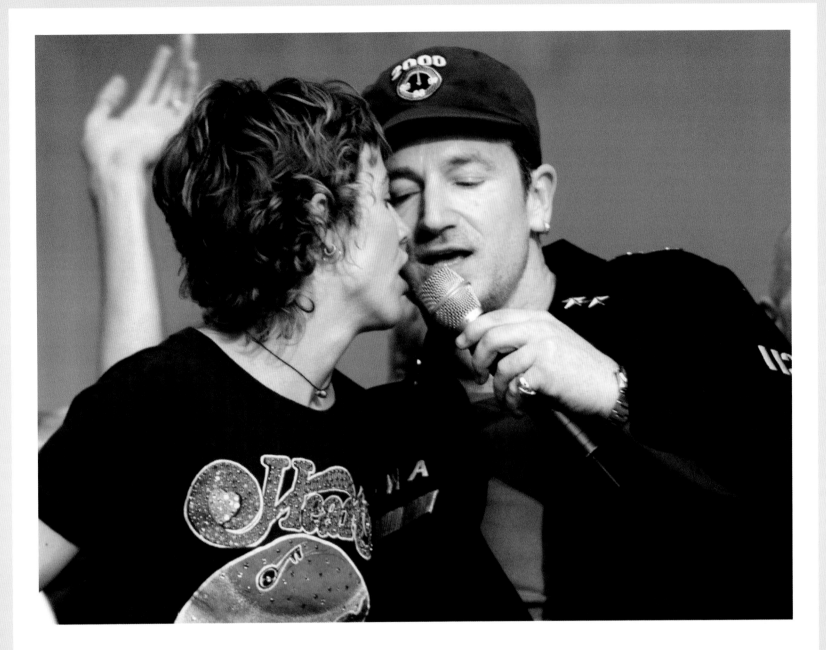

Campaigning

Above: Bono duets with Sheryl Crow at the NetAid concert, 9 October 1999.

The relatively quiet period of 1998 did the band no harm with its fanbase who were happy to reconnect their memory with the pre-PopMart U2 thanks to the compilation albums. Always busy, the band enjoyed their appearance on the long-running TV animation series *The Simpsons* in a show involving stadiums and politics!

Opposite: At the G8 Summit in Cologne, 19 June Bono prepares to hand

over a petition to German Chancellor Gerhard Schroeder demanding that the poverty of third-world nations should be alleviated by cancelling their debt to the rich western nations in a gesture to usher in the new millennium. During 1999 Bono gave much of his time to supporting Jubilee 2000 – the international campaign to cancel the national debt of third-world countries. This took him round the world for a variety of engagements from attending the G8 summit in Cologne where he presented a petition signed by 17m people, to later in September when he met with Pope John Paul II.

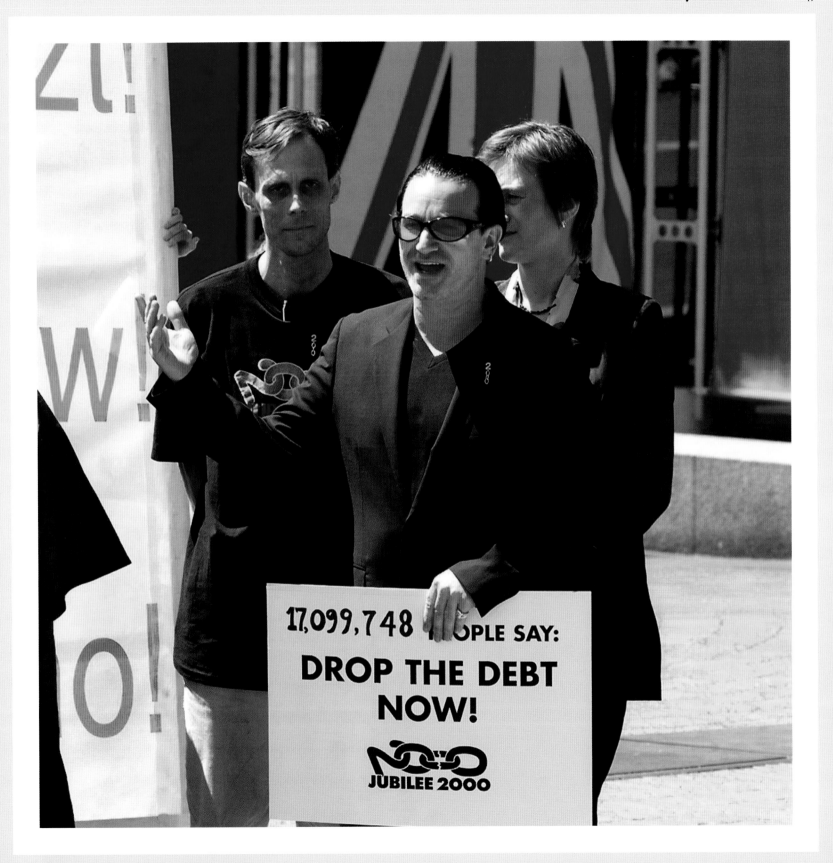

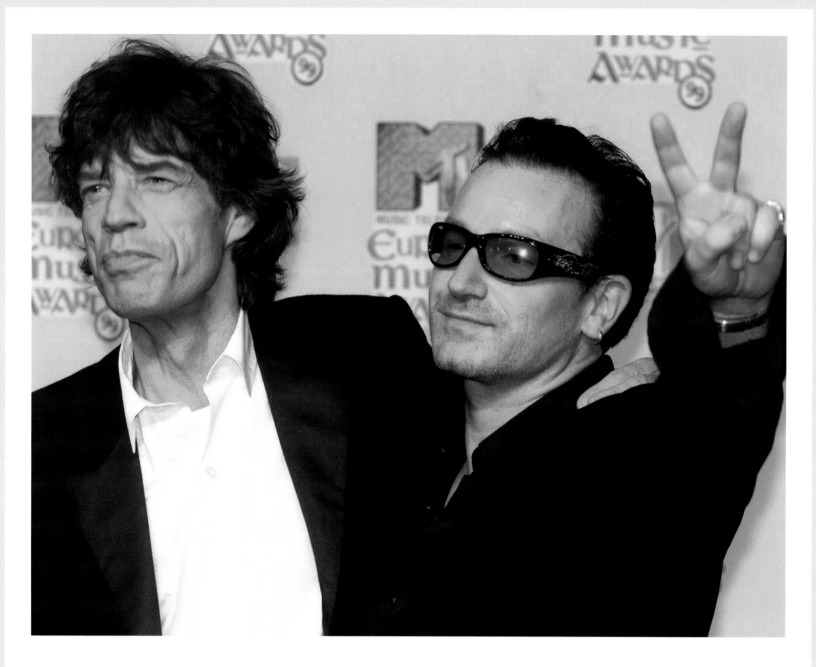

Front men

Above: Mick Jagger and Bono pose for the cameras at MTV Europe Awards at The Point, Dublin, on 11 November 1999.

Between the high profile events of 1999 – that included his third Rock and Roll Hall of Fame inauguration, this time of Bruce Springsteen – Bono did some work on the next album and became a father once more. His third child, his first son, was born on 17 August 1999 and was named Elijah.

Opposite: Bono and Larry at the 2000 MTV Video Music Awards at Radio City Music Hall in New York City on 7 September 2000 where they introduced Rage Against the Machine.

Larry Mullen's suggestion that U2 reinvent themselves as "four people working in a room" provided the keynote for the next album and by returning the band to their roots ensured that they came up with more tuneful ballads than was needed for one album. With much groundwork in 1999 the album received finishing touches in 2000.

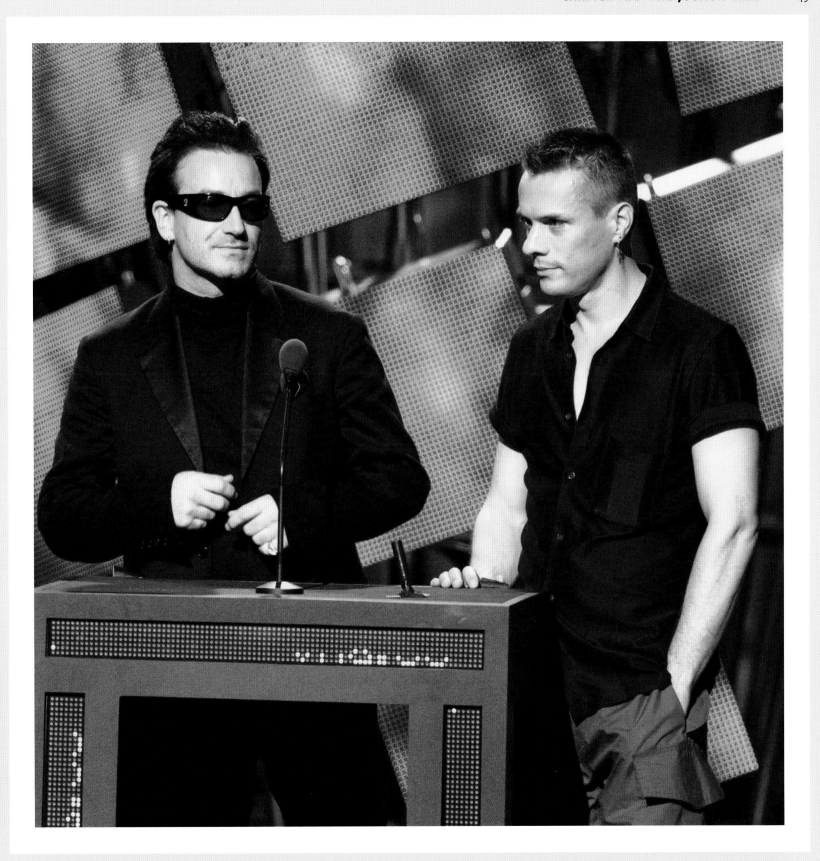

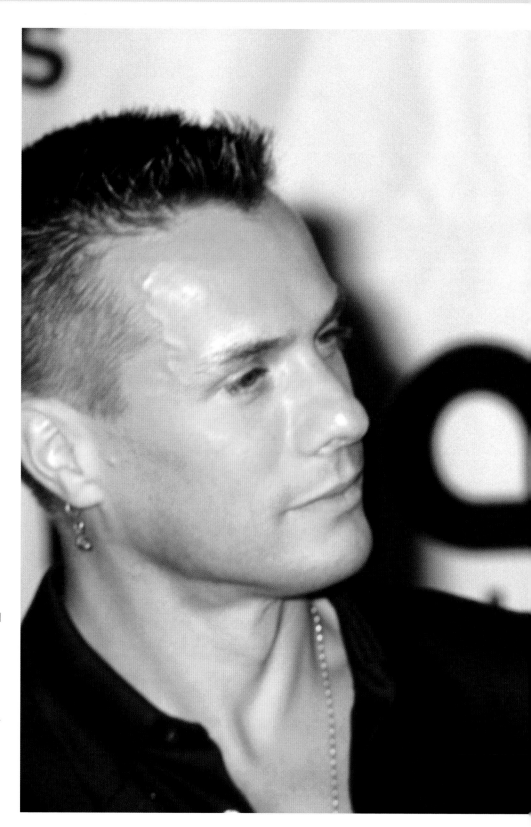

Freemen of Dublin

Right: Larry and Bono at the 2000 MTV Music Awards.

While the band spent the early part of 2000 in Dublin recording studios, Bono worked to complete his longstanding project *Million Dollar Hotel*, a story he had written some years before with the idea of making it a film. The story was taken up by director and friend, Wim Wenders and a script written by Nicholas Klein. The soundtrack was largely performed by Bono, U2 and Daniel Lanois with Bono credited as co-producer. The movie premiered at the Berlin Film Festival 9 February.

In March Paul McGuinness and U2 were honoured by receiving the Freedom of Dublin; at the same ceremony Burmese freedom campaigner Aung San Suu Kyi received the same honour. On hearing her story U2 wrote the song "Walk On" which appeared on the new album. Bono's typical offbeat take on tokens of fame was to exercise his new status which included the right to graze sheep on the grass of Dublin centre's St Stephen's Green.

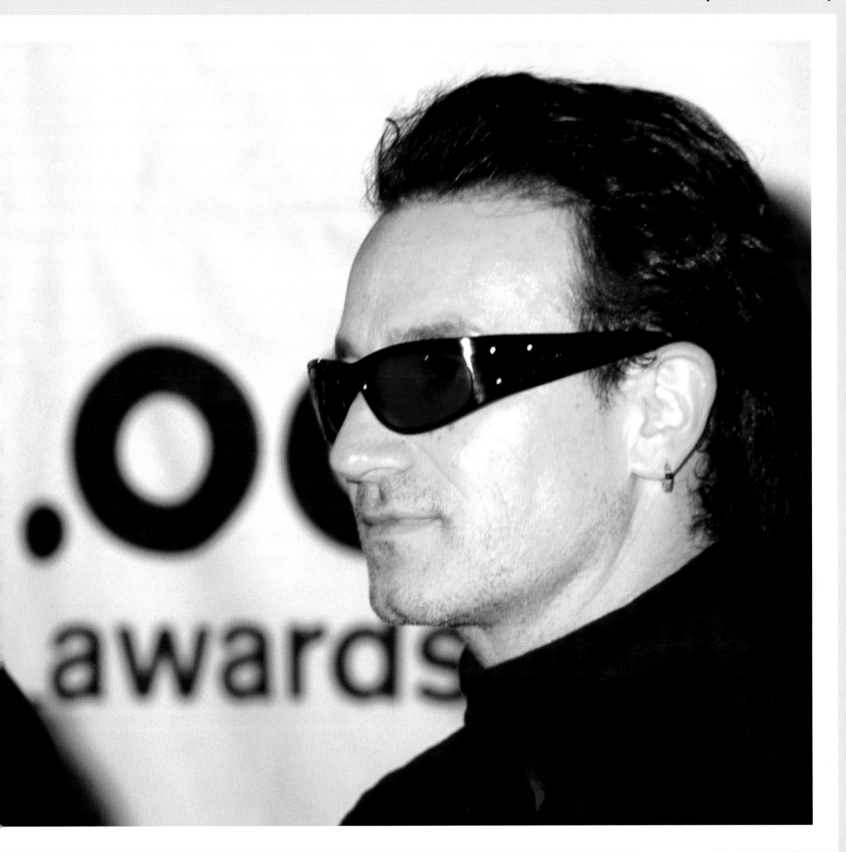

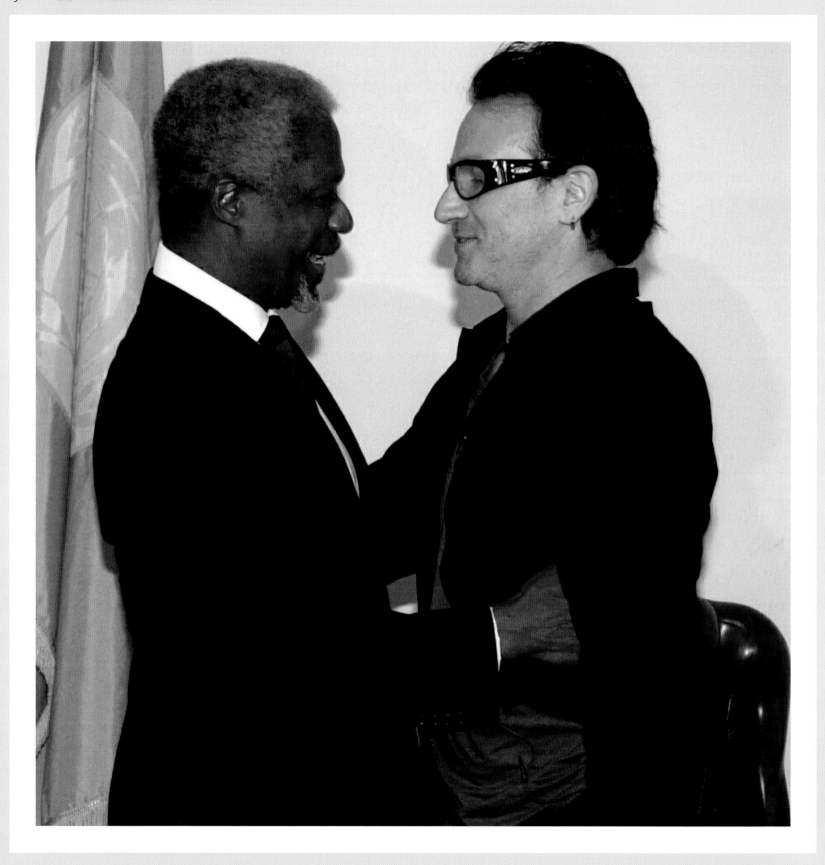

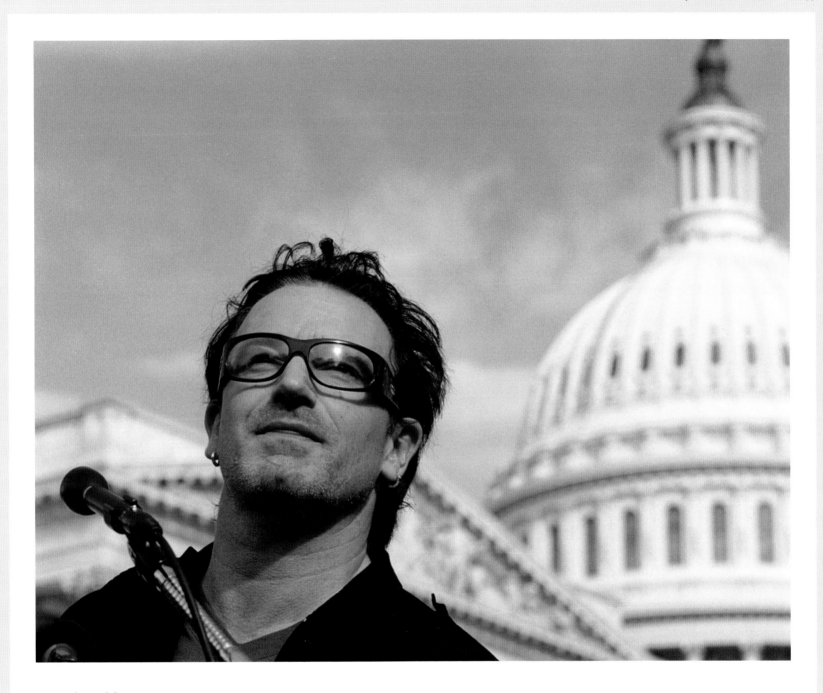

Summit petition

Opposite: UN Secretary General Kofi Annan and Bono embrace when meeting at the United Nations Millennium Summit, New York City, September 2000. Bono and Nigerian president Olusegun Obasanjo presented a petition to the summit, signed by 21 million people around the world, urging G8 leaders to cancel the global debt.

Above: Bono speaks during a press conference on third-world debt relief at the US Capitol on 21 September.

Bono turned 40 in May and seemed at ease in his dual role of rock star and campaigner for social justice which continued vigorously in 2000; on 25 May, soon after his birthday, at a sports awards ceremony in Monaco he finally met the inspirational figure Nelson Mandela, whom he had supported for many years.

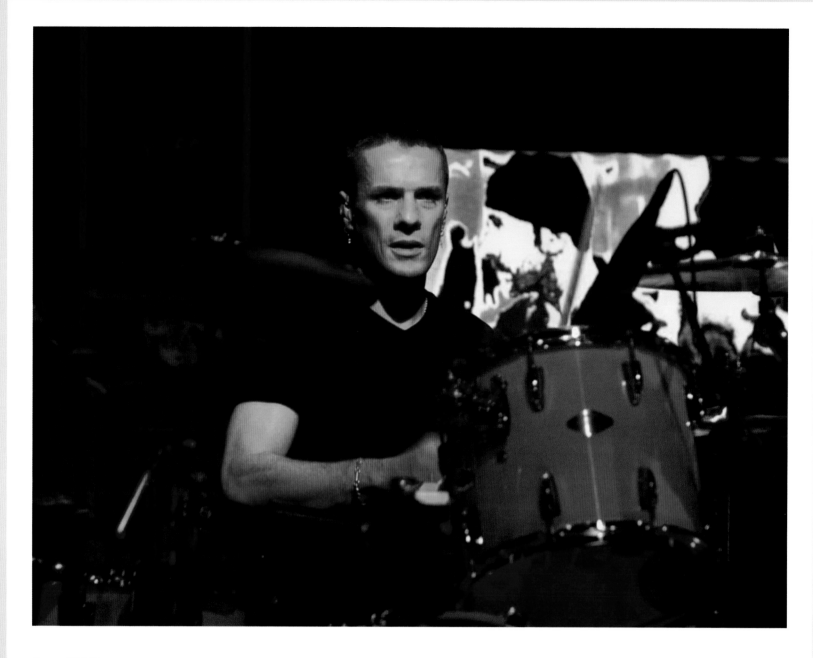

Beautiful Day

Above: Larry drums during U2's performance on *Farmclub.com* TV show filmed at LA's Universal Studios on 27 October. Watching the show are celebs Sheryl Crow, Dr Dre, Winona Ryder and Kevin Spacey.

In August the band revealed the title for their new album will be "All That You Can't Leave Behind". Despite the possible different readings of the title, The Edge is clear about the content; "It's us playing together, very simple, perhaps back to like our first few records with guitar, bass, drums."

Opposite: U2 perform at the inaugural My VH1 Awards, 30 November 2000, at Shrine Auditorium, Los Angeles.

In late September Bono sang at the funeral of Paula Yates, partner of Michael Hutchence. A few days later the band recorded three songs for BBC's *Top of the Pops*: they played live on the roof of the Clarence Hotel in Dublin. Returning to more conventional promotion of their music is part of the message behind the new album and with the release of "Beautiful Day" on 9/10 October the countdown to the album release began.

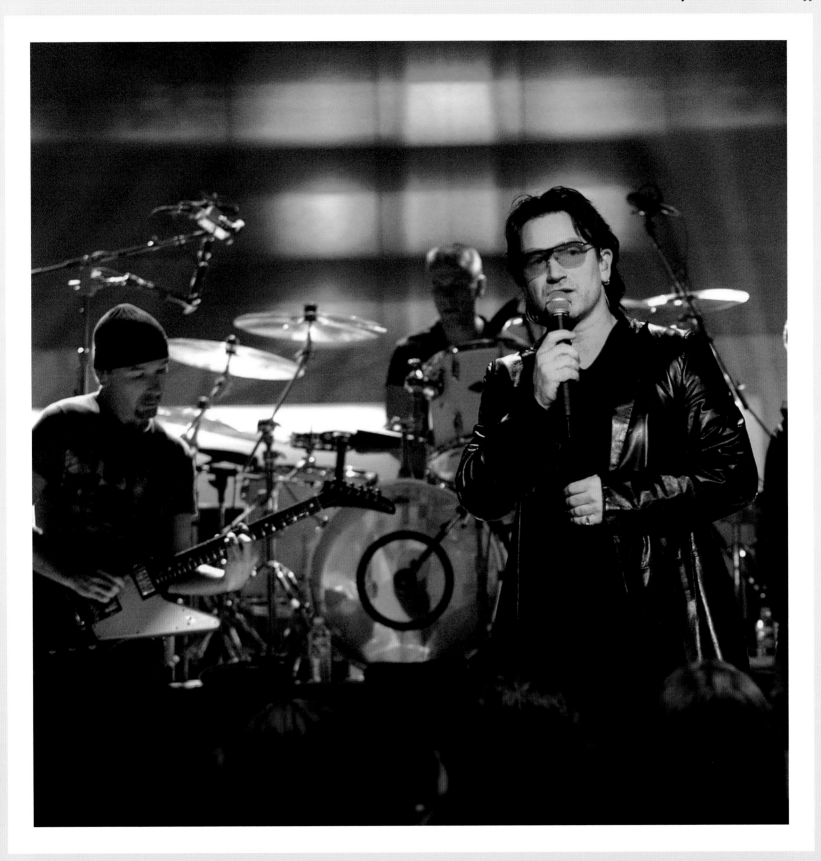

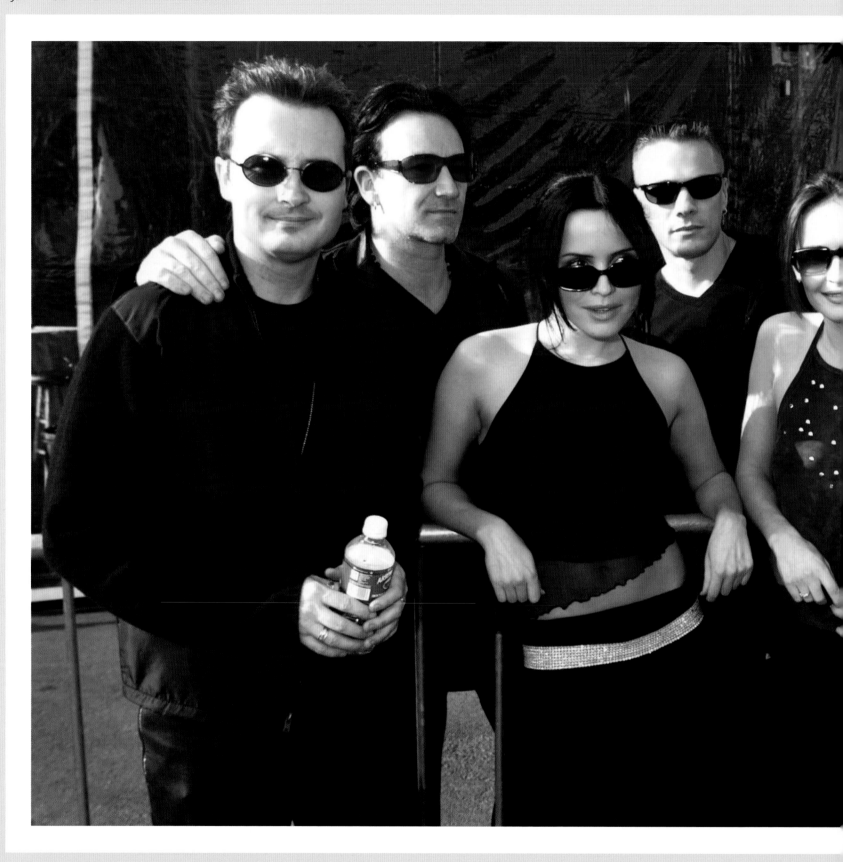

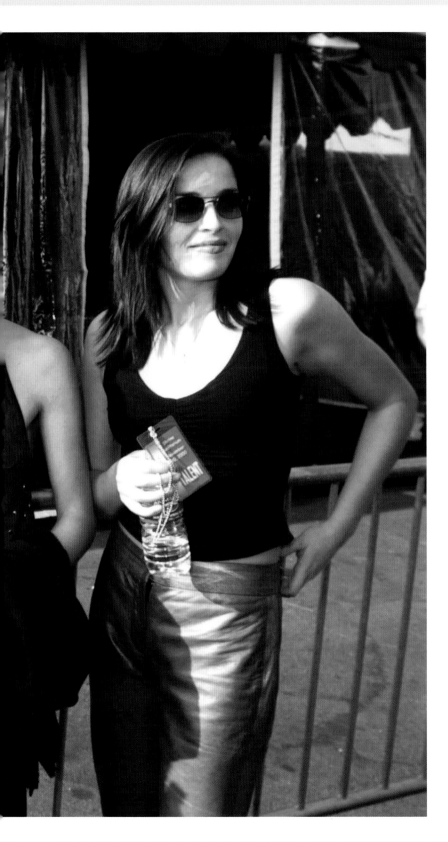

"Third masterpiece"

Left: Bono and Larry at the My VH1 Awards pose for photographers backstage with their fellow Irish band The Corrs.

The new album was released worldwide on 30 October to a wave of acclaim and positive reviews: James Hunter in his *Rolling Stone* piece calls it their third masterpiece after *The Joshua Tree* and *Achtung Baby*. The self-conscious pop-art elements of *Pop* may have disappeared but the album cover still is a work of symbolic meaning. The front cover picture was taken by Anton Corbijn during the video shoot for "Beautiful Day" at Charles de Gaulle Airport, Paris. The band stand isolated in the cavernous interior that seems to evoke an acoustic quality. For the ultra-observant, Bono asked for the departure board to carry J33-3 – a reference to the Bible where the book of Jeremiah reads "Call to me and I will answer you and will tell you great and hidden things which you have not known." By mid-December *All That You Can't Leave Behind* has been certified Platinum in the US. For the band the heartfelt praise for the album must have been a huge vote of confidence in their core musical style.

Bono had an extra bonus for his sustained campaigning when on 6 November 2000 Bill Clinton cited Bono's passion in persuading both political parties to pass legislation cancelling the debt of the world's poorest countries to the US, a bill that President Clinton signed that day.

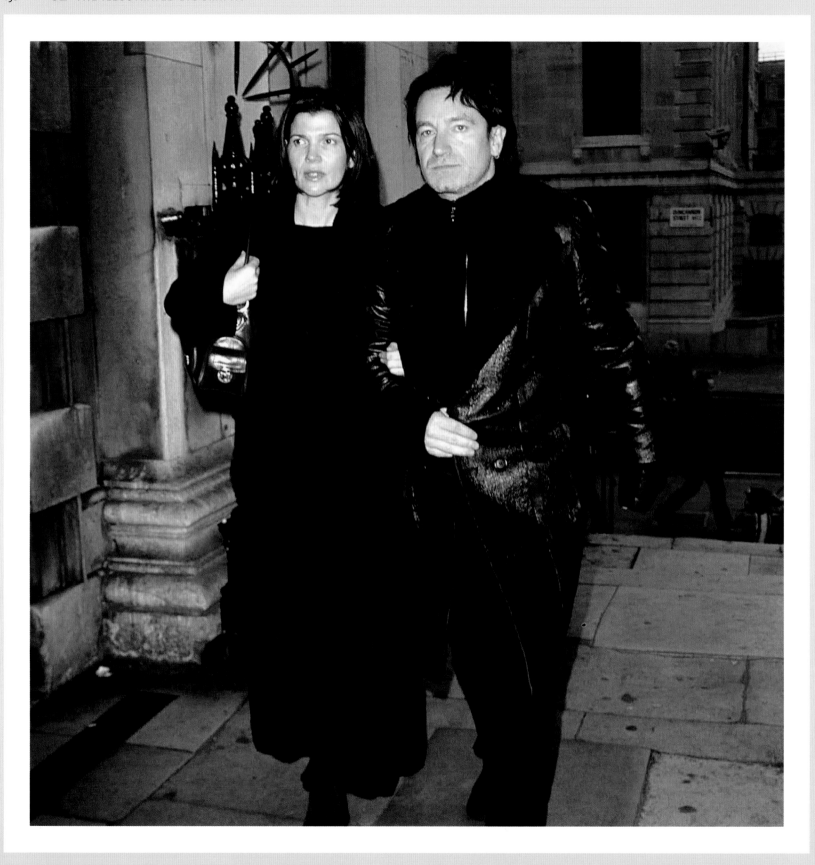

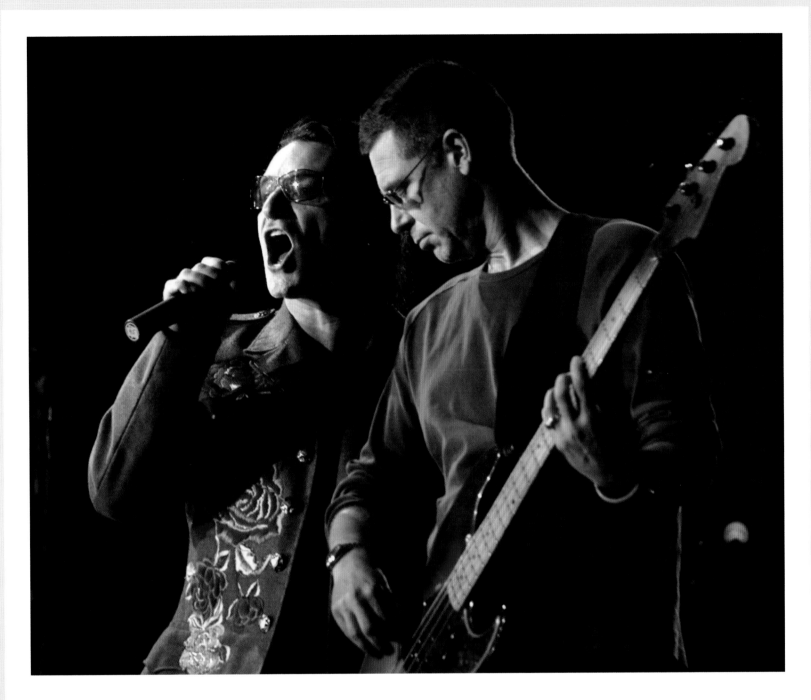

2001

Opposite: Bono and Ali photographed in London, February 2001.

The new year of 2001 starts out well for the band with three Grammy nominations and tickets selling out fast for the first shows in their Elevation tour announced in January.

Above: Bono and Adam rehearse their set for the 43rd Annual Grammy Awards at the Staples Center, Los Angeles, on 20 February.

On 7 February the band played a warm-up show for their forthcoming tour at London's West End Astoria Theatre. The small venue only held about 2,000 and the audience was either there by invitation or winners of a competition that brought them from Europe as well as the UK. Many music business celebrities were in the audience.

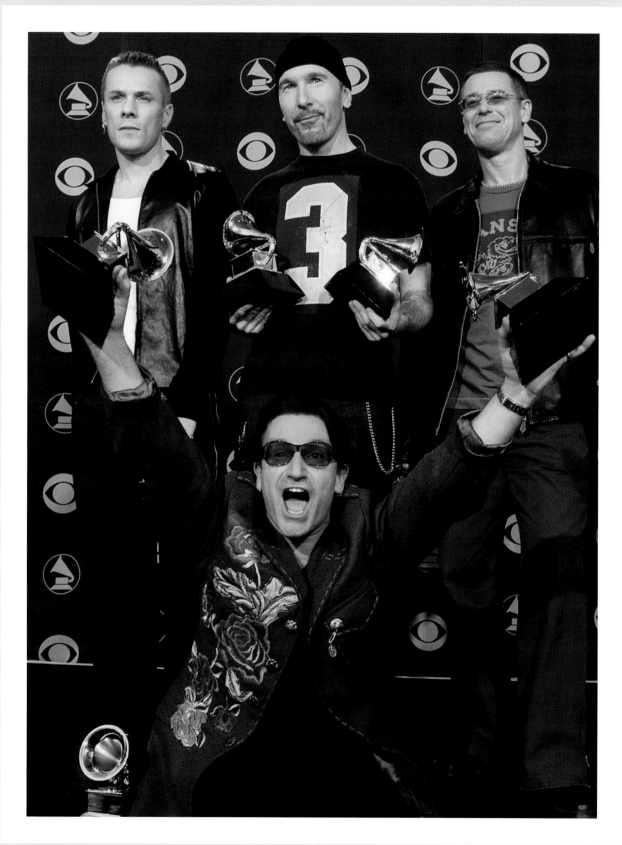

Grammy triple

Left: Celebrations are in order at the 2001 Grammy Awards in Los Angeles, 21 February. "Beautiful Day" ends up winning all three Grammys in its nominated categories: Record of the Year, Song of the Year and Best Performance by a Rock Group or Duo with Vocal. Owning up to feeling humility – Bono told the audience that the band have gone back to scratch and are re-applying for the job of "Best band in the world."

Opposite: Bono sings with Mary J. Blige, performing Bob Marley's "Could You Be Loved" at the 16th Annual Rock and Roll Hall of Fame Induction Ceremony where Bono inducted Chris Blackwell, founder of Island Records, into the Hall of Fame in New York on 19 March.

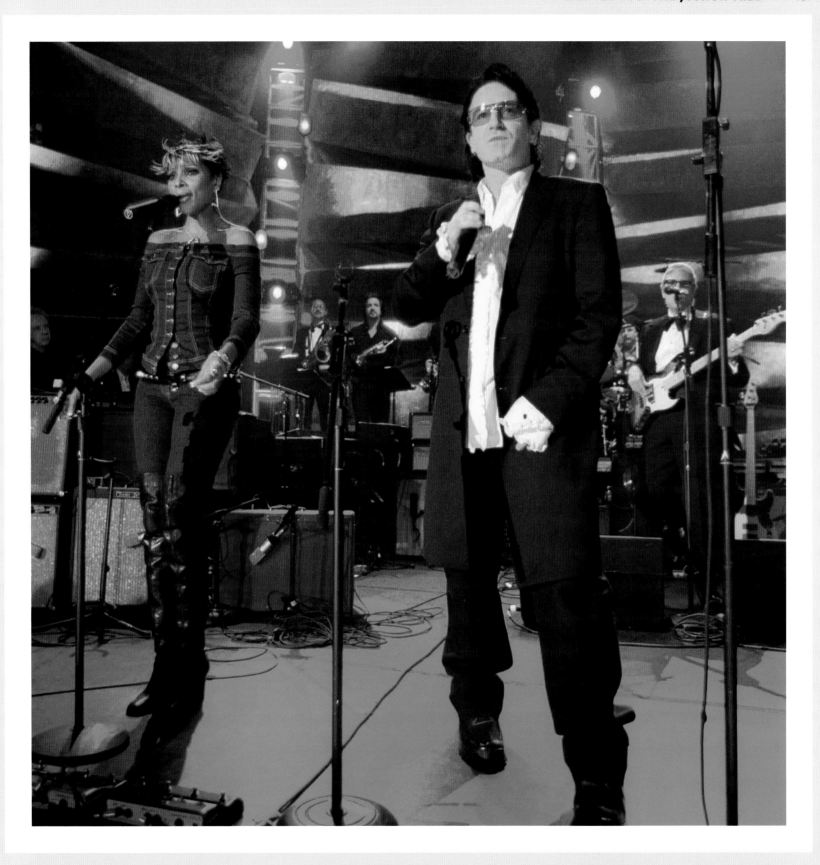

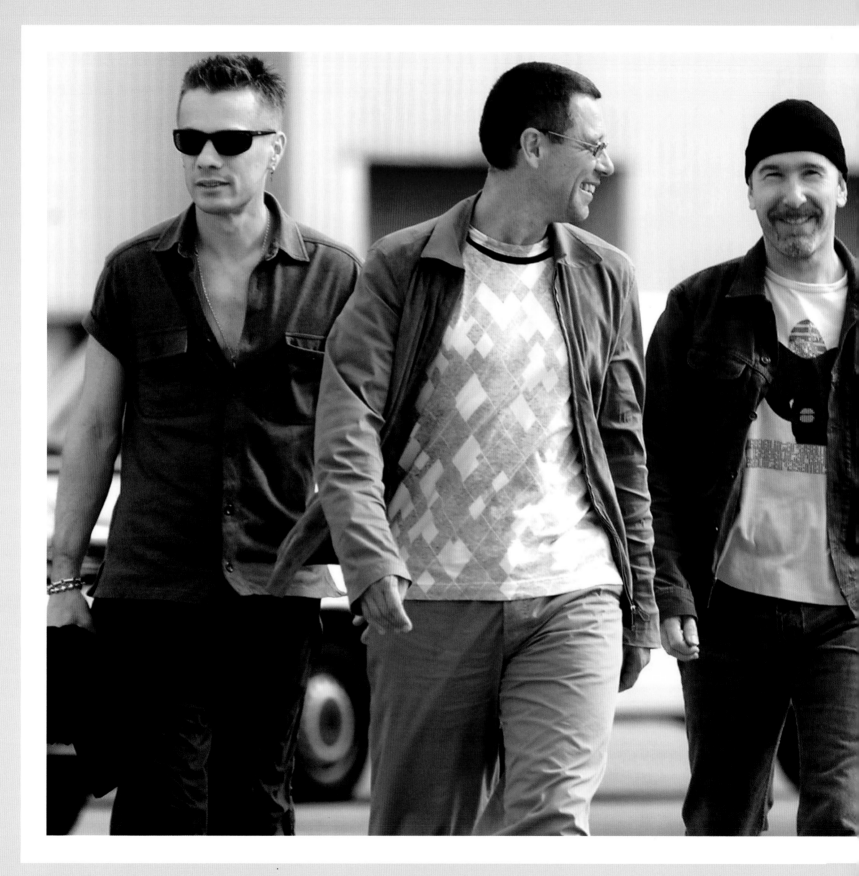

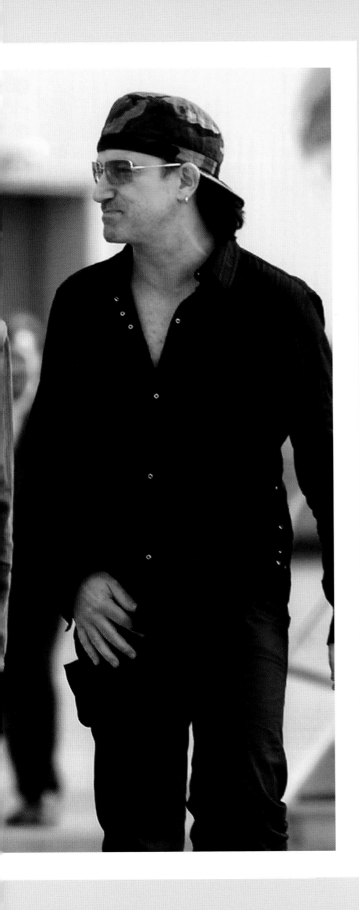

Chapter Three
Elevation

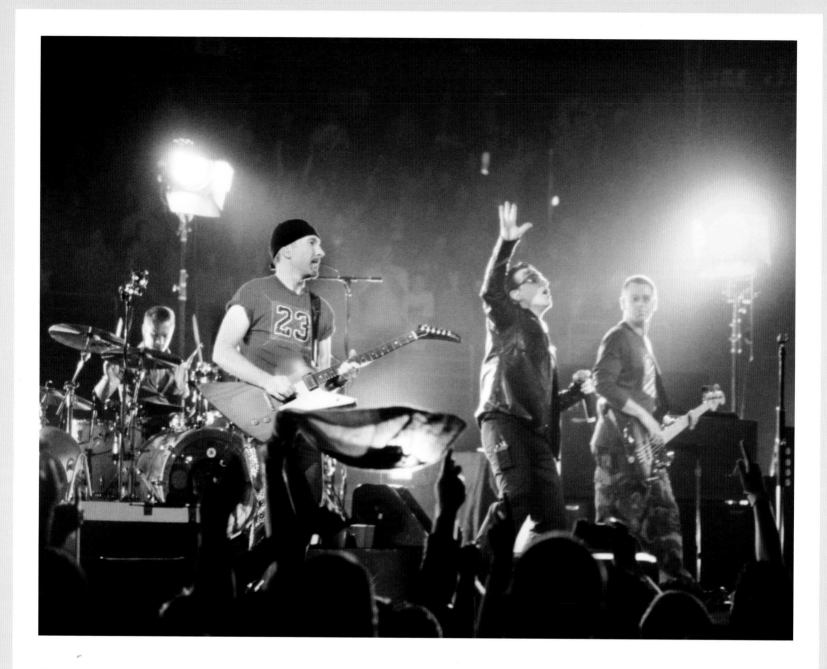

Elevation moves out

Above and opposite: April 2001: U2 photographed on stage at Arrowhead Pond, Anaheim, where they played three dates.

The Elevation tour set out with two dates at the glitzily named National Car Rental Center, Sunrise, Florida on 24 and 26 March. Any fan attending one of these concerts after the PopMart tour would have been astonished. For a start the prime seats at ground level had been removed and "General Admission Tickets" made available for standing only. The equivalent of the best view of the band had now been made cheapest. The stripped-down stage bore no likeness whatsoever to the excesses of PopMart with just four relatively small video screens adding up to a total lack of sensory overload other than light and sound. A new feature was a heart-shaped catwalk and its enclosed area which could hold 300 standing fans. The opening show was a resounding success, receiving good critical reviews as well as enthusiasm from fans. The opening date's after-show was buzzing with industry stars including Lenny Kravitz and Elvis Costello.

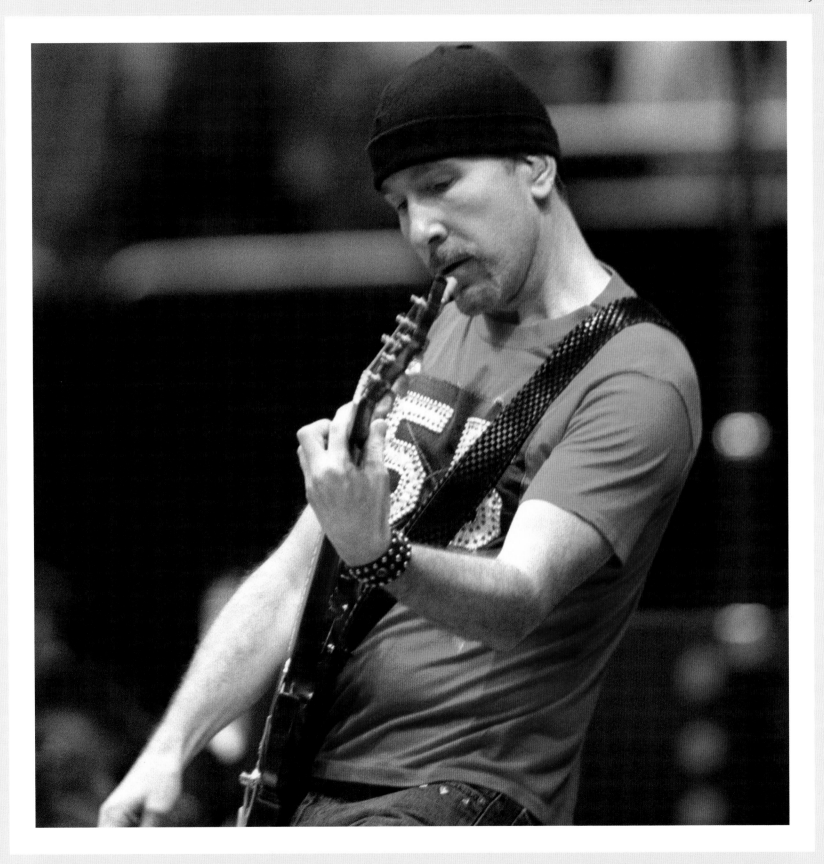

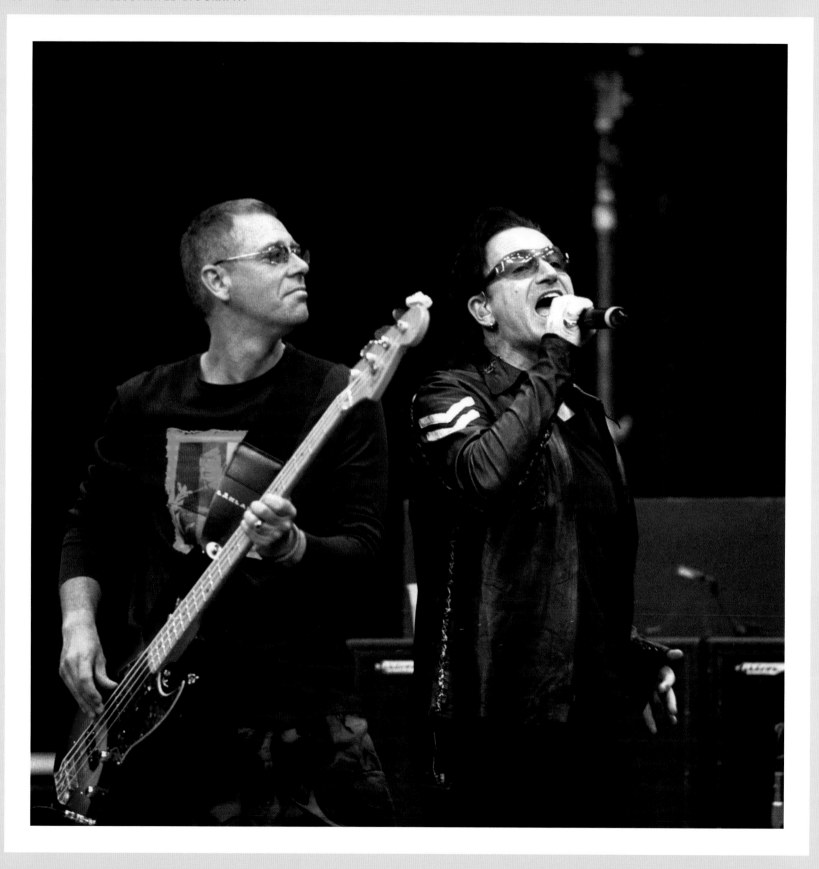

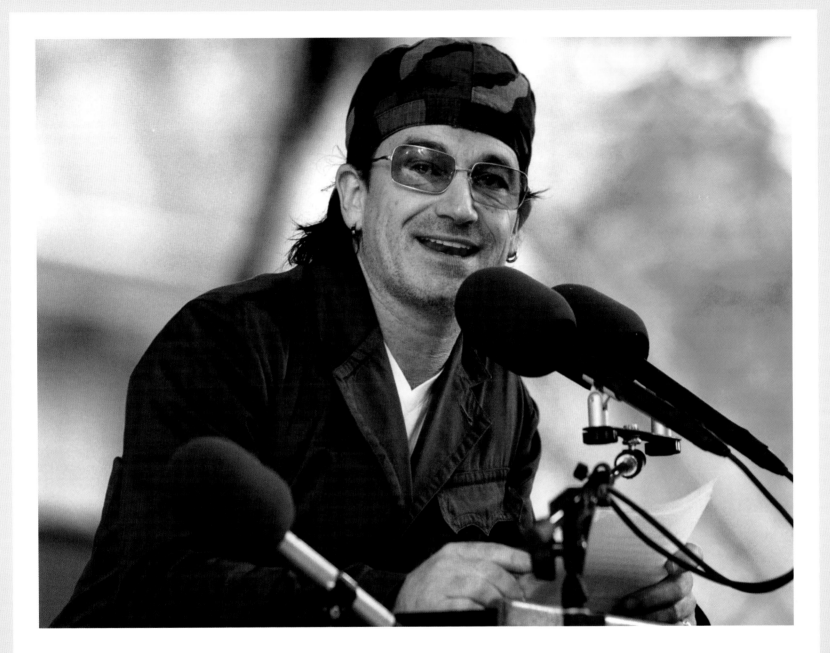

Bono graduates from Harvard

Opposite: Bono and Adam perform at the Nationwide Arena, Columbus, Ohio on 7 May 2001.

The band took a two-day break 7-8 April to shoot a video for their song "Elevation" which in a remix version will accompany some of the most exciting action footage in the forthcoming movie *Tomb Raider*. The U2 music video cleverly substitutes the band into key points of the movie's action. The remix demanded a heavier prog sound which required the services of Nine Inch Nails drummer, Chris Vrenna, who did the mix with new guitar lines from Edge.

Above: Bono addresses the 2001 graduating class of Harvard University, 6 June, Cambridge, MA. The audience of 15,000 heard him say "I'm not here to brag or take credit. I've come here to ask your help," referring to the current AIDS crisis in Africa, which he called "The biggest health crisis since the bubonic plague wiped out a third of Europe." The class conferred an honorary degree on Bono for his efforts.

After U2's four-date appearance at United Center, Chicago, Bono flew back to Dublin on 16 May to be with Ali who gave birth to their fourth child, another son, John Abraham, on 20 May.

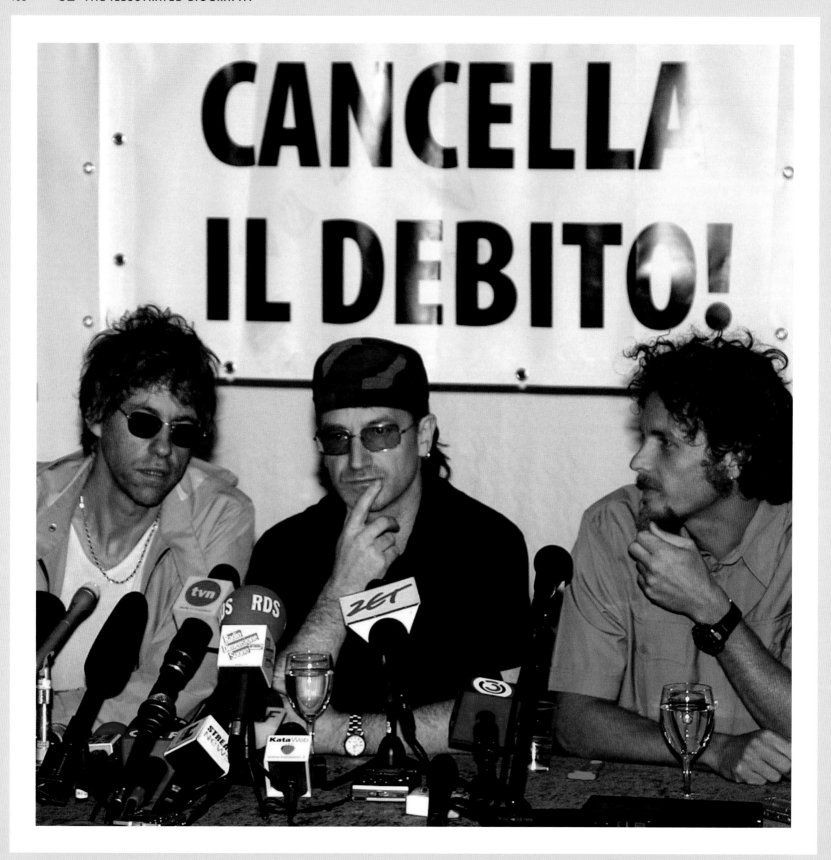

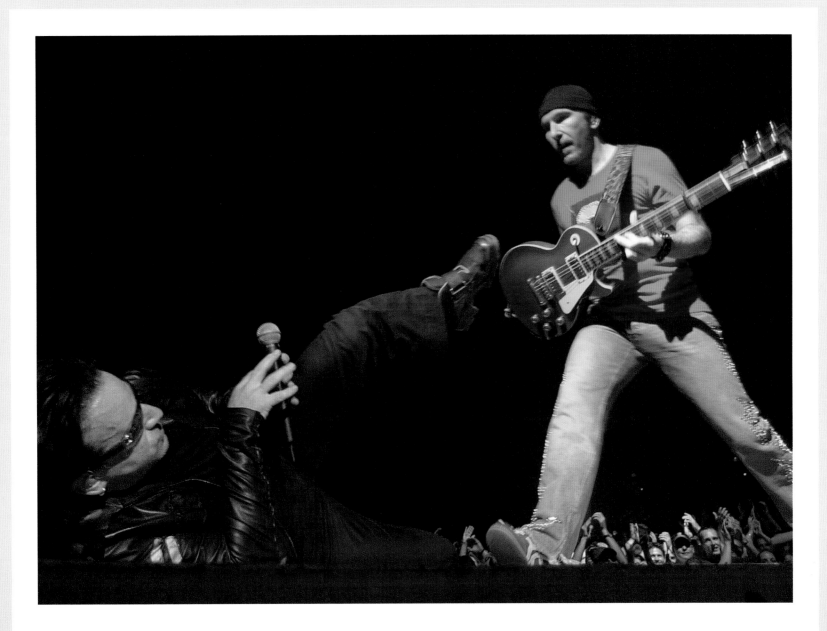

On to Europe

Opposite: Left to right Bob: Geldof, Bono and Italian rap star Lorenzo Jovanotti put on a press conference on 21 July during the G8 Summit in Genoa, Italy, in which they demand that rich countries of the world cancel the poorest countries' crippling debt.

The first leg of the Elevation tour ended with dates in the New York area: two nights at Madison Square Garden, 17 and 19 June, followed by two dates on 22 and 25 June at Continental Airlines Arena, East Rutherford, New Jersey.

Above: Bono and Edge engage in a bit of stage drama at the Gelredome Arnhem gig on 31 July 2001. The European leg of the Elevation tour set out from the Forum, Copenhagen, Denmark, with two dates on 6 and 7 July. Just because Bono was in the middle of a world tour with his band didn't take him away from his passionate campaigning. Earlier in the tour in June he did some serious lobbying in Washington, winning support from the US Treasury Secretary. In July with fellow campaigner Bob Geldof, Bono attended the G8 summit in Genoa to put personal pressure on the leaders of the richest countries of the world to do more for the poorest third-world countries.

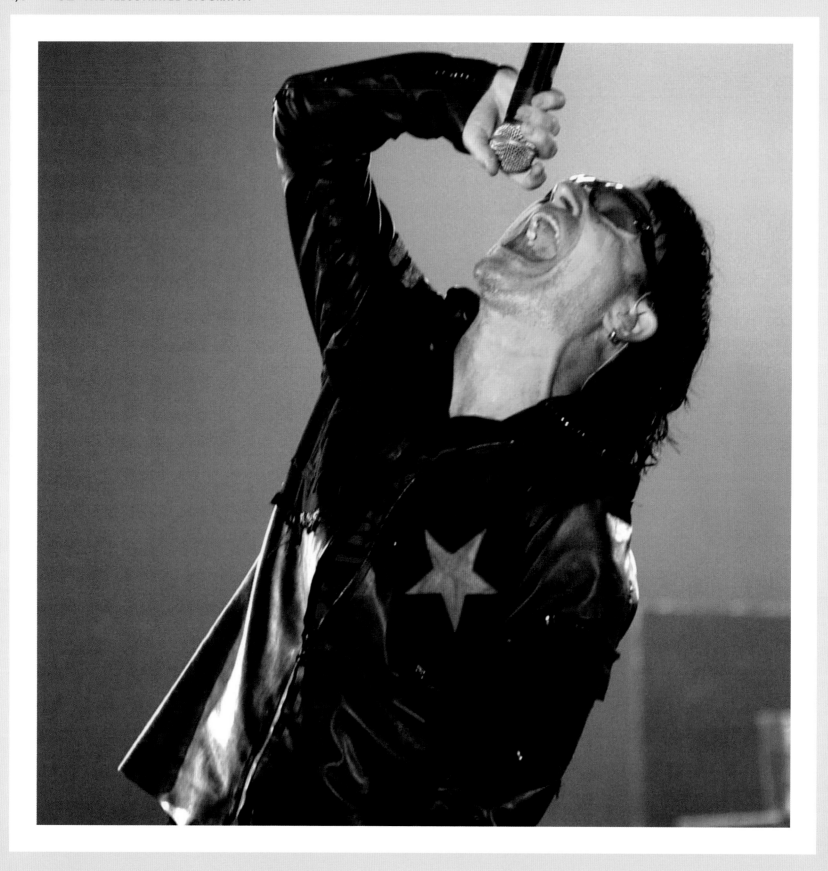

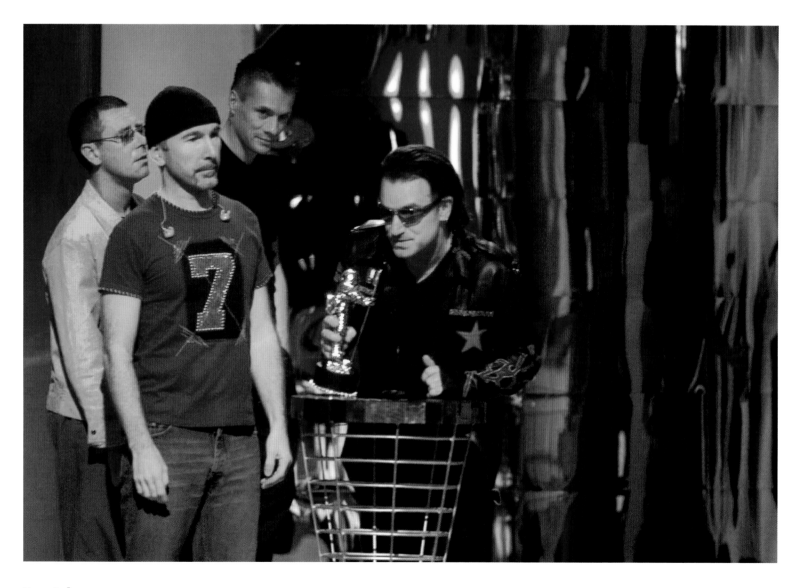

Bono's loss

Opposite: Bono sings his heart out during a performance at SECC Glasgow on 27 August 2001.

Tickets for the European tour had sold swiftly and the band performed to full houses in Scandinavia, Germany, France, Italy, Switzerland, Austria, The Netherlands, Belgium and Spain in swift succession then arrived in the UK for gigs starting on 11 August in Manchester. During this time Bono had to cope with his father being in hospital with terminal cancer and in the middle of four shows at Earls Court 18, 19, 21, 22, Bob Hewson finally lost the battle against cancer, dying in the early hours of 21 August. Bono went onstage the same night and spoke of his father to the audience, introducing "Kite" as the song he had written for Bob. Bono nursed his grief at the loss of his father after his funeral on 24 August,

sharing moments with the 80,000 audience at Slane Castle, Dublin on 25 August. The mood of loss continued at the second Slane Castle gig when the names of the 29 dead from the Omagh bombing scrolled up a video screen.

Above: U2 accept the Video Vanguard Award at the 2001 MTV Video Music Awards held at the Metropolitan Opera House on 6 September 2001 in New York City. U2 were in New York in early September for the MTV Video Music Awards but Bono had departed to Venice for the Film Festival and was wandering its labyrinths when he heard the news of the Twin Towers attack and, in shock, watched the catastrophe with American tourists in a local hotel.

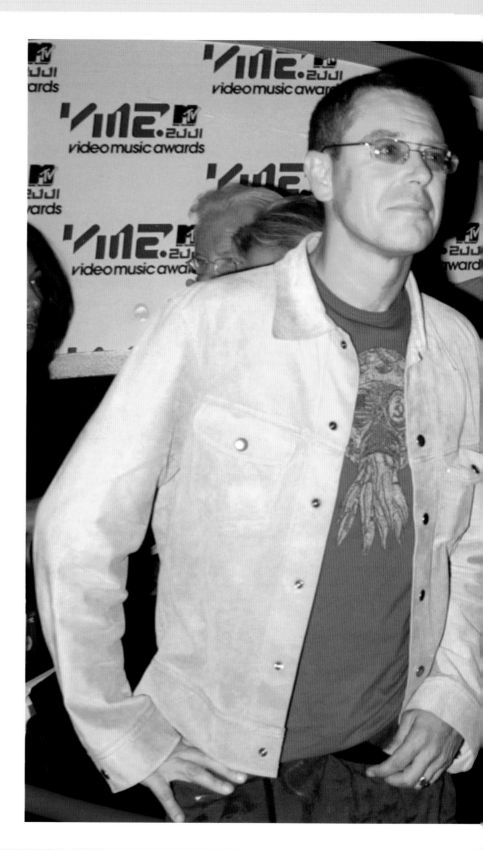

9/11

Right: U2 arrive at the MTV Video Music Awards, New York City 6 September 2001.

The band acted quickly out of respect for the 9/11 tragedy, cancelling all advance ticket sales scheduled to begin the following weekend. The title of *All That You Have To Leave Behind* and numerous songs from it chimed with the shocked and mourning population of the USA. The close connection of U2 with America in general and New York in particular kept them reaching out during the third leg of the Elevation tour.

On 21 September U2 performed in a live broadcast BBC TV programme, *A Tribute To Heroes*, at 2.15 am London time; it was a fundraiser for the victims of 9/11 and the worldwide broadcast succeeded in raising around $150 million.

In late September/early October Bono took time out in Bali to mourn his father and therapeutically started working on new songs.

The next leg of the Elevation tour started out on 10 October in South Bend, Indiana, at the University of Notre Dame whose sporting teams are known as the Fighting Irish. It was U2's first gig in the USA since 9/11 and the band were well aware of the association of Irish-Americans with the New York Fire Department; small adapations made the show a tribute to those who were killed in the attack and those who died trying to rescue them. At their performance in Hamilton, Ontario on 13 October the names of the passengers on the four hijacked flights were scrolled on video screens as the band sang "One". Future shows had the list of victims expanded to include New York's police and firefighting personnel.

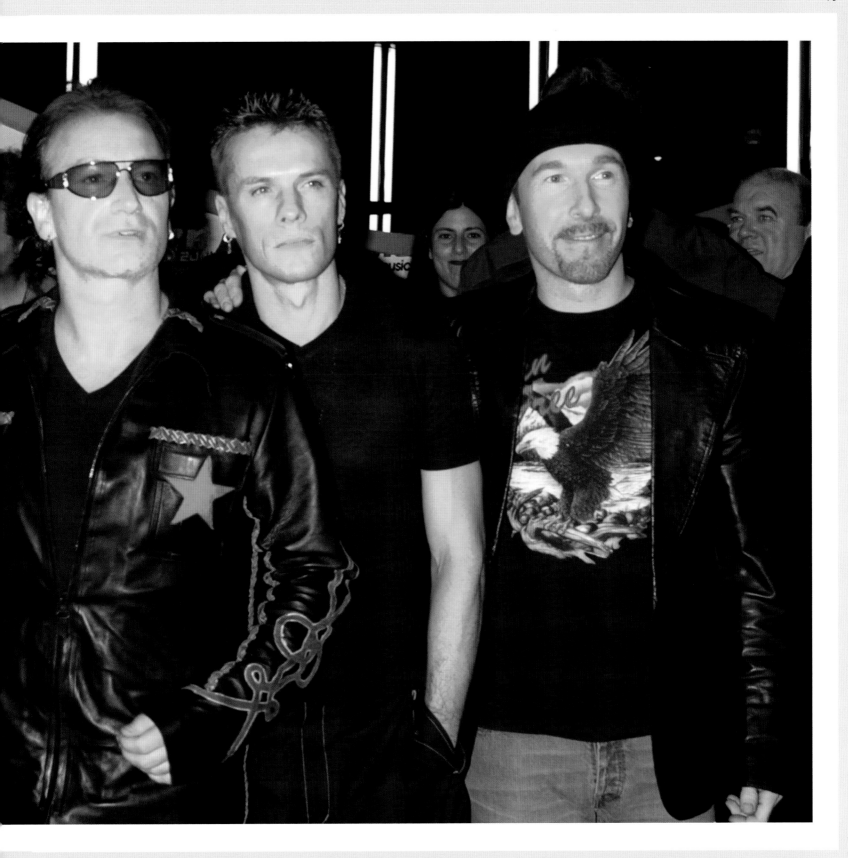

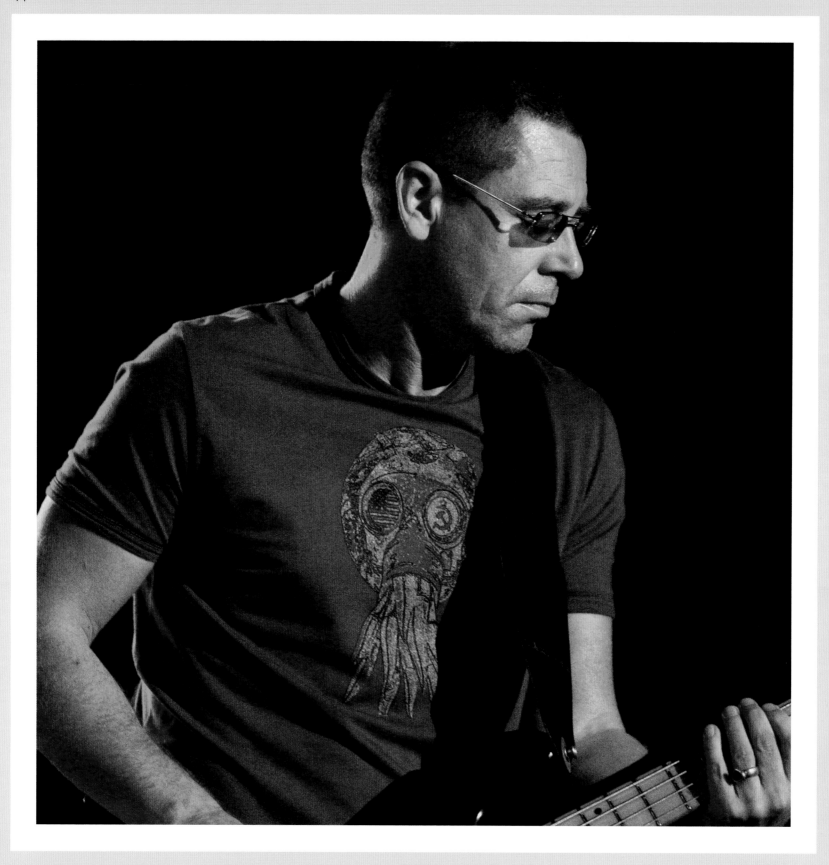

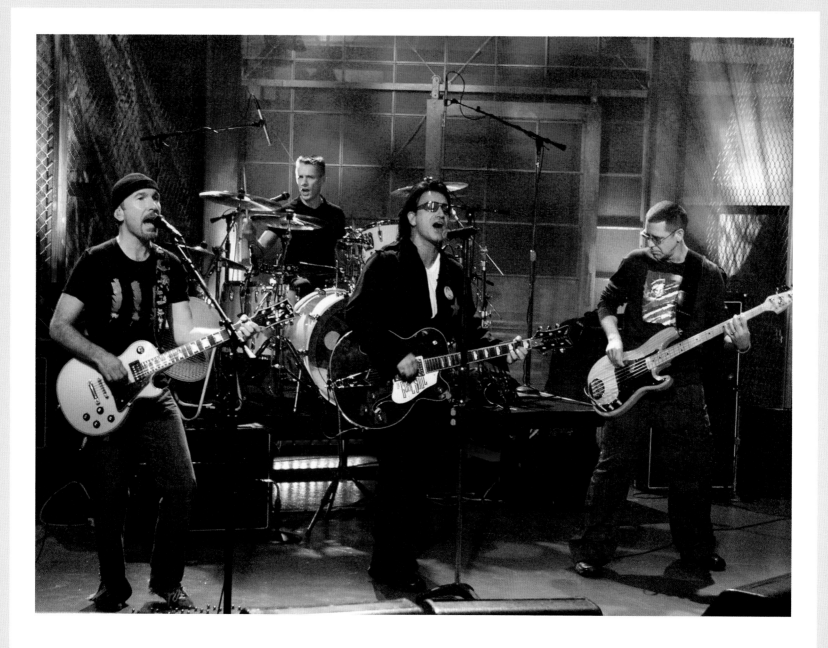

Tears in the Garden

Opposite: Adam on stage at the Staples Center, Los Angeles, California.
On 24 October U2 played Madison Square Garden; it was a highly charged show, bringing the audience to tears. The experience had a big impact on the band which was reinforced by a visit to Ground Zero on 28 October. The band appeared on the *Late Show with David Letterman* the following day and significantly performed full versions of "New York" and "Stuck In A Moment You Can't Get Out Of"; normally guest music was limited to less than five minutes on the Letterman show.

Above: U2 performs on *The Tonight Show with Jay Leno* at the NBC Studios in Los Angeles on 21 November 2001. The show is a special Thanksgiving night broadcast honouring the US military with the live studio audience comprising military personnel in its entirety. The programme is broadcast around the world to watching US Armed Forces.

Piano man

Right: Bono and The Edge performing at
the Oakland Arena in Oakland, California, on
16 November 2001.

The last gig of the Elevation tour took place on
1 December at Tampa, Florida. Geographically the
tour finished close to where it started but without a
doubt the world had changed completely.
In early December the band started working on new
material, spending a week in a London recording
studio around 10 December.

Bill Clinton was in London with daughter Chelsea;
Bono and Ali attended his lecture at the Institute of
Education, the four of them have dinner afterwards
joined by Ronan Keating and they ended up with
an impromptu performance for Chelsea by Bono
at the piano of the Groucho Club. Bono's last
campaigning meeting of the year was with Prime
Minister Tony Blair, discussing the problems of
African nations' debt, poverty, disease and famine.

2002 again started well for the band who in
January were already working on their next album
when they received eight Grammy nominations,
going on to win four of them in March, taking their
tally to 14 with *All That You Can't Leave Behind*
responsible for seven.

Bono's campaigning was top of his agenda during
the year and although he commented that the band
was doing well in his absence, time will bring this
into question. A big step forward for Bono was
setting up DATA with Bill Gates to manage his
campaigning for the end of third-world poverty.

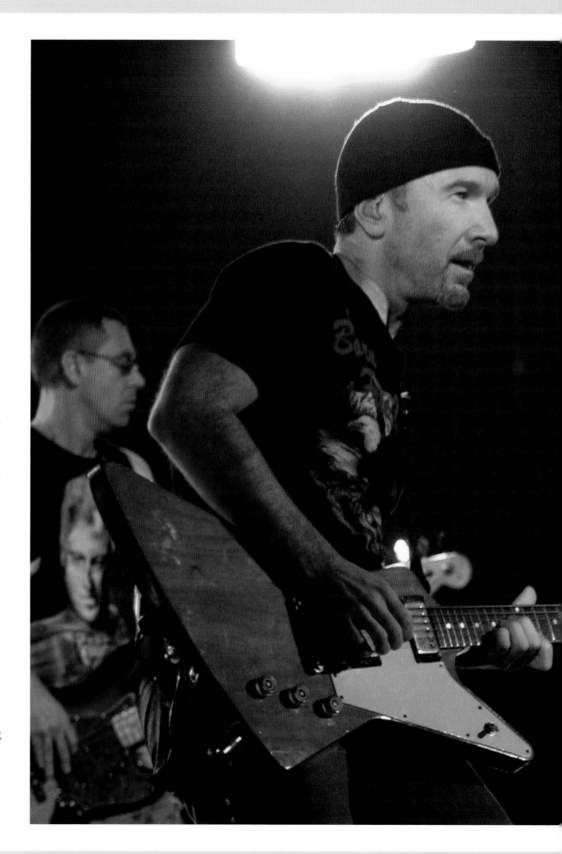

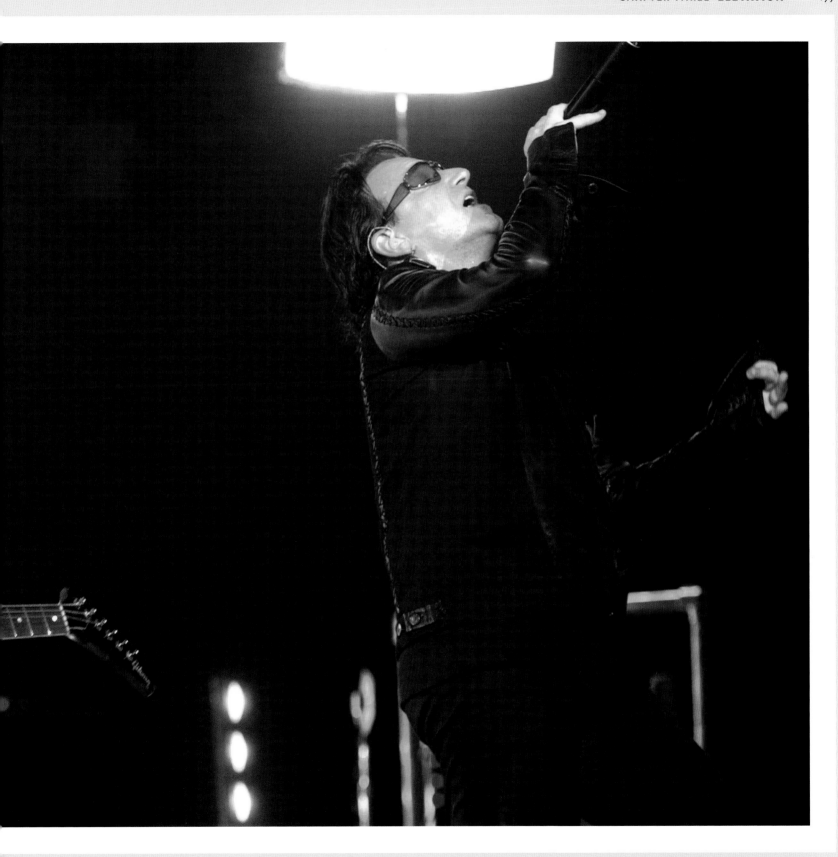

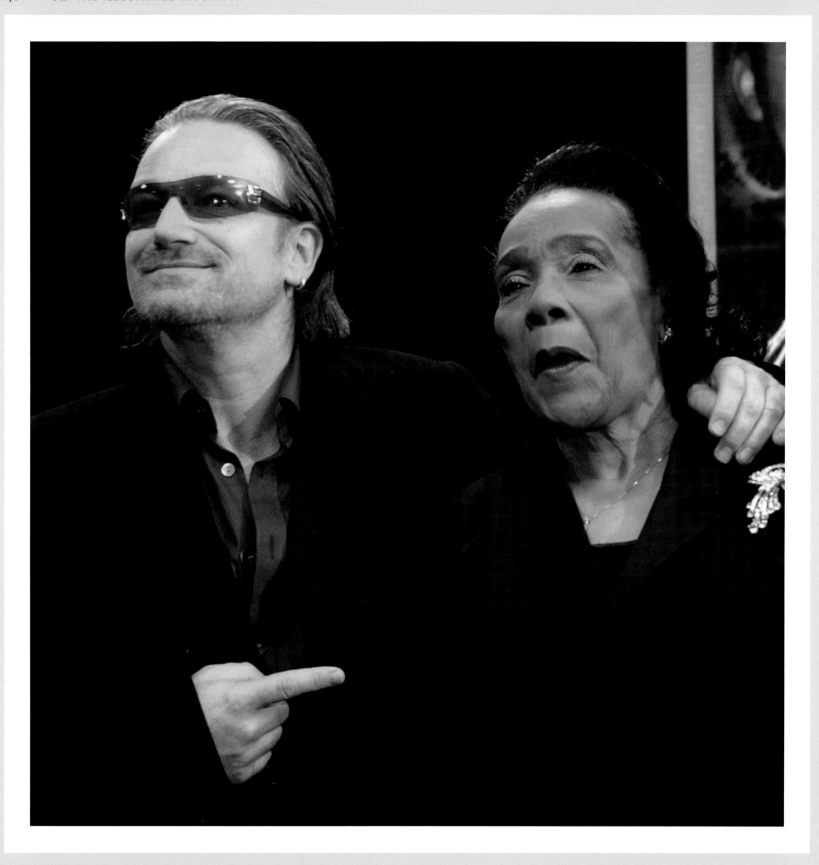

2002

Opposite: Bono points to his "mother" Coretta Scott King, widow of civil rights leader Martin Luther King Jr., during a news conference on 17 January 2004 in Atlanta, Georgia. Bono was honoured by the King Center during their annual Salute to Greatness awards dinner as a part of the 36th King Holiday Observance.

Right: Bono gives the crowd a peace sign at the launch of The "One" Campaign to Fight Global Aids and Poverty on 16 May 2004 in Philadelphia, Pennsylvania. Activists including New York Knick Dikembe Mutombo, Christian musician Michael W. Smith, Reverend David Beckman and Philadelphia 76ers' General Manager Billy King were among the attendees at the rally in front of Independence Hall.

In early summer 2002 Bono toured Africa with US Treasury Secretary Paul O'Neill; after 11 days the pair had differing opinions.

On a musical note, the compilation album *The Best of 1990-2000* was released in early November 2002 and sold strongly and a long-running project came to fruition in December with the premiere of Martin Scorsese's movie *Gangs of New York*: Bono and The Edge sang "The Hands That Built America" live for the first time at an after-show party; written for the movie soundtrack, the song will win them a Golden Globe the following January.

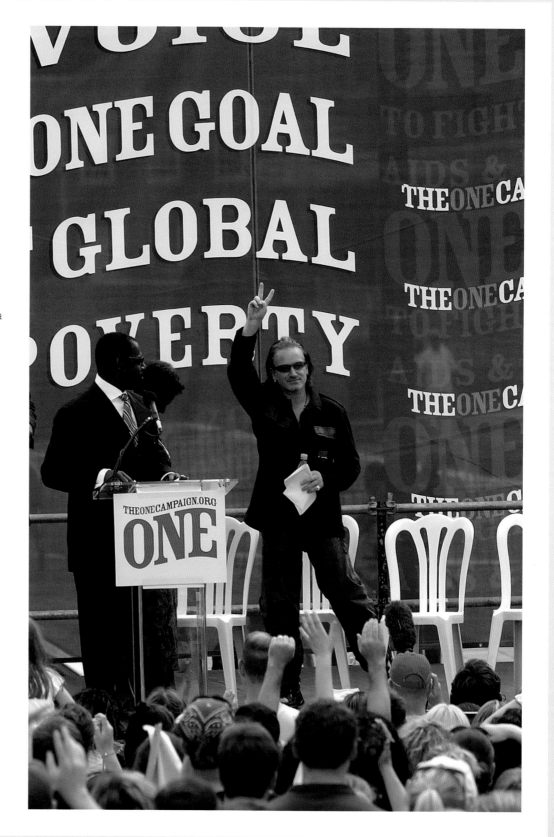

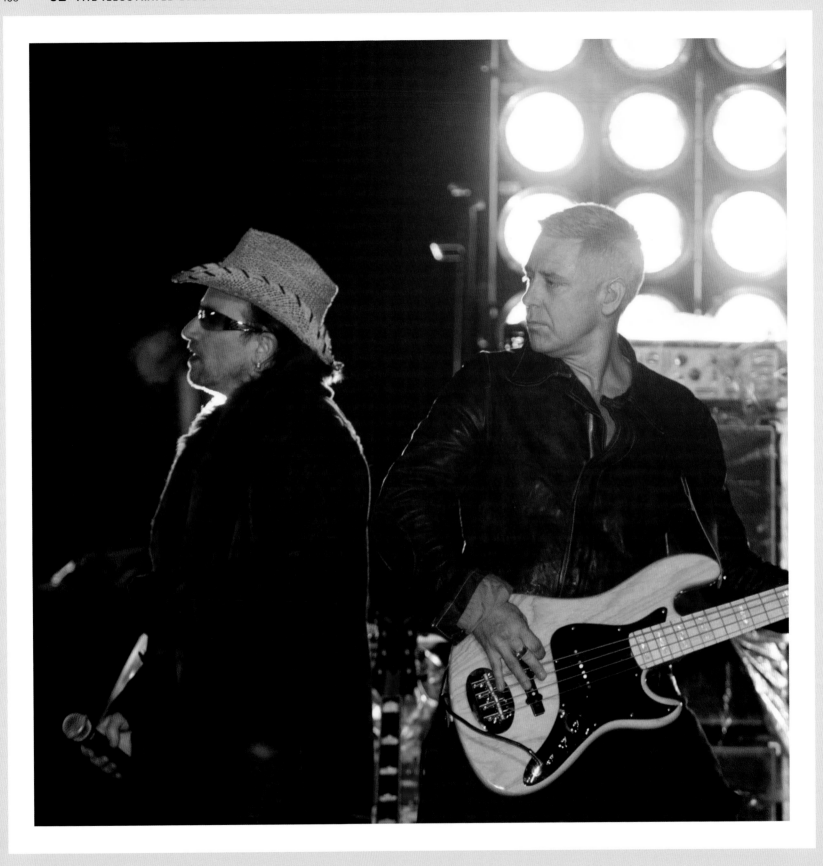

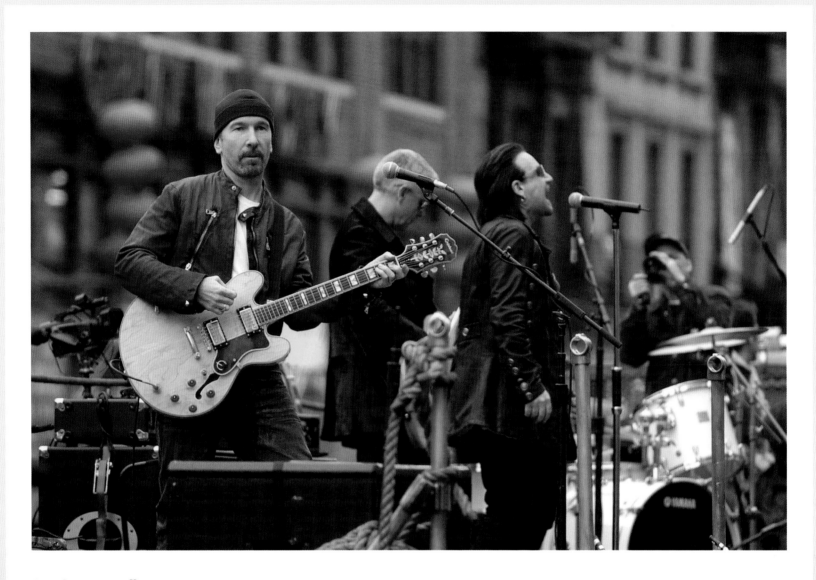

Creating a new album

Opposite: Bono and Adam perform on stage for *Top Of The Pops* at BBC
Television Centre on 15 October 2004 in London.
2003 dawned with U2's next album as a priority – especially for Bono; In
February they began work in their Hanover Quay studio in Dublin with
producer Chris Thomas. Looking for change, Eno and Lanois were not in
the frame and the band had high hopes for the veteran producer who had
previously worked with the likes of Roxy Music and the Sex Pistols.

Ever interested in new media developments, U2 started an association
with Apple's nascent iTunes whose online store launched on 28 April
2003; Bono appeared in the launch announcement and early on U2 ran
iTunes exclusives.

Bono's crusading continued earning him accolades including France's
Legion of Honour and honorary Doctor of Laws from Trinity College Dublin.

Above: U2 perform from a flatbed truck as it passes through Chinatown,
New York City, during filming of the promo video for their second single
release from the new album; Phil Joanou is directing and fans follow the
band around Manhattan as they go up and down the city on 22 November
2004, the date of the album release.

In November 2003 the new album was apparently nearing completion
but all was clearly not well and after a disastrous studio session in London
with a 50-piece orchestra, Daniel Lanois arrived in U2's Dublin studio to
listen to the current mix. The outcome of Lanois' visit was not revealed
until news broke in mid-February that Steve Lillywhite had been called in
to take over from Thomas. In Edge's words, "The record felt finished one
day and then, suddenly, it wasn't finished."

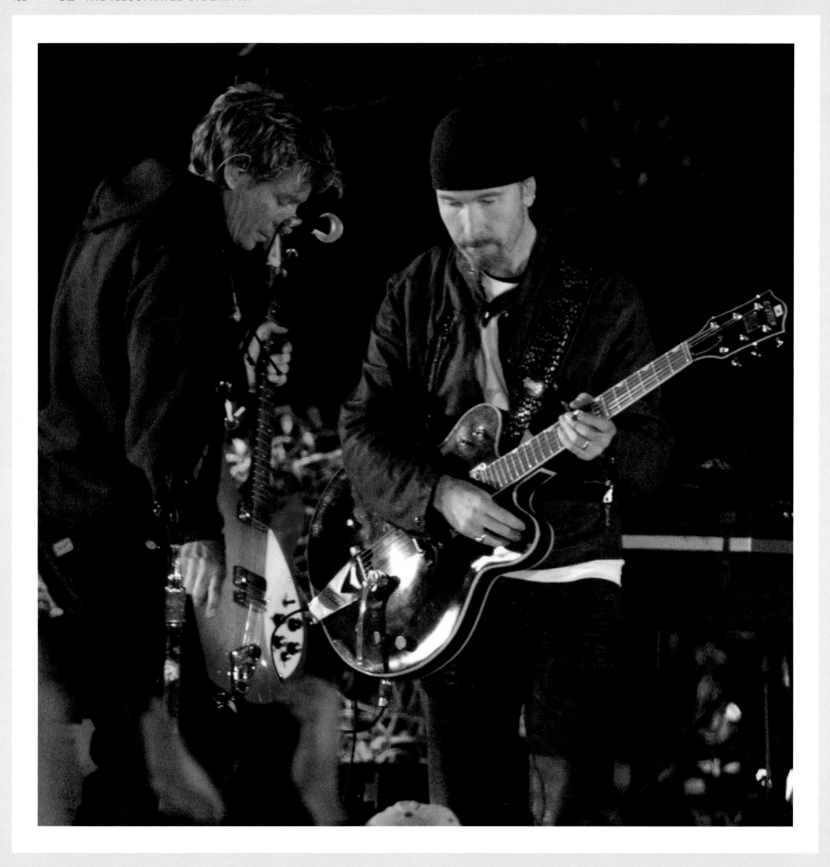

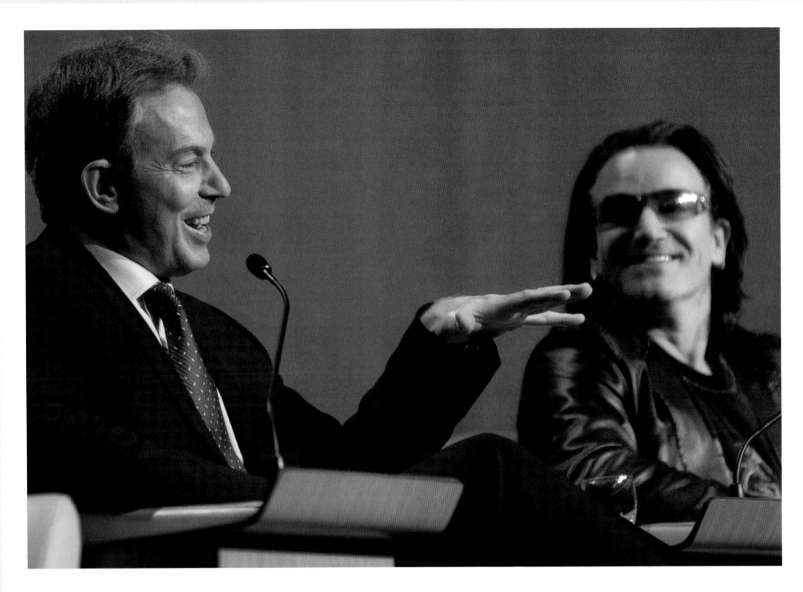

Dealing with Vertigo

Opposite: After shooting the promo, the same evening U2 staged a free concert to be taped for MTV at Empire-Fulton Ferry State Park in the New York City borough of Brooklyn. Not formally announced, news of the concert spread rapidly via the internet bringing crowds from all over the city.

By 4 July the new album was complete and given the title *How To Dismantle An Atomic Bomb*. Willie Williams was called in to discuss ideas for the staging of the promotional tour which will be called Vertigo – the title of the album's opening track. Willie's ideas for the set revolved around the effigy of a bomb but in Bono and Edge's thinking the bomb was much more metaphorical and about relationships rather than the threat of mutually assured destruction.

Above: UK Prime Minister Tony Blair, left, shares a laugh with Bono, during a session on the G8 and Africa at the World Economic Forum in Davos, Switzerland, 27 January 2005. Blair said the G8 industrialized nations should consider all options for fighting poverty and disease in Africa, including a French proposal to tax capital flows.

In the run-up to the release of the new album, U2 were busy using iTunes as a promotional vehicle, recording exclusive video adverts and announcing the first "digital boxed set" – *The Complete U2*, which will be exclusive to iTunes, retailing at $149 with over 400 tracks. In October Apple announced a version of the iPod to tie in with *How To Dismantle An Atomic Bomb*. U2's 11th studio album was released worldwide on 22/23 November 2004, going immediately to number 1 in many countries, including the US.

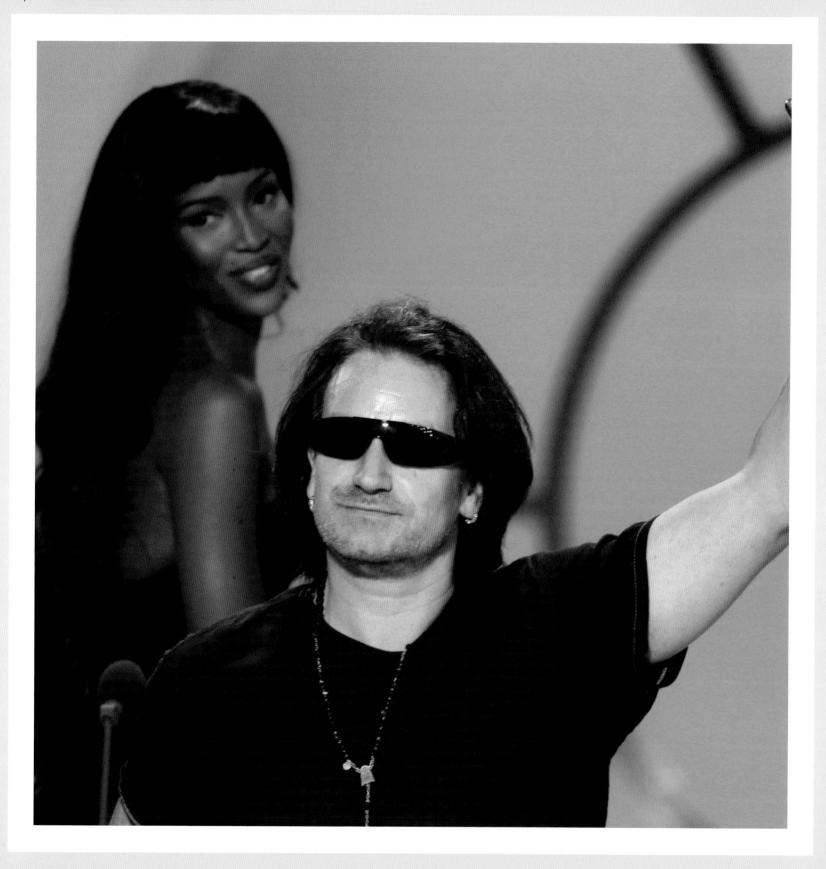

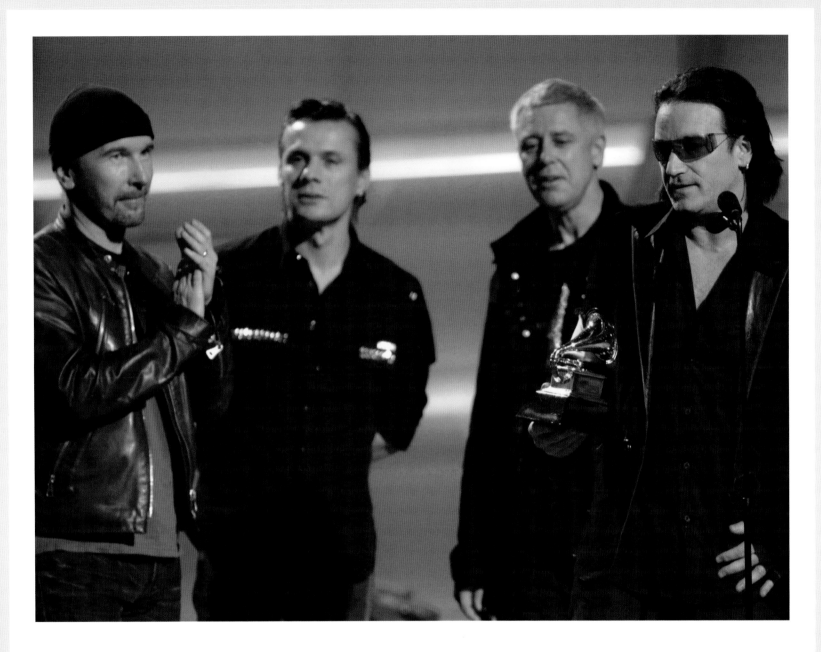

Personal pain for The Edge

Opposite: Naomi Campbell looks on during the NRJ music awards ceremony in Cannes on 22 January 2005 having presented a Special Achievement Award to Bono who accepted on behalf of the band.
The first single from the new album was "Vertigo", released in the first half of November 2004 and reaching the top slot on both sides of the Atlantic in the singles charts.

Above: U2 accept the award for Best Rock Performance by a Duo or Group With Vocal on stage during the 47th Annual Grammy Awards at Staples Center, Los Angeles, 13 February 2005.
In mid-December 2004, just as they were on the point of releasing the forthcoming tour dates and tickets going on sale, Edge learned his daughter Sian was seriously ill, delaying the release by about 6 weeks. With this personal dark cloud over The Edge, the following February's Grammy Awards brought better news as "Vertigo" scooped U2 another three Grammies.

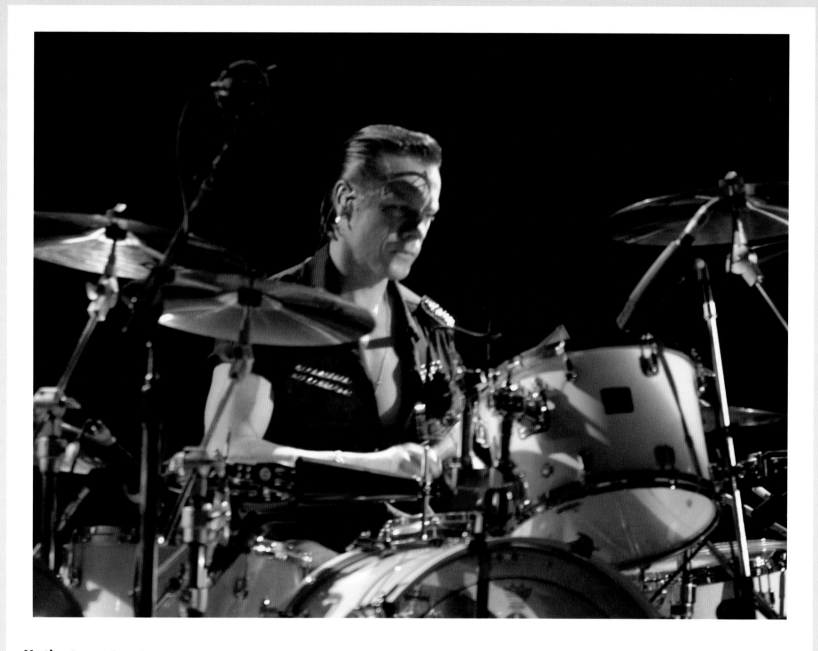

Vertigo tour sets out

Above: Larry drums during the Vertigo tour at Fleet Center, Boston, on 28 May 2005.

With *How To Dismantle An Atomic Bomb* already having reached number 1 in the UK and US album charts in December, the first US leg of the Vertigo tour began in San Diego's iPayOne Center on 28 March. The stage featured curtains of LED lights as a backdrop and with the actual stage based on concentric circles and a circular enclosure to replace the heart shape of the Elevation tour.

Opposite: U2, performing live onstage at Twickenham stadium just outside London on 19 June during the Vertigo tour. The picture shows the stage set and lighting of the outdoor set-up brought in for the European leg of the tour.

Bono's campaigning didn't falter during the Vertigo tour but it had to fit in with the band's commitments. During May he finally persuaded Bob Geldof to join him in organizing a sequel to Live Aid to be timed to coincide with the forthcoming G8 summit in Edinburgh in July.

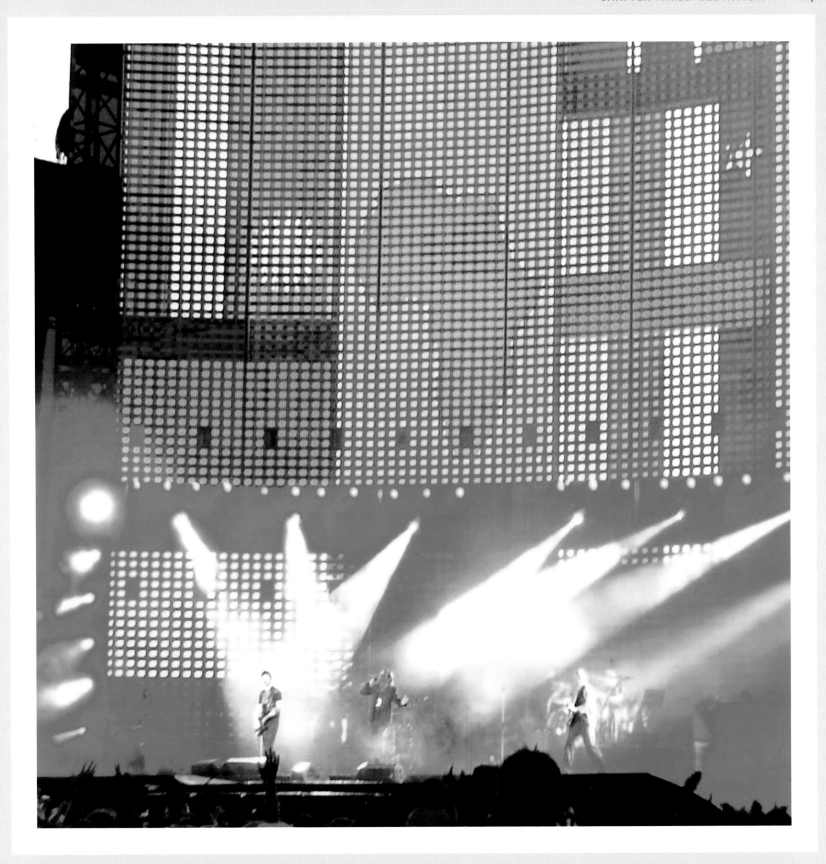

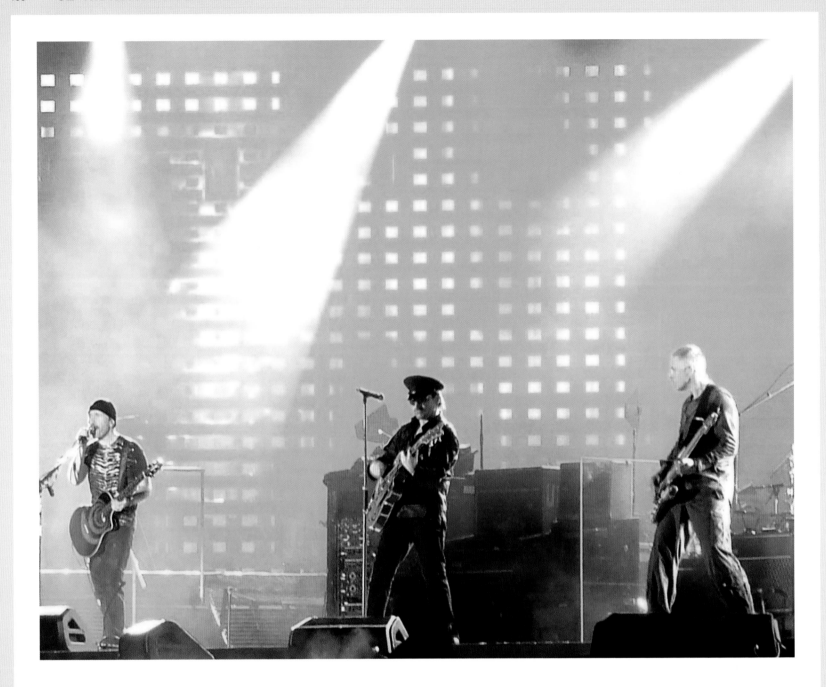

Make Poverty History

Above: U2 perform at Twickenham in June 2005.

The European leg opened in Brussels on 10 June with the band returning to Ireland and the UK for shows in Manchester, London and Glasgow followed by three sold-out shows in Dublin's Croke Park on 24,25 and 27 June. But the big one was Live 8 in Hyde Park on 2 July which U2 opened with Paul McCartney, performing a version of "Sgt Pepper's Lonely Hearts Club Band".

Opposite: The Edge and Bono perform on stage at Live 8 London in Hyde Park, 2 July 2005. Simultaneous shows are taking place in Philadelphia, Berlin, Rome, Paris, Barrie, Tokyo, Cornwall, Moscow and Johannesburg with the same goal – to raise awareness of poverty in the world's poorest countries. On the day U2 are unable to wait around for the extensive shows to play out as they rush off to a Vertigo gig that evening in Vienna.

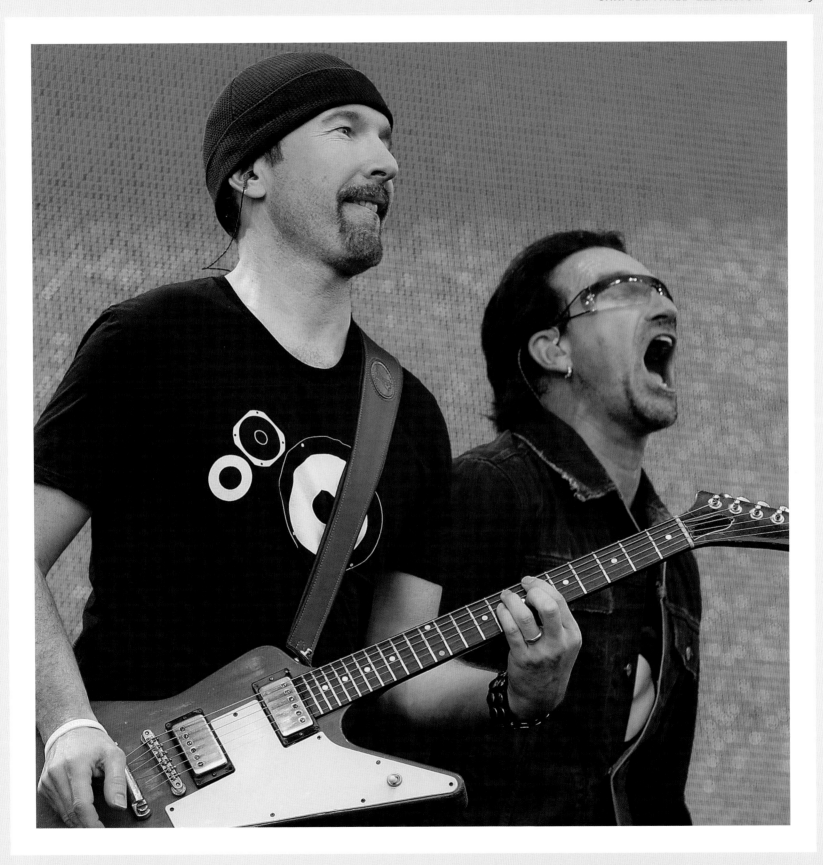

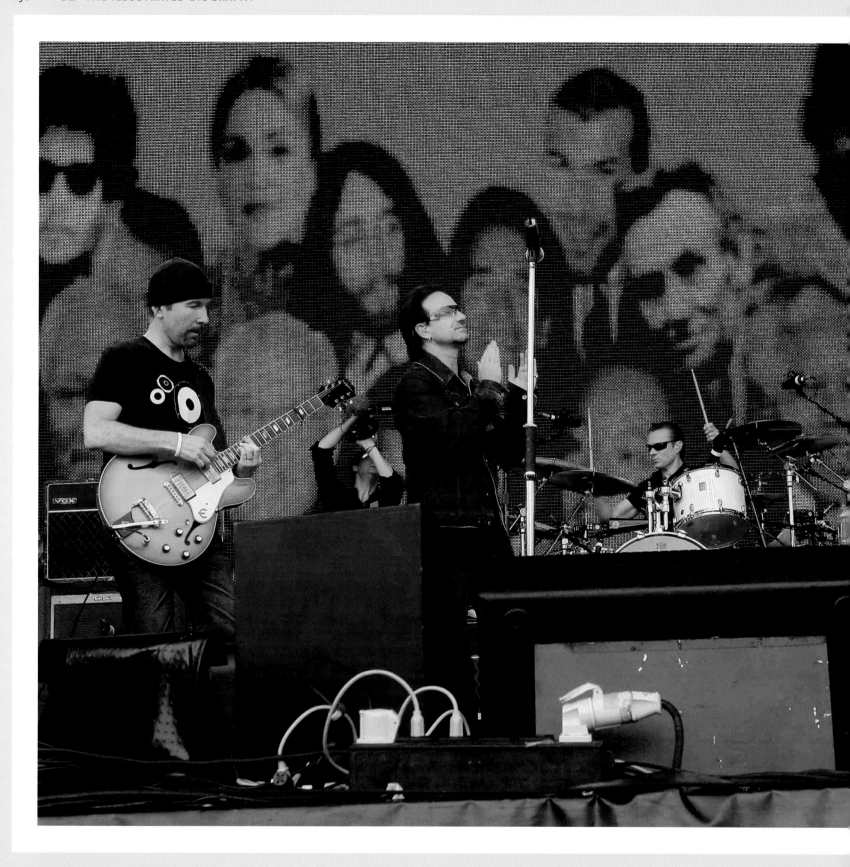

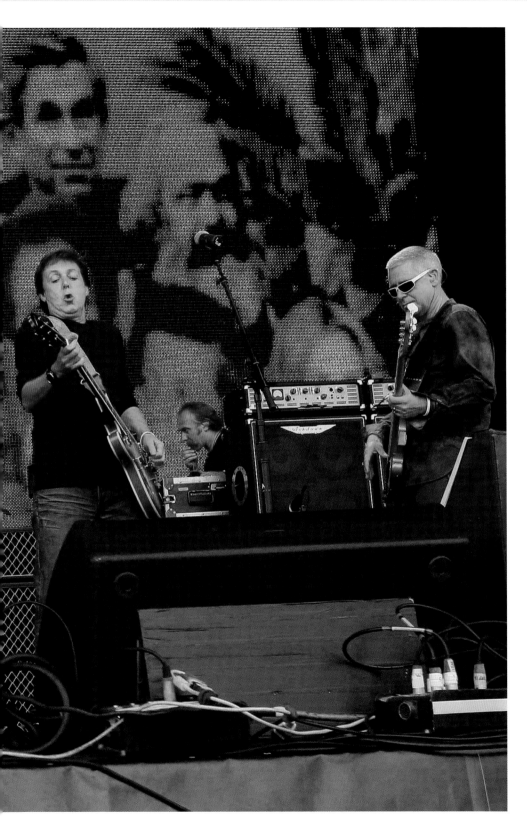

Joining together

Left: U2 with Paul McCartney open proceedings at Live 8 in Hyde Park, London, on 2 July.

The strength of the music world's commitment to making the world better was summed up by Pink Floyd's decision to reunite to play Live 8 after years of rancour between Roger Waters and the rest of the band. Likewise Madonna's performance while holding the hand of the (now grown-up) child whose plight during the Ethiopian famine had triggered Bob Geldof's determination to mount Live Aid 20 years earlier gave evidence of what had actually been achieved.

Four days after Live 8 London Bono flew back from Poland for the opening day of the G8 Summit in Edinburgh; as well as speaking at a press conference he held meetings with four of the heads of state attending – UK Prime Minister Tony Blair, Germany's Chancellor Gerhard Schroeder, Canadian Prime Minister Paul Martin and US President George W. Bush.

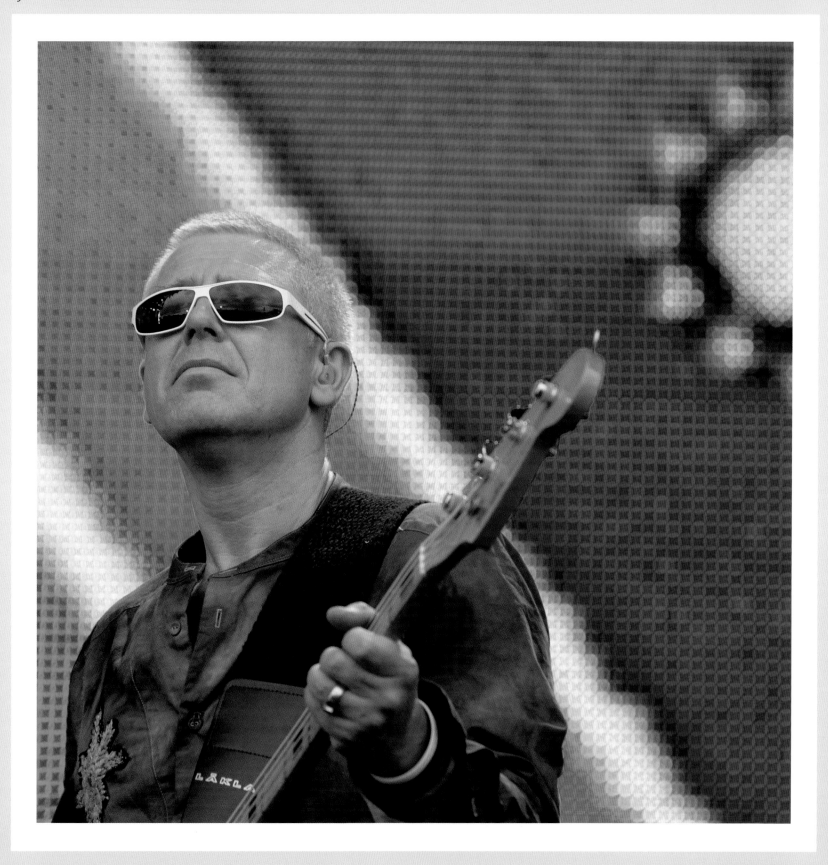

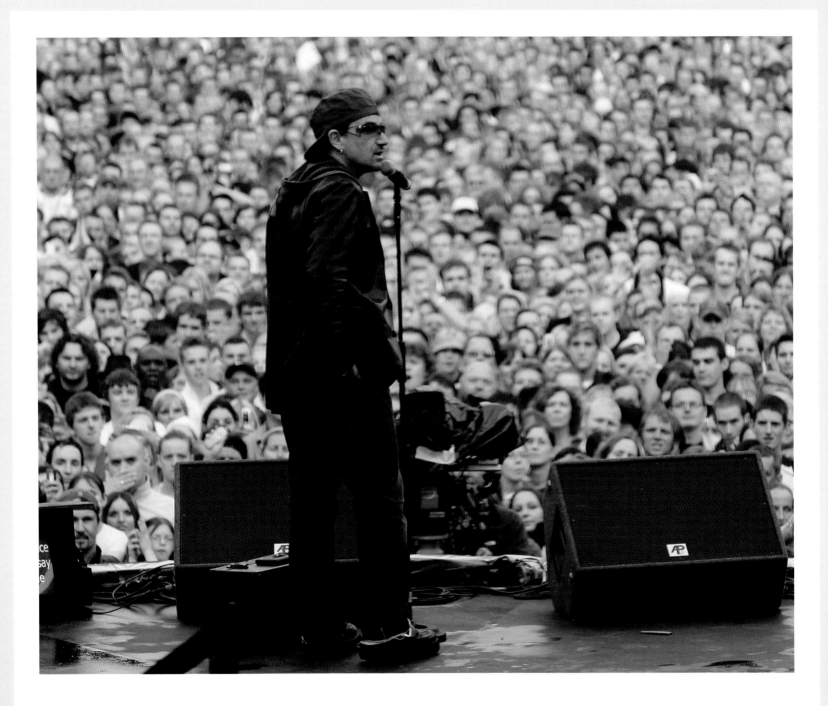

The shades are on

Opposite: Adam performs on stage at Live 8 London looking extra cool against the brightly lit stage backdrop.

Above: Bono addresses the crowd at the Live 8 concert at Murrayfield Stadium on 6 July 2005 in Edinburgh, Scotland. The free gig, labelled Edinburgh 50,000 – The Final Push, was a culmination of generally peaceful protest to the G8 by 225,000 supporters of Make Poverty History. Bono performed at the concert singing "When The Stars Go Blue" with The Corrs.

On 7 July the G8 announced they would double aid to the poorest countries but events in London overshadowed the successes of the campaign as more than 50 people died in bomb attacks.

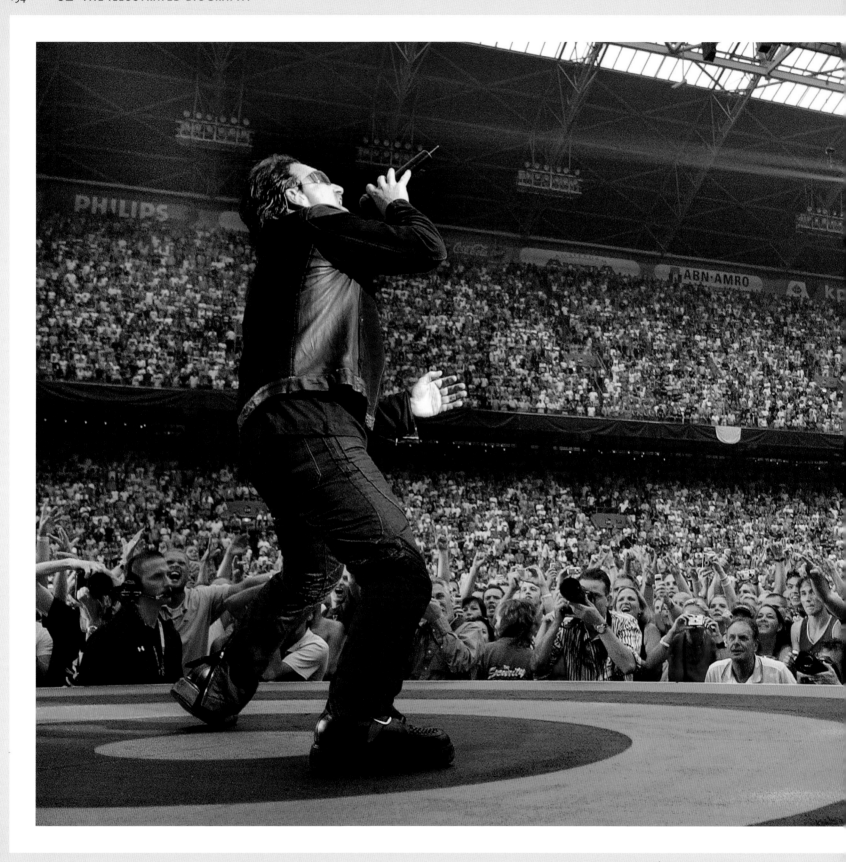

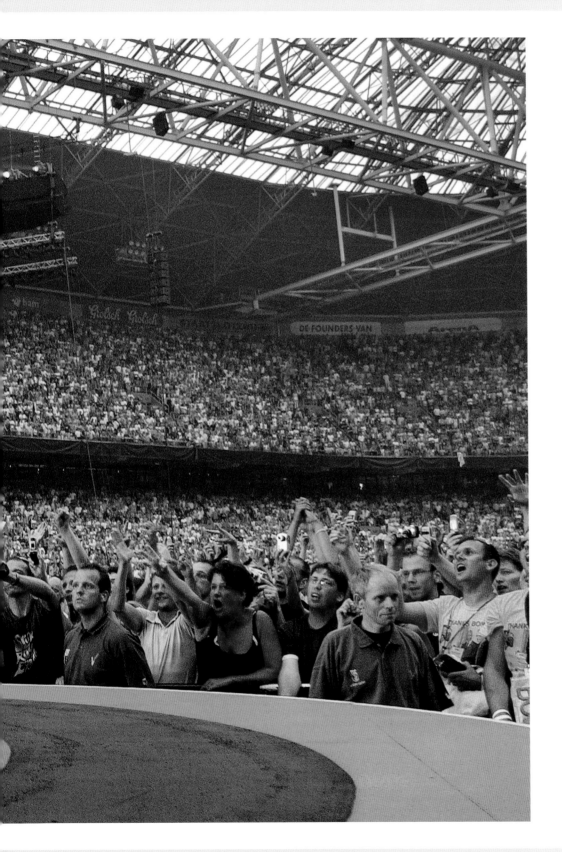

European Vertigo

Left: Bono performs live on stage in front of a capacity crowd at the Arena, Amsterdam on 13 July – the first of three dates at the huge venue. The European leg ended in Lisbon on 14 August and the tour took up again in Toronto on 12 September – another North American leg with many more dates than the first one. In the aftermath of August's Hurricane Katrina, U2 were keen to support the aid programme with Edge's Music Rising charity particularly involved in a campaign to replace the thousands of instruments lost by musicians during the catastrophic flooding of New Orleans in the wake of the storm. Edge visited the ravaged city on 17 November.

At the Wachovia Center show in Philadelphia on 17 October, Bono announced they needed an extra guitarist to help play "People Get Ready"; the audience expected that, as on previous occasions, a volunteer would be called up from the crowd. Instead Bruce Springsteen walked on to play in the song; soon after that The Boss's wife, Patti Scialfa joined the party to sing some more stanzas. The audience was suitably wowed. In November U2 announced an extension of the Vertigo tour with extra dates in Central and South America and Oceania added for 2006.

December 2005 brought news of five Grammy nominations and Bono's appearance on the cover of *Time* magazine with Bill and Melinda Gates who were jointly named *Time*'s Persons of the Year for 2005 as a result of their campaigning for social justice.

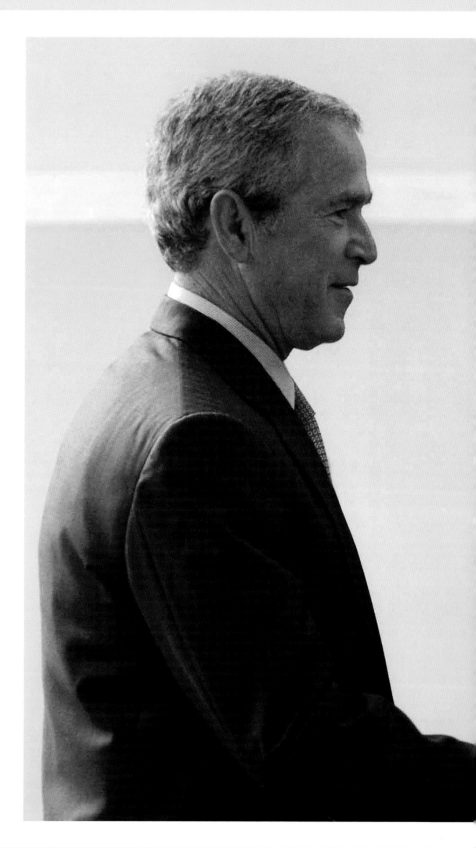

Better Red

Right: US President George W. Bush shakes hands with Bono under the piercing gaze of Bob Geldof on 6 June 2007 before a meeting of the G8 summit at the Baltic Sea resort of Heiligendamm, northeastern Germany. Bono, who also met summit host, German Chancellor Angela Merkel, lobbied the US President on aid to Africa from the sidelines of the G8 conference.

February's Grammy awards was another rich harvest for U2, winning in all five nominated categories. However, good news was tempered by bad when later in the month, with the Vertigo tour reaching full throttle, as the band completed the next leg in Latin America and were moving to the next stage in Australia, Edge's daughter's illness forced them to postpone the next 10 dates leaving fans up in the air for much of the rest of the year.

In January of 2006 Bono had launched his (Product) RED initiative which contributed aid funding from consumer spending, bringing on board major brands like Motorola and Gap during the year. The band's downtime in touring gave Bono a window to tour Africa in May, visiting six countries over ten days.

Finally, in July, new tour dates were announced for the postponed gigs in October through to December. Wrapping the tour with a big party jammed with celebs in Honolulu on 9 December the tour ended up as the second-highest grossing tour in the history of rock; they had sold the best part of 5 million tickets for $389 million. With a knighthood promised to Bono and the Vertigo tour a huge success the vexing matters of Sian's health and the next album remained on the horizon.

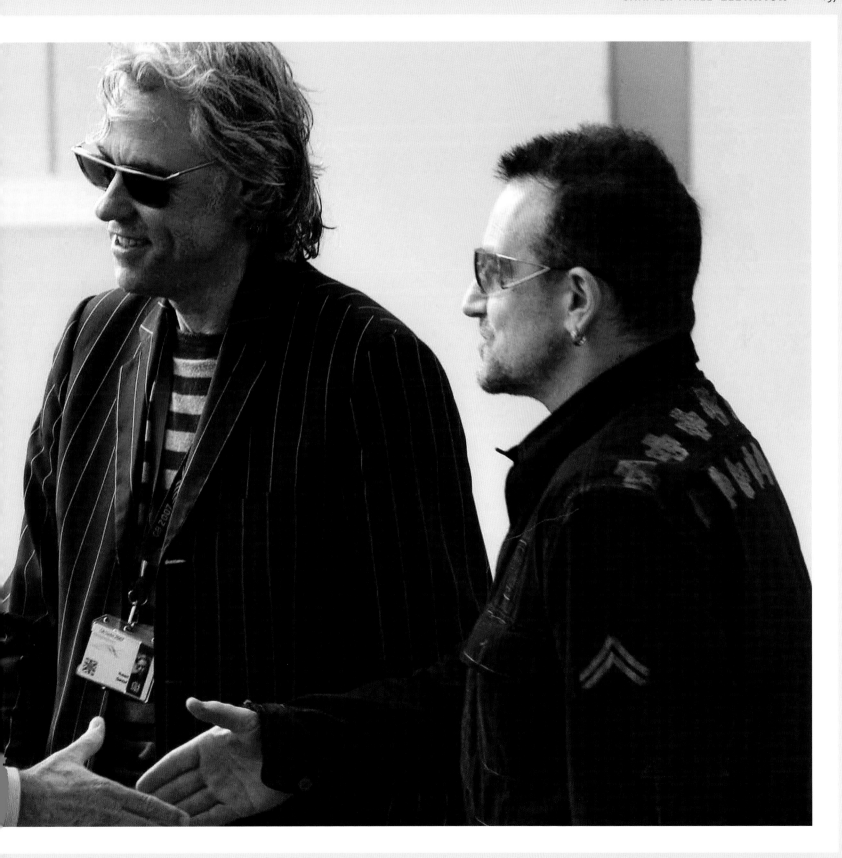

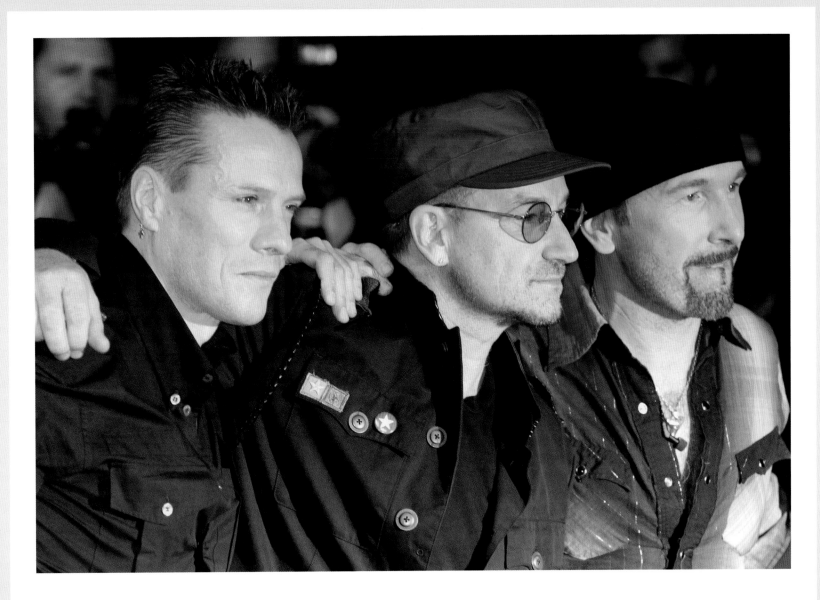

Another dimension

Above: Larry, Bono and The Edge attend the premiere of the film *U2 3D* at the Palais des Festivals during the 60th International Cannes Film Festival on 19 May 2007.

Work on a new album was already in hand: the band started recording with producer Rick Rubin in September 2006 but that work was abandoned. In May while they were working in their Dublin studio, Adam warned a fan that the album would not be released before 2008. Later that month U2 spent two weeks in Morocco with Daniel Lanois and Brian Eno, this time with the pair collaborating in writing rather than production. Fans have to survive on a diet of singles for some time ("Window in the Skies" released 1 January) or re-masters –*The Joshua Tree* remix went on sale in November.

Opposite: Bono acknowledges the crowd following his receiving the 2007 Liberty Medal during a ceremony at the National Constitution Center, in Philadelphia, Pennsylvania on Thursday 27 September 2007. The medal and $100,000 prize recognized Bono and DATA's (Debt, AIDS, Trade for Africa) work in spurring a positive global response to the crisis of AIDS and poverty in Africa.

In June Bono had taken the G8 world leaders to task for falling behind in their commitments which he insisted had to be measurable and within a timetable.

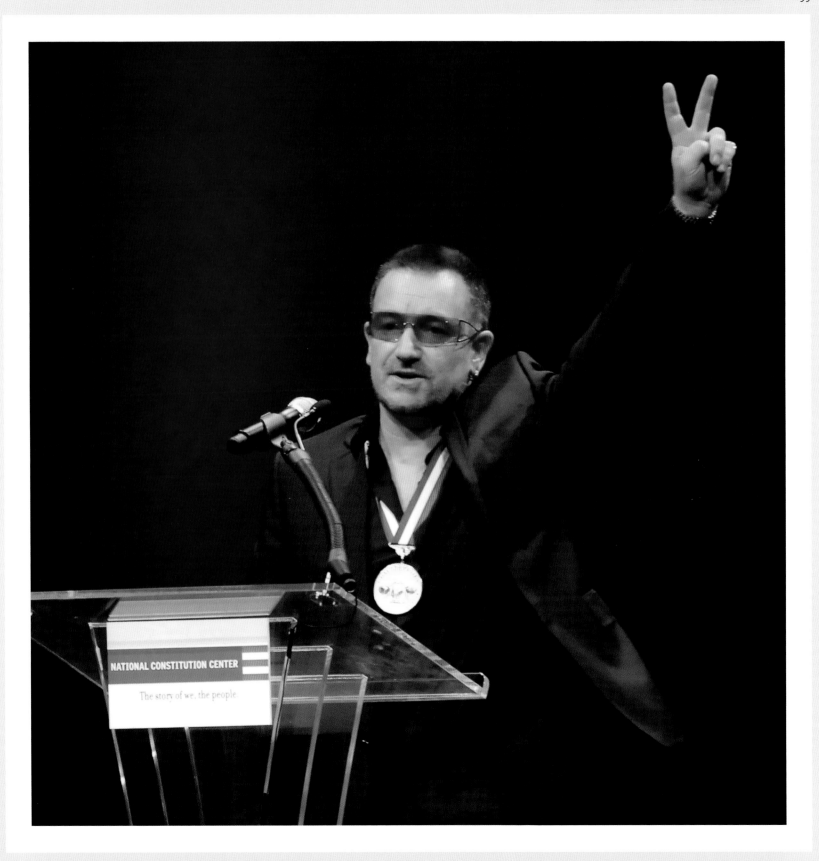

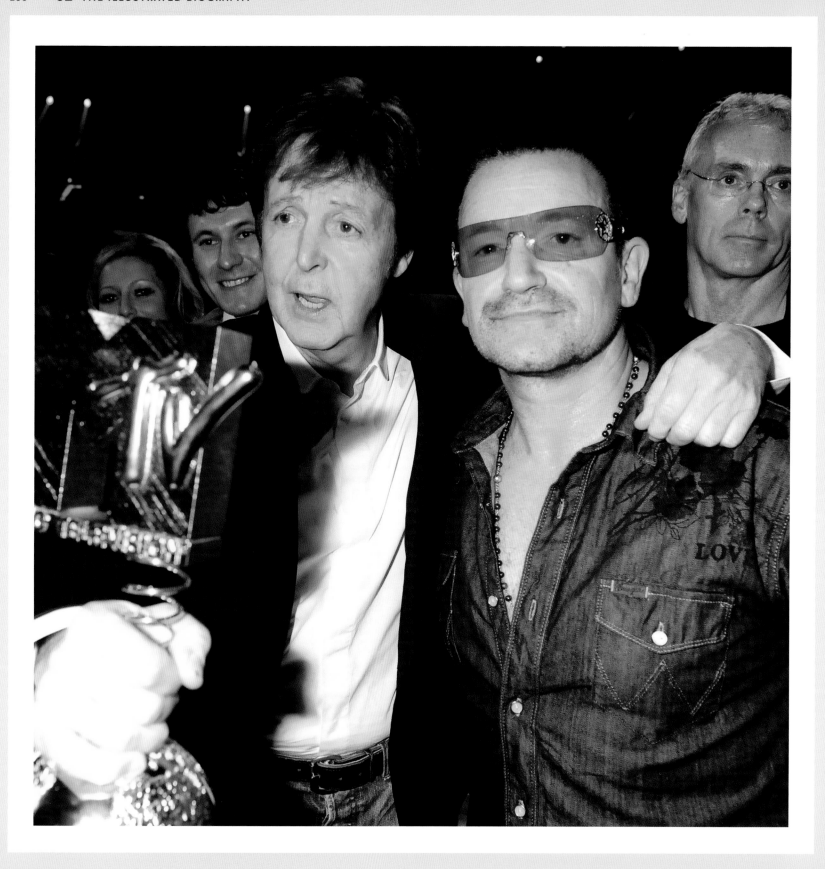

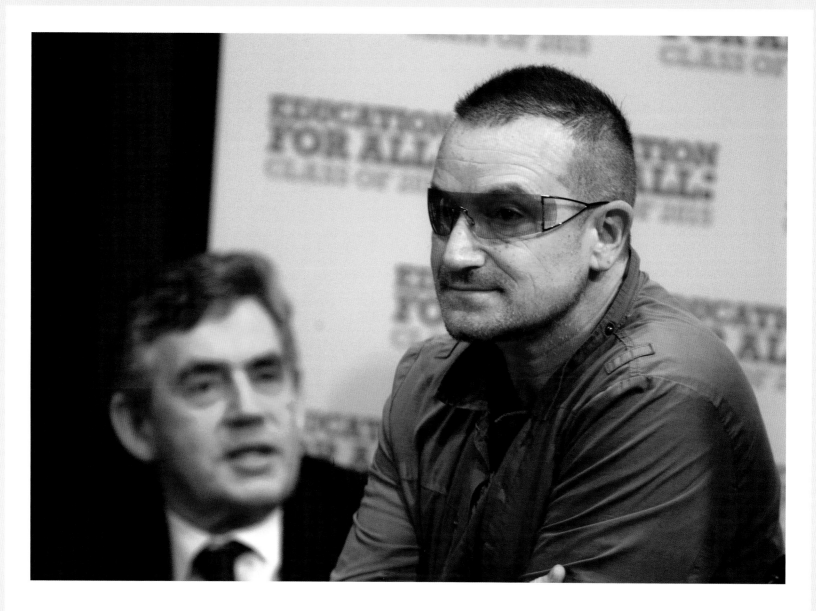

Knights of rock

Opposite: Sir Paul McCartney with his Ultimate Legend Award presented to him by Bono at the 2008 MTV Europe Music Awards held at the Echo Arena on 6 November 2008 in Liverpool, England. As he handed over the award Bono bowed before Macca and quipped: "You can call him Sir. I call him Lord." Bono received his honorary knighthood in March 2007.

Re-mastering of U2's early catalogue continued with *Boy, War, October* and *Under a Blood Red Sky* released in various formats in mid-2008. Work on the new album finished in December 2008 and they announced that *No Line On The Horizon* would be released in spring 2009.

Above: UK Prime Minister Gordon Brown and Bono attend a conference on education at the 63rd annual United Nations General Assembly at the UN in New York on 25 September 2008. Bono continued to hold world leaders to account: earlier in the year he met with French President Sarkozy who not only promised Bono he would restore €20 million cut from the Global Fund to fight AIDS, TB and malaria, he also committed to a plan to restore promised future French aid.

Having kept secure aid for the poorest nations, Bono and the band looked after their own finances with a 12-year merchandising agreement signed with Live Nation in March 2008.

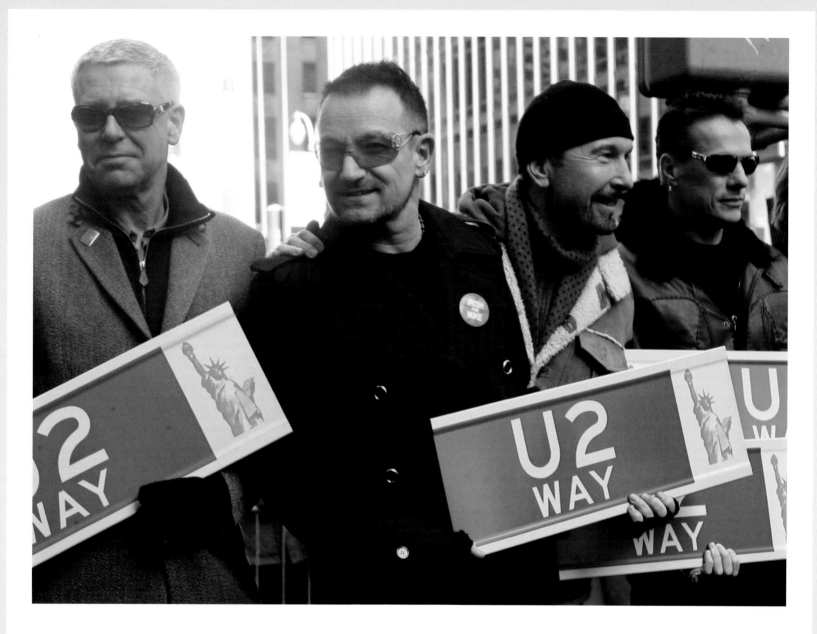

Where the Street has their name

Above: U2 attend the unveiling of a portion of West 53rd Street to be temporarily renamed "U2 Way" on 3 March 2009 in New York City. "Get on Your Boots", released on 23 January, was the first single from the new album which was launched on Interscope Records on 27 February 2009.

The U2 360° Tour set out from Barcelona, Spain, on 30 June 2009. Designer Willie Williams returned to an earlier idea that had been shelved as impractical – to place the stage in the middle of the audience so that the band was completely surrounded. To do this a claw-like structure carried the stage lighting and sound while a highly innovative LED screen

that could retract and unfold projected video content. The investment in the high-tec stage was immense and the structure was too large to freight from continent to continent so the band planned three of them at a cost of $15m each, partly funded by a sponsorship deal with phone company, Blackberry.

Opposite: U2 play a special live gig on top of the BBC building, Portland Place, London, on 27 February 2009. The exclusive performance for the BBC marked the release of their 12th studio album, *No Line On The Horizon*.

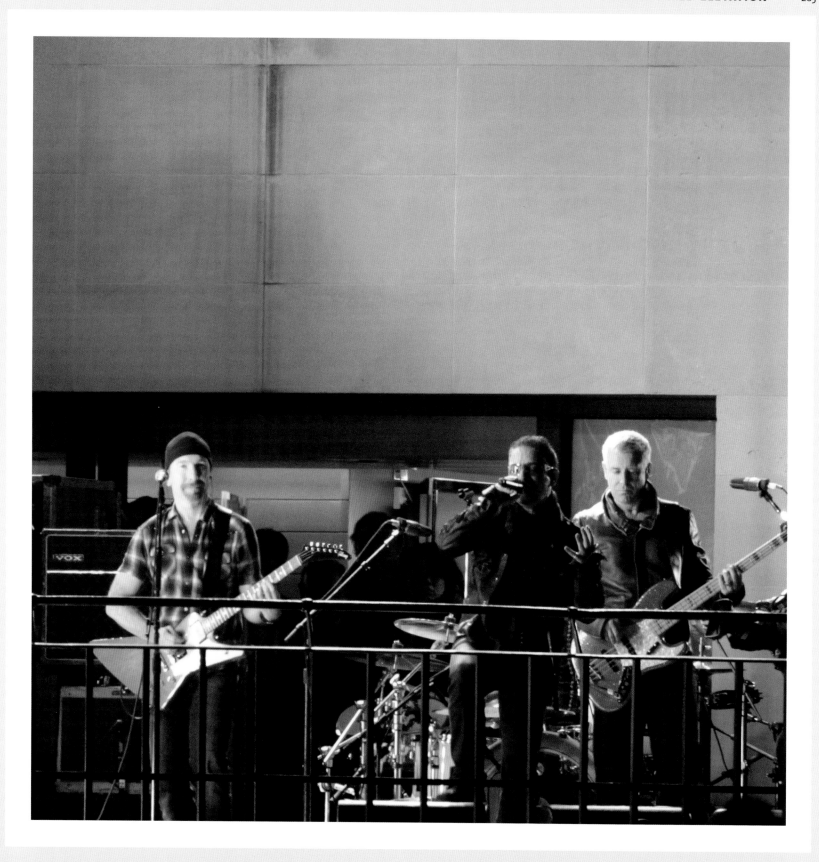

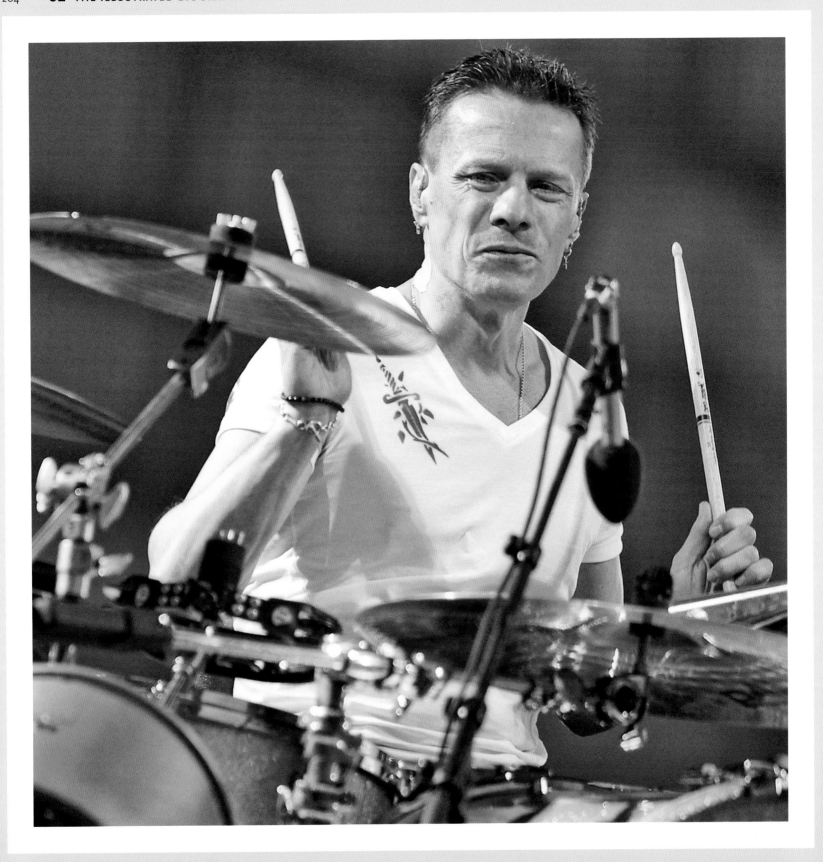

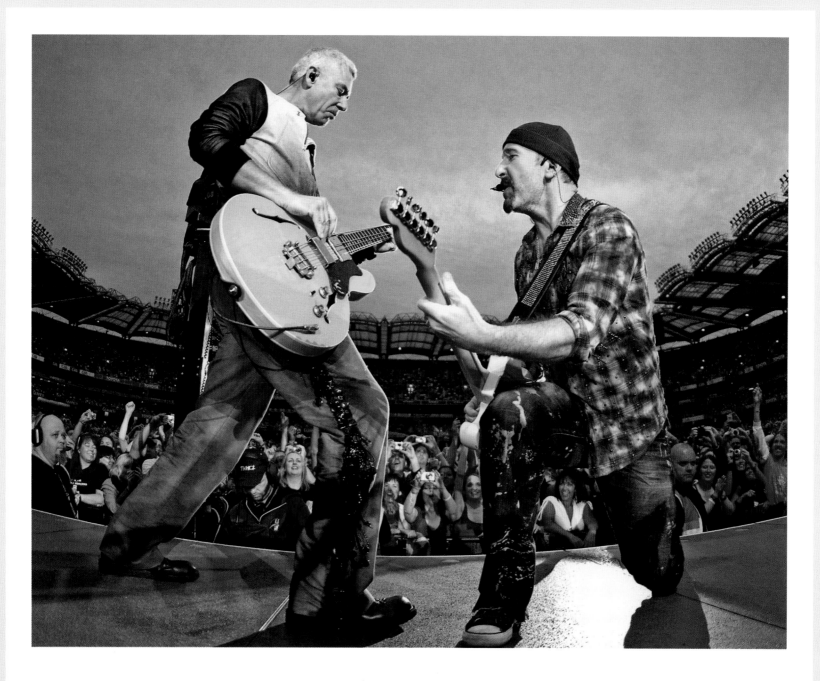

U2 YouTube

Opposite and above: Larry (opposite), Adam and The Edge (above) perform on stage at Croke Park, on 25 July 2009, the second date of three, in their home town Dublin, during U2's 360° World Tour.

Earning $311 million for the 44 shows in 2009, the U2 360° Tour was the highest-grossing tour of the year. The seven legs continue into July 2011 with 100 per cent sell-out to the end of the sixth leg in Sao Paulo, April 2011; the value of ticket sales up to that point was almost $600 million. The 25 October 2009 Rose Bowl concert in Pasadena, California, was broadcast live on YouTube and filmed in HD for a future video release This was the first time a concert streamed live on YouTube, and it was reported that almost 10 million people in 188 countries were watching. The concert itself, with over 90,000 people present in the Rose Bowl, broke previous US attendance records.

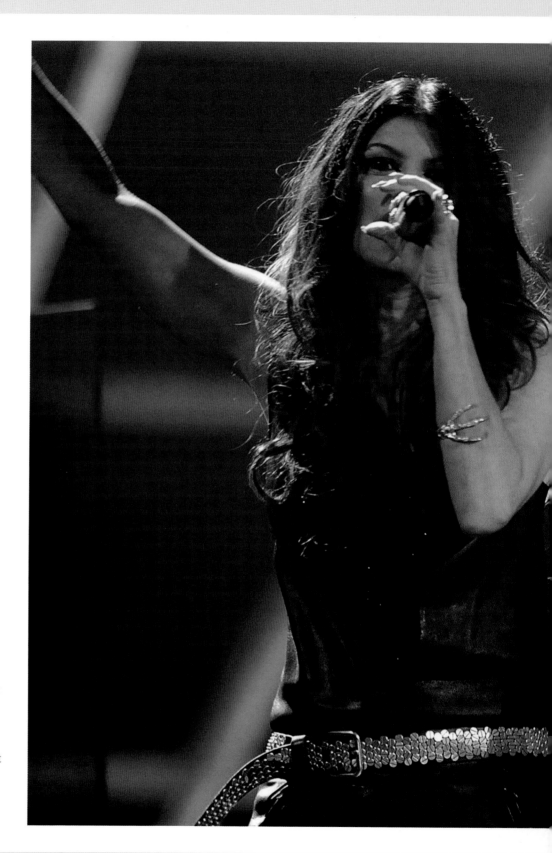

Unforgettable Fire remastered

Right: Fergie of Black Eyed Peas and The Edge
perform onstage at the 25th Anniversary Rock and
Roll Hall of Fame Concert at Madison Square Garden
on 30 October 2009 – a few days after the release
of a 25th anniversary remastered edition of *The
Unforgettable Fire* by Mercury Records.The slick timing
of the record company assured that, as the second leg
of the tour came to an end, there was the opportunity
to buy another of U2's re-mastered classics. With the
band's extensive back catalogue, some of their greatest
earnings successes were achieved by sales of already-
released albums being refreshed by touring and new
album promotional campaigns.

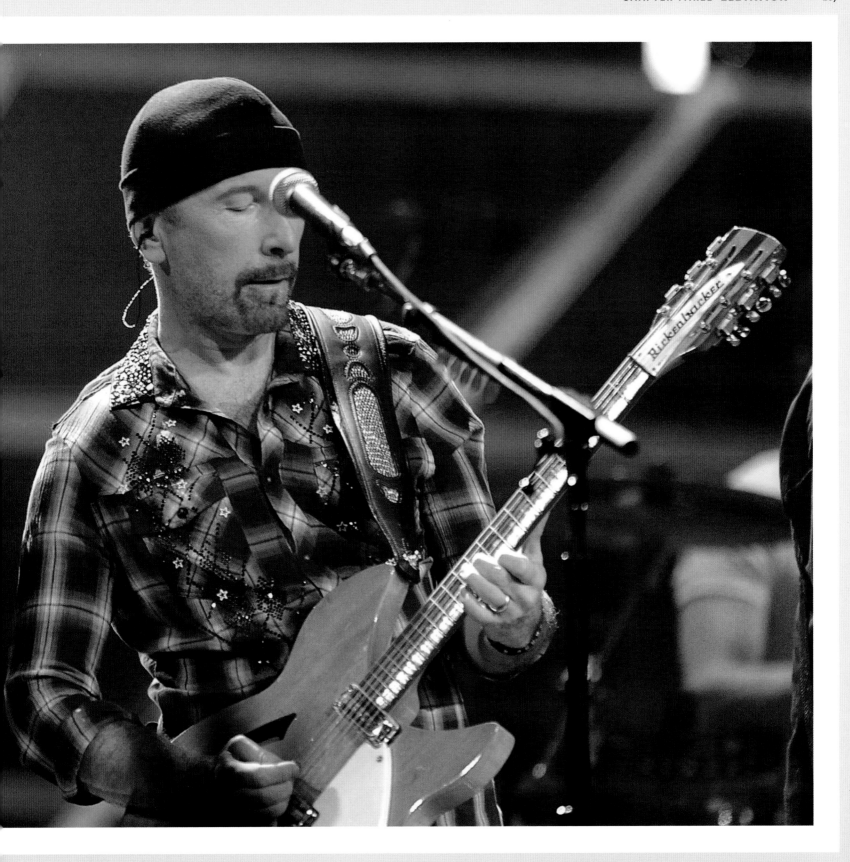

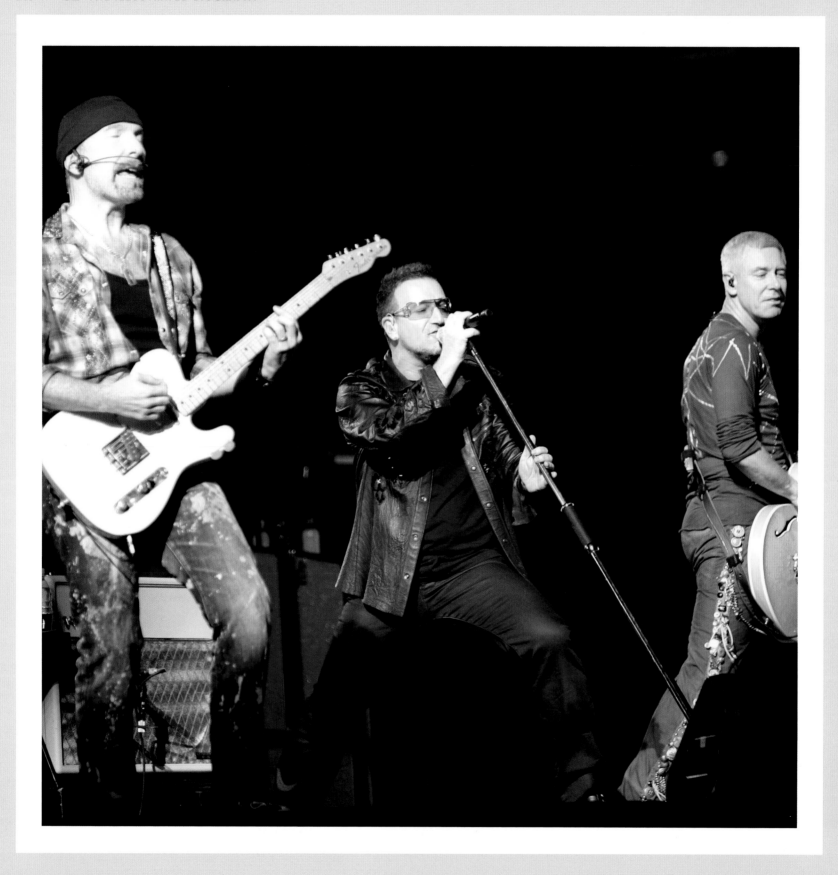

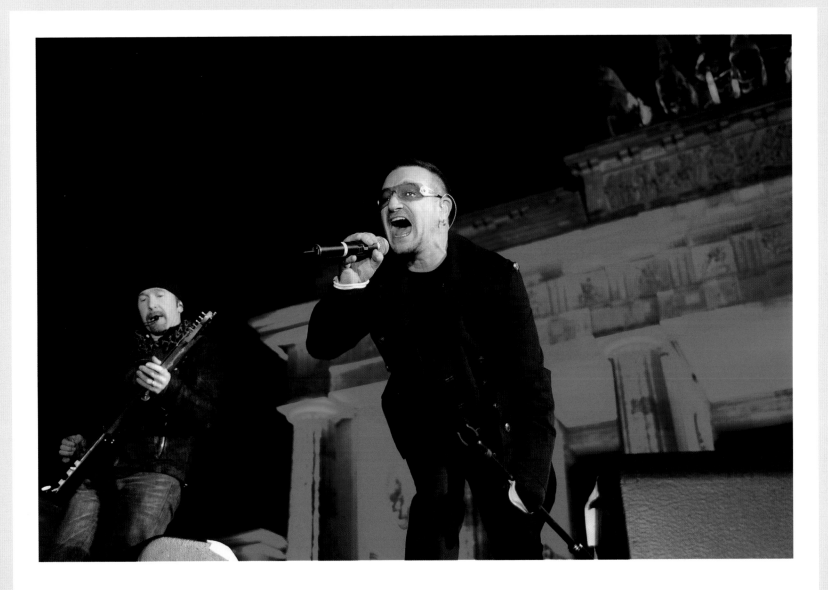

Forced to cancel

Opposite: The Edge, Bono and Adam perform at the Reliant Stadium in Houston, Texas on 14 October 2009.

For some years Bono had been troubled by intermittent back pain. In 2010 the problem became critical and he had to have emergency surgery on 21 May while in the USA, preparing for the third leg of the 360° Tour. This led to the entire leg being postponed until 2011 and U2's headlining of Glastonbury 2010 was cancelled. Damon Albarn's Gorillaz stepped in and Muse were joined by The Edge when they performed "Where The Streets Have No Name" while headlining the Pyramid Stage on Saturday night.

Above: The Edge and Bono perform in front of the Brandenburg Gate Berlin, Germany, on 5 November 2009 in. At the invitation of the city's Lord Mayor, U2 performed a free concert in collaboration with MTV Europe as part of the city's celebration of the 20th anniversary of the fall of the wall that bisected post-war Germany as well as its capital, Berlin. Ten thousand fans watched the band play a six-song set.

Despite many musical incarnations, the band stays close to its original artistic style, taking music and staging to high conceptual levels, their experimentation often taking them to the boundary's edge. The Spiderman musical, still in development by Bono and The Edge on Broadway, has had numerous delays but their determination and demand for perfection is likely to prevail here as it has elsewhere in the past.

U2 shows little sign of slowing down: the music still intrigues and astonishes fans old and new; the live shows still thrill.

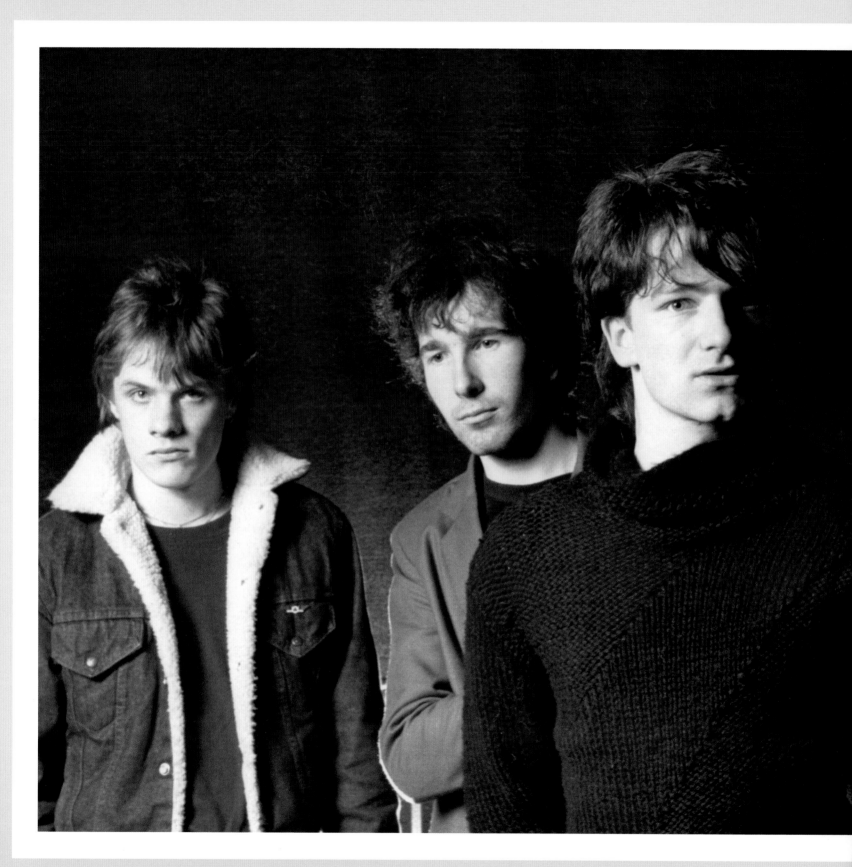

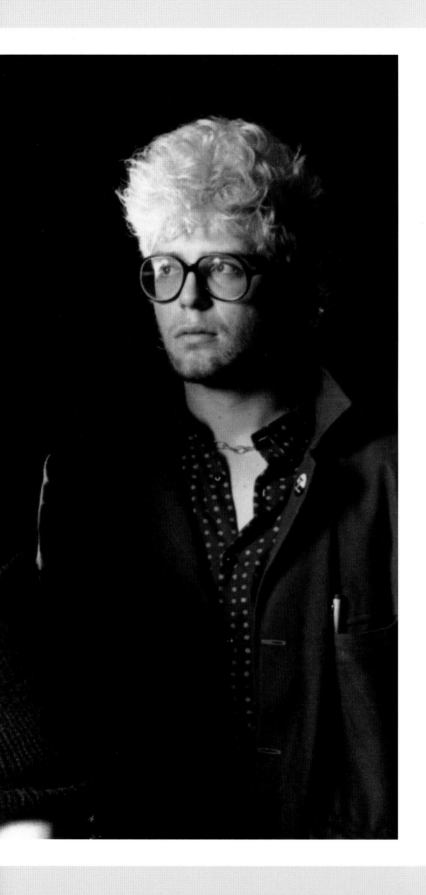

Chronology & Discography

Pre-1980

March 13, 1960: Adam Clayton is born in Chinnor, Oxfordshire.

May 10, 1960: Paul Hewson (Bono) is born in Dublin.

August 8, 1961: Dave Evans (The Edge) is born in East London.

October 31, 1961: Larry Mullen, Jr. is born in Artane, Dublin.

September 12, 1974: Bono's mother Iris Hewson dies of a brain tumour in Dublin four days after collapsing at her father's funeral.

September 12, 1976: Embryo band forms in Dublin after Larry advertises on their school notice board for musicians to form a band. Larry was on drums, Bono on lead vocals, The Edge and his older brother Dik on guitar, Adam Clayton, a friend of the Evans brothers, on bass guitar; initially Ivan McCormick and Peter Martin, friends of Larry's, were also in.

September 1976: The group settle on the name "Feedback".

April 11, 1977: The band's first serious performance was on Easter Monday, St Fintan's School Assembly Hall, Dublin. Afterwards they rename as "The Hype".

February/March 1978: The band record a performance of their song "The Fool" in February for the RTÉ programme, *Our Times*. It is the band's first TV appearance.

March 17, 1978: On St Patrick's Day, the band win a talent show in Limerick, Ireland. The prize is £500 and studio time to record a demo for CBS Ireland.

April 28, 1978: Bill Graham writes his first interview with U2 in Irish music paper, *Hot Press*.

April 1978: The band record their first demo tape at Keystone Studios, Dublin.

May 25, 1978: Paul McGuinness agrees to become U2's manager.

September 9, 1978: U2 support The Stranglers at the Top Hat Ballroom. It is their biggest gig so far and they are paid £50.

November 1978: Larry's mother, Maureen Mullen, is killed in a car accident.

February 1979: Using borrowed money, Bono travels to London to plug U2 at the offices of record companies and music magazines.

September 1979: U2's first release, an Ireland-only EP entitled *U2-3*, becomes the band's first Irish chart success.

October 5, 1979: U2 play their first television performance on RTE at a televised concert in the Cork Opera House.

December 1, 1979: With £3,000 borrowed from family and friends, U2 begin a two-week tour of London clubs, their first shows outside Ireland. They play two nights at the Electric Ballroom, Camden, they open for Talking Heads and Orchestral Manoeuvres in the Dark. Rob Partridge of Island Records attends one of their better shows.

1980

February 26: National Boxing Stadium, Dublin – a gig to which U2 invited friends and family. Nick Stewart of Island Records is also there. Their second single "Another Day" is released on the CBS label for the Irish market only.

March 19: U2 share the bill with Berlin and The Virgin Prunes at the Sense of Ireland festival. Record company executives attend and four days later U2 sign an international deal with Island Records – £50,000 advance and £50k tour support in a four-year, four-album deal with three singles to be released in the first year.

April: Early in the month The Edge buys an Electro Harmonix Memory Man Deluxe echo box.

May 22: First UK tour with Island kicks off at the Hope & Anchor in Islington, London, and wraps at The Half Moon on June 8.

May 23: "11 O'Clock Tick Tock/ Touch" single released.

July 11: The band meet Chris Blackwell for the first time.

September 6 - December 3: A 56-date tour of the UK and Europe supporting first album, *Boy*.

October: "I Will Follow" released as a single – peaks at no. 20 on *Billboard* Mainstream Rock chart.

October 15: First continental Europe gig at Melkweg Amsterdam.

October 20: *Boy*, released to good reviews, peaks at 52 in UK.

December 6: An unfriendly audience at their first US gig in New York's Ritz Club is won round by the band; promoter Frank Barsalona watches for the first time and is impressed.

December 7-15: Eight East Coast gigs. After learning of the assassination of John Lennon, their inspired and emotional performance wins them rave reviews in Toronto.

1981

March: "I Will Follow" single released in USA.

March 3: *Boy* released in North America on Warner, reaches no.94.

March 4: Next leg of the Boy tour sets out in N. America from Philadelphia playing almost 60 dates across the country and ending May 31 at Asbury Park.

July: Recording of next album *October* starts in Dublin. "Fire", the first single of the album reaches no. 35 in UK charts.

October 12: *October* released, enters UK album chart at no.11.

November 4: Final show of October European tour at Metropol, Berlin. Bono and Edge tell McGuinness they want to quit the band. Paul explains their legal and moral commitments and they realize they can be rock stars and be Christian.

November 20-22: Three consecutive sell-out shows at New York City's Ritz.

December 20-21: Two sell-out shows at the Lyceum, London. Island executive Neil Storey presents the band with a gold disc for *October*.

1982

February 11: The US October tour reprises. Dutch photographer Anton Corbijn is with an *NME* journalist and the band initiate a friendship which will be very influential in their artistic development.

May 17: U2 begin recording their third album.

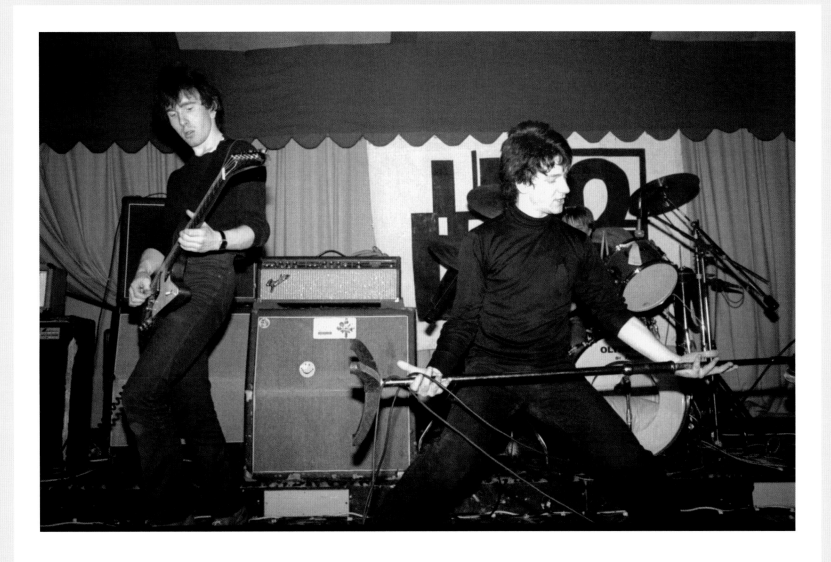

August 8: Edge's birthday; work starts on *War* in Dublin; Steve Lillywhite is producer.

August 21: Bono marries Alison Stewart in Dublin. They honeymoon at Blackwell's home in Jamaica.

December 20: At a Belfast gig Bono introduces "Sunday Bloody Sunday", telling the audience that if they don't like it they'll never play the song again.

1983

January: The new album's first single, "New Year's Day" is released becoming the band's first hit outside Ireland and the UK.

February 28: Third studio album *War* is released. It enters the UK chart at no 1 and reaches no.12 in the US.

April 23: War Tour opens at Kenan Stadium, Chapel Hill, N.C.

June 5: Red Rocks Amphitheater Denver: U2 decide to film a live show and fly in a video crew from UK and a sound team from NYC. The weather turns really bad but 5,000 fans brave the poor weather and come out to watch a stunning show. Pleased with the video the band release a mini LP with with eight tracks – two taken from the Red Rocks show: *U2 Live – Under a Blood Red Sky*.

July 12: Edge marries girlfriend Aislinn O'Sullivan; Bono is best man.

November 16: Honolulu NBC Arena – the War tour continues in the Pacific

November 21: *U2 Live Under a Blood Red Sky* is released and peaks at No2 in UK and 28 in US.

November 22: First of six shows in Japan at Osaka, Nagoya and finally Tokyo.

December: U2 is voted "Band of the Year" in the *Rolling Stone* magazine writer's poll.

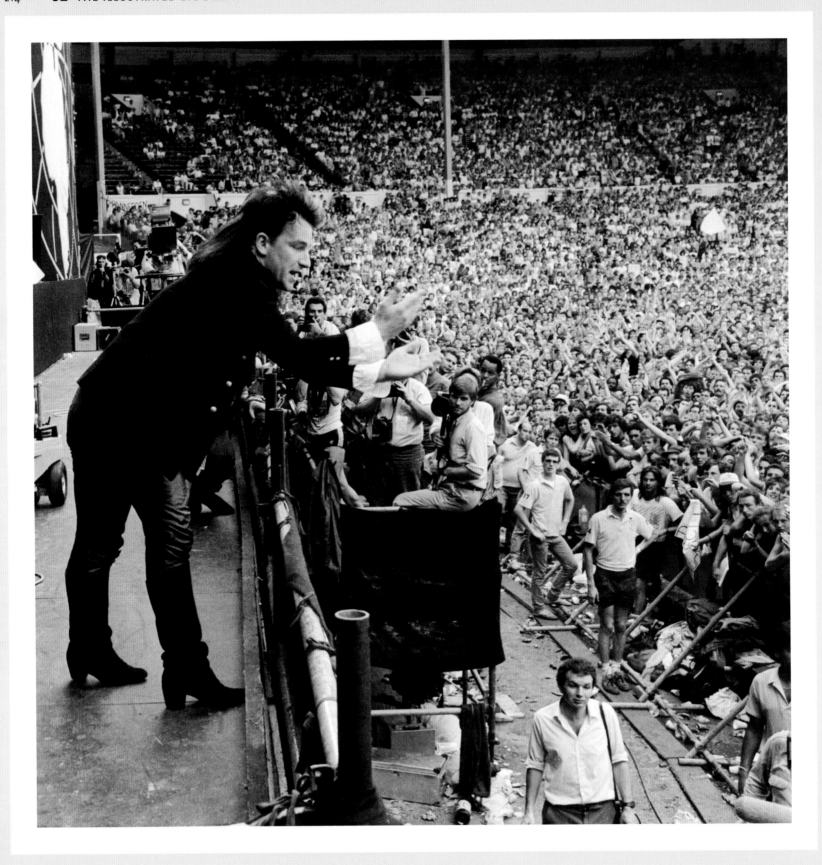

1984

July 4: Edge's wife Aislinn gives birth to their first child, Hollie.

July 8: Dylan in town for a gig admonishes Bono for not knowing more Irish folk music history.

August 29: Under Australian Skies tour opens in Christchurch, NZ.

September 1-2: In Auckland they hire a local called Greg Carroll who stays on as crew for the rest of the tour; he takes Bono to see a local landmark called One Tree Hill.

September 4: The tour moves to Australia opening at Entertainment Centre, Sydney

October 1: *The Unforgettable Fire,* produced by Brian Eno and Daniel Lanois, is released. It is a conscious choice to move U2's sound on. It reaches no. 1 in the UK but peaks at 12 in US chart.

October 18: European tour kicks off from Lyon playing 21 shows in halls and arenas in Western Europe.

November 21: At a German festival they are called by Bob Geldof to record Band Aid's "Do They Know It's Christmas?". Bono and Adam join Band Aid to record the song four days later.

December 1: 10 dates in major United States cities. Demand for tickets outstrips supply– U2 will no longer be able to play smaller theatres and halls.

December 3: Band Aid single goes straight to no.1 in UK and 12 other countries, raising £8m.

December 31: Final *Rolling Stone* magazine issue of the year puts three U2 albums in its top 100 of 1984 chart.

1985

January 23: European leg of the tour resumes in Norway, ends in Paris, February 10 after 13 shows.

February 25: US tour continues in Austin Texas; 40 shows follow in 29 cities in the US and Canada – their first tour played solely in arenas.

March 14: *Rolling Stone* magazine calls U2 the "Band of the 80s".

April 1: First perfomance at Madison Square Garden.

April: The album's second and final single, "The Unforgettable Fire", is released.

May 4: Tour wraps at Hollywood Sportarium, Fort Lauderdale.

Late May – mid-July: Nine gigs in the European festival season.

June 29: Homecoming Concert at Croke Park, Dublin, playing to an audience of 57,000.

July 13: U2 give one of the most memorable performances of Live Aid at Wembley Stadium, London.

September: Bono and Ali fly to Ethiopia to spend time with relief workers – staying a month in one of their feeding centres has a profound effect on both.

October 15: Birth of Edge and Aislinn's second child, Arran.

December: Musical collaboration with Clannad broadens Bono's musical education.

1986

January: Recording starts on the next album at Danesmoate House south of Dublin.

February: First issue of new fanzine *Propaganda*.

May 17: Benefit concert at Self Aid festival in Dublin intended to create jobs and raise money in Ireland's unemployment crisis.

June 4: The first of 6 shows in the 11-day Amnesty International Conspiracy of Hope tour is at Cow Palace, San Francisco. The finale brings all artists on stage to sing Dylan's "I Shall Be Released".

June 11: The Omni, Atlanta – The Police reunite here and for the last two shows of the tour.

June 15: Amnesty tour ends with an all-day concert attracting 55,000 people. It is broadcast live on MTV. The tour has raised $3m and tripled US membership.

July 3: Kiwi Greg Carroll dies in a motorbike accident in Dublin.

July 10: Band members perform at Carroll's burial in New Zealand. Bono writes "One Tree Hill".

Mid July: Bono and Ali fly to Nicaragua to visit a mission dedicated to human rights and economic development. While travelling on to El Salvador, government troops fire in their direction.

August 1: Back to recording in Dublin. The conflicts in Central America are a central influence on songs such as "Bullet The Blue Sky" and "Mothers of the Disappeared". The influence of Dylan, Van Morrison, and Keith Richards, connects the band to the roots of rock music.

December 14-16: The band are in the California desert with Anton Corbijn – *The Joshua Tree* album cover is shot at Zabriskie Point in Death Valley.

1987

March 4: "With or Without You" released for radio play, enters the *Billboard* chart at no. 64 then rises to no.1 in early May. Achieves no.4 in UK.

March 9: *The Joshua Tree* is released to become the fastest-selling album in British music history – 300,000 sold in 48 hours – taking it to no. 1 in the album chart. Debuts in US album chart at no.7 then goes to no.1 soon after. It is the first album to sell a million CDs in the US.

March 21: "With or Without You" goes on sale and becomes the band's first no.1 single in the US.

April 2: The Joshua Tree tour sets out from Arizona State University, Tempe, but Bono has voice problems.

April 12: Performing in Las Vegas the band go out on the streets to film the video for "I Still Haven't Found What I'm Looking For" which will be the second single from *The Joshua Tree.*

April 17-22: Five dates at Sports Arena, Los Angeles. On the 20th Dylan joins U2 onstage to sing "I Shall be Released" and "Knockin' on Heaven's Door".

April 27: U2 headline the front cover of *Time* magazine: "U2: Rock's Hottest Ticket". At the same time they are on the cover of *Rolling Stone* – a first for any band.

April 30: 51,000 tickets sold at Pontiac Silverdome, Detroit – U2's first stadium headline in USA.

May: "I Still Haven't Found What I'm Looking For" is released and hits no.1 in the US, no.6 in UK.

May 7,8,9: At the Hartford gig U2 are approached by Phil Joanou, a 25-year-old film director wanting to make a movie with them. He is invited to spend the summer with them to develop ideas.

May 16: US leg closes at Brendan Byrne Arena, East Rutherford. They return to Dublin with Joanou and start planning *Rattle And Hum*.

May 27: The European leg begins at the Stadio Flaminio in Rome: most of the 31 shows are in outdoor stadiums.

July 4: The Paris show is filmed for Island Records' 25th birthday celebrations.

July 15: U2's first show in Spain at the Bernabeu, Madrid, draws an audience of 115,000, the largest crowd of the year.

August: Island is in financial trouble and cannot pay the $5m *Joshua Tree* royalties. McGuinness negotiates a stake of 10 per cent of the label against the unpaid royalty.

August 8: European leg concludes at Cork, Ireland.

August: "Where the Streets Have No Name" is released as *The Joshua Tree*'s third single.

September: Joanou starts filming *Rattle And Hum*.

September 10-11: Third leg of The Joshua Tree Tour opens with two shows in New York City.

17-18/9/87: Two dates in Boston – Mayor Raymond Flynn confers honorary citizenship on the band.

September 20: At RFK Stadium, Washington, Bono slips and injures his shoulder – he will wear a sling for the next dozen shows.

September 26: U2 visit Harlem with Joanou's film crew to meet Dennis Bell's New Voices of Freedom gospel choir; they rehearse "I Still Haven't Found What I'm Looking For" for the Madison Square Garden concerts in two days' time.

November 29: A visit to Graceland and then on to Sun Studio in Memphis to work on new songs.

December 21: The Joshua Tree tour ends and the band returns to Dublin. The album is ranked no.3 in *Rolling Stone*'s list of top albums of 1987.

1988

January: Australian tour is postponed to start work on the *Rattle And Hum* album.

February: U2 move to Los Angeles to work with Phil Joanou on the *Rattle And Hum* documentary. They also record new songs at A&M and STS Studios.

March 2: U2's first two Grammy Awards: Best Performance by Group or Duo for "I Still Haven't Found What I'm Looking For" and Best Album for *The Joshua Tree*.

March: U2 sweep the board at the *Rolling Stone* 1987 Music Awards, taking Best Band and Artist of the Year; each band member wins their individual category.

May: Back to Dublin to work on *Rattle And Hum* (album and film).

June: Work continues in LA.

September 19: "Desire", the new album's first single – U2's first UK no.1. It reaches no.3 in US.

October 10: *Rattle And Hum* part live, part studio, double album released.

October 22: *Rattle And Hum* goes to no.1 on the UK album chart.

October 27: *Rattle And Hum* Movie world premiere at Savoy Cinema, O'Connell St, Dublin. A week later it is released in the US. It grosses $3.8m in its first weekend.

December 17: "Angel of Harlem" is the second single release from *Rattle And Hum*.

1989

February 22: Two more Grammys.

March 11: Bono and Edge join B.B. King on stage in Dublin to perform "When Love Comes to Town" – the following month it is released as *Rattle And Hum*'s third single.

May 10: Bono's daughter, Jordan is born on his 29th birthday.

June 16: Adam arrested on suspicion of drunken driving.

June 26: Aislinn gives birth to third daughter Blue Angel.

August 1: Chris Blackwell announces the sale of Island Records for $300m.

August 6: Adam is arrested in Dublin for possession and intent to supply marijuana. In court a month later he gets away with a telling-off and a £25,000 donation to charity.

September 15: U2 are in Sydney about to embark on the Lovetown Tour with B.B. King. The following day King turns 64; U2 organize a party on a yacht in the harbour.

September 21,22,23: The tour sets out with 3 dates in Perth.

November 23: Japan leg of the tour begins in Yokohama – the band's kit arrives late when a plane with their gear hit a flock of birds.

December 11-12: The tour continues back in Europe with Bono's voice deteriorating; two Amsterdam shows are cancelled.

December 26,27,30,31: Four long-awaited shows in Dublin – their first indoor shows here since 1982. Bono says onstage "this is just the end of something for U2...we have to go away and ... and dream it all up again".

1990

January 17: Bono inducts The Who into the Rock and Roll Hall of Fame in New York City.

March: Bono and family rent a van and travel across the US, spending two weeks in New Orleans where Bono writes two songs with the Neville Brothers.

Summer: The band gathers at STS Studio in Dublin to prepare material for the next album.

August 9: U2 watch Bowie perform in Dublin: Bono hosts a party for him.

October 3: U2 arrive in Berlin as Liberation Day kicks off and they join the celebrations walking from East to West and back. They start to record the next album at Hansa Tonstudio where Bowie recorded *Low* and *Heroes* in the 1970s. The equipment isn't in great shape and Lanois and Eno have to ship in their own gear.

December: It's tough going in the studio but Eno tells them they're doing better than they think and they get inspired by "One" and decide to continue in Dublin.

December 12: U2 is named Best Act in the World at the *Q* magazine awards.

1991

January 16: Back in Berlin, the Gulf War unfolding on TV stirs Bono's imagination.

February 9: To Tenerife in time for Santa Cruze festival where U2 don masks to mingle with the crowds. Bono calls stage designer Willie Williams and invites him to the island. Bono repeats the words 'ZooTV'. Willie has just finished the Bowie Sound and Vision tour which uses massive video screens.

Late March: Edge and Aislinn separate, affecting the album material he is writing.

July 7: Bono's second child, Eve, is born.

September 21: Studio work on *Achtung Baby* wraps but last minute work takes them into the early hours. The next morning Edge takes the tapes to Los Angeles for final mastering.

October 21: "The Fly" – the first single from the new album is released and goes straight to no.1 in the UK but no higher than no.61 in the US.

November 13: The forthcoming tour will be called ZooTV.

November 18,19: *Achtung Baby* is released worldwide and goes straight to no.1 on *Billboard* but is held off the UK top spot by Michael Jackson's *Dangerous*.

November 24,25: "Mysterious Ways" is released, reaching no.9 in the US singles chart and no.13 in the UK.

1992

January 15: Edge flies to New York to inaugurate The Yardbirds into the Rock and Roll Hall of Fame.

February 15: Tickets go on sale for ZooTV concerts in North America. A 7,000-seat arena in Lakeland, Florida sells out in 4 mins.

February 29: At Lakeland Civic Center, Florida, ZooTV goes live using many forms of media to capture the MTV generation. TV screens show different angles on band members and there are daily hook-ups to the war in the Balkans. The tour is a success with fans and critics.

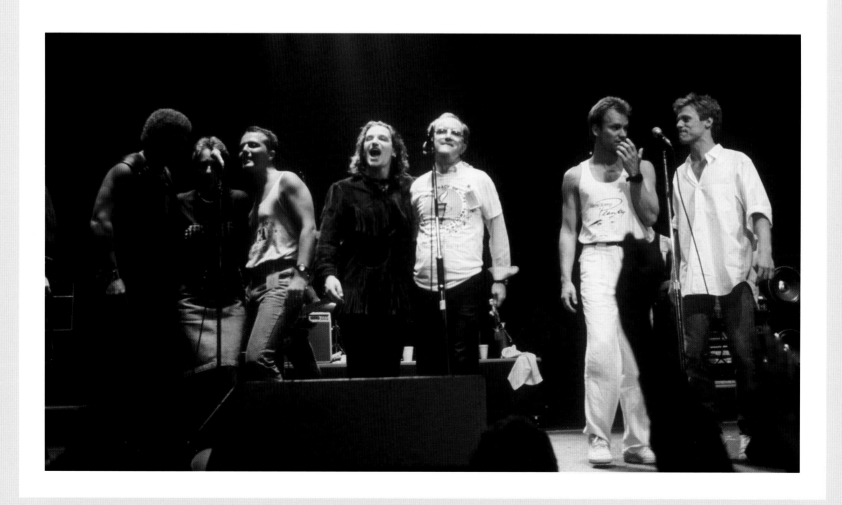

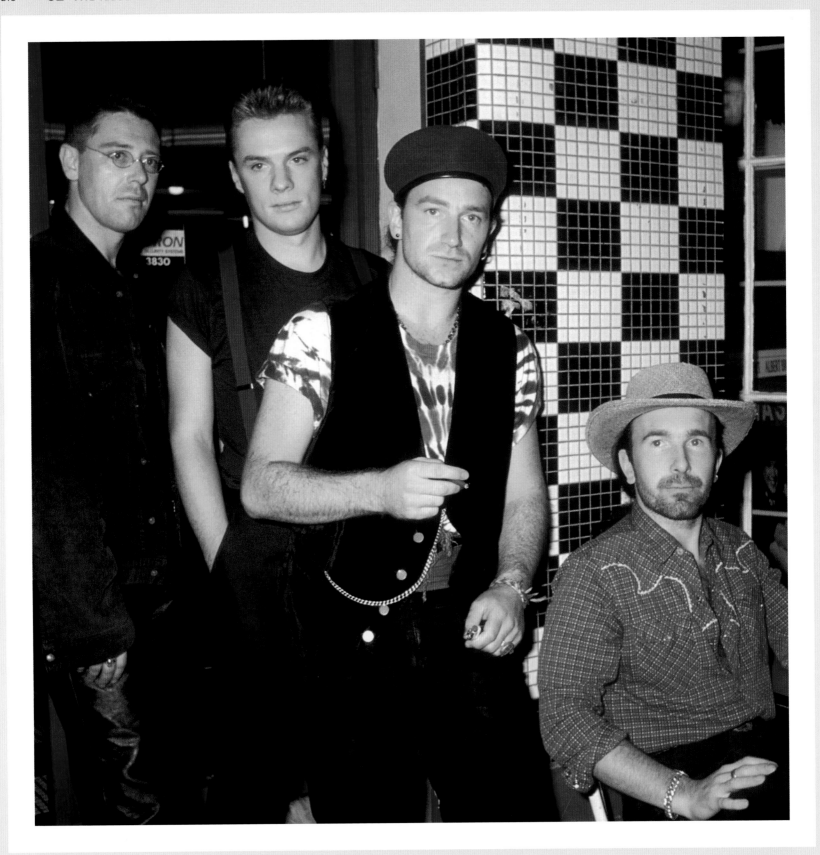

March: The third single from *Achtung Baby*, "One", is released.

April 23: Last date of the American leg of the tour in Vancouver.

May 07: The European leg of the ZooTV tour sets out from Paris, France.

June 8: The tour continues in Scandinavia. Bjorn & Benny of ABBA join the band on stage on the 11th to perform "Dancing Queen".

June 20: At Sellafield Power Station in the north of England, U2 go ashore with other protesters opposing the opening of a second nuclear plant.

August 12: U2 are back in USA and after the inaugural ZooTV outside broadcast show at Giants Stadium, N.J., Adam meets Naomi Campbell for the first time. Morleigh Steinberg makes her debut as the belly dancer in "Mysterious Ways".

August: The fifth and final single from *Achtung Baby*, "Who's Gonna Ride Your Wild Horses", is released.

September 14: They meet Presidential candidate Bill Clinton in Chicago. He invites them to play at his inauguration.

1993

January 20: Larry and Adam attend President Clinton's inauguration in Washington, DC. In MTV's Rock n Roll Inaugural Ball, they play with Michael Stipe and Mike Mills of R.E.M.

February: In a break from the tour, U2 start their next album *Zooropa*.

February 24: Adam and Naomi meet again during a flight from NYC to LA for the Grammy Awards where *Achtung Baby* wins Best Rock Vocal Performance.

April 27: Adam proposes to Naomi and is accepted.

May 9: Now known as "Zooropa", the tour recommences with a European stadium leg in Rotterdam. 2m people enjoy over 43 shows. During May, the band routinely fly back to Dublin to work on the *Zooropa* album.

June 2: U2 extend their deal with Island with a $60m advance and 25% royalty rate, making U2 perhaps the highest-paid rock act in history.

July 5-6: *Zooropa* goes on sale worldwide.

September 1: Edge and Morleigh Steinberg have become close; she returns to LA to tell her boyfriend.

October: Adam and Naomi seem to be cooling off.

November 12-13: Australian leg of ZooTV tour "Zoomerang" sets out from Melbourne.

December 5: Tour moves to Japan after dates in New Zealand; it wraps in Tokyo. The costly two-year tour has made no money and without $30m merchandising sales would have made a loss.

1994

January 19: Bono inducts Bob Marley into Rock and Roll Hall of Fame.

March 1: At Radio City, New York, U2 receive their 5th Grammy Award, for *Zooropa*. Bono gives a fulsome introduction to Frank Sinatra who receives a Living Legend Award.

Summer: Larry and Adam move to New York City to study music.

1995

June 5: "Hold Me, Thrill Me, Kiss Me, Kill Me" from *Batman Forever* is released around the world.

Summer : U2, Brian Eno, and Howie B. form alternative band, Passengers, and spend five weeks recording in Dublin.

September 9: Bono, Edge and Eno are in Modena to perform in the Pavarotti and Friends charity concert attended by Princess Diana.

November 07: The Passengers album *Original Soundtracks 1* is released world-wide. On the same day, Tina Turner releases "Goldeneye", the theme for the new James Bond film of the same name, written by Bono and Edge.

1996

January: Work begins on a new album in Dublin.

May 11: Bill Graham of *Hot Press* dies from a heart attack. The band fly back to Dublin from America to attend the funeral.

November 20: Studio recording of *Pop* is completed and goes to mixing in New York.

1997

February 12: In a Manhattan K-Mart U2 announce the dates for their next tour – PopMart.

March 3: World release of *Pop* which sells well initially but sales are not sustained.

April 25: The PopMart tour opens at Sam Boyd Stadium, Las Vegas.

July 14: "Last Night on Earth" is the third single release from *Pop*.

August 31: The second of two shows in Dublin is overshadowed by the death of Princess Diana but the effect is to energize their performance.

September 6: After a flying visit to New York for the MTV awards, U2 start another Europe stint in Paris.

September 23: An epic gig in Sarajevo marks a return to normality for the city and fulfils U2's dream to perform there.

October 1: Morleigh Steinberg gives birth to daughter Sian.

October 26: The third leg of the PopMart tour kicks off in Toronto.

December 12: PopMart wraps in Seattle.

1998

January 27: Back to the PopMart tour, performing seven dates in South America for the first time.

February 17: Performance in Perth, one of just four dates across Australia.

March 5,11: Two dates in Japan.

March 21: The PopMart tour concludes in Johannesburg.

September 20: U2 shoots video for "Sweetest Thing" on the streets of Dublin.

Autumn: Bono's father is diagnosed with cancer and Bono suffers serious vocal cord problems.

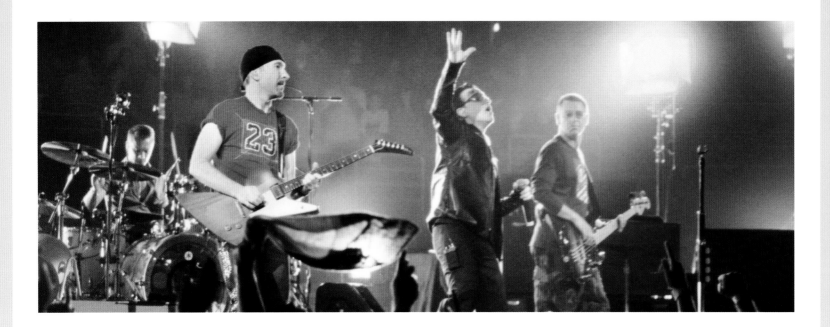

November 9:*The Best of 1980-1990* compilation album is released.

December 23: Larry and partner Ann Acheson have a baby girl.

1999

February 16: Bono helps to launch Jubilee 2000 campaign with an article in the *Guardian* newspaper.

March 15: Bono inducts Bruce Springsteen into the Rock and Roll Hall of Fame in New York City.

June 19: Bono appears at the G8 Summit in Cologne, Germany, to present 17m signatures supporting the cancelling of Third World debt.

August 17: Bono and Ali have a baby boy named Elijah Bob Patricious Guggi Q.

September 9: Bono gives a speech to the UN Assembly in New York to mark the launch of NetAid to raise awareness of global poverty.

October 25: Edge and Morleigh have their second child, Levi.

2000

May 25: Bono meets Nelson Mandela for the first time.

September 7: Bono and Nigerian President Olusegun Obasango present 21m signatures from 155 countries to the UN Millennium Summit calling for global debt relief

October 30: *All That You Can't Leave Behind* is released and regarded as a welcome return to form.

2001

February 21: The single "Beautiful Day" wins three Grammy Awards.

February 29: "Stuck in a Moment You Can't Get Out Of" is the second single release of the album.

March 19: Bono inducts Chris Blackwell into the Rock and Roll Hall of Fame.

March 24: American Leg of the Elevation Tour starts in Miami, Florida, returning to arenas after years of stadium productions.

June 12: "Elevation" is released as the third single from the album.

May 20:Ali & Bono's fourth child John Abraham is born in Dublin

July 7: European leg of the Elevation Tour starts in Copenhagen, Denmark.

August 21: Bono's father dies of cancer.

October 10: The second American leg of the Elevation Tour. Following 9/11 attacks, the album gained extra meaning in the US.

December 2: Elevation Tour wraps in Miami and the band is immediately working on new material for the next album

2002

January 2: Bono attends World Economic Forum in NY; later in the day launches DATA with Bill Gates – Debt AIDS Trade Africa.

February 27: U2 win four Grammy Awards out of eight nominations. Their Grammy total is now 14.

June 17: Edge and Morleigh marry in Dublin register office.

October 21: "Electrical Storm" is released as a single.

December 9: Bono and Edge perform "The Hands That Built America" for the first time live after the premiere of Scorsese's movie *Gangs Of New York*; it was written for the soundtrack.

2003

February: Work starts on a new album in Dublin with producer Chris Thomas.

March 23: U2 performs "The Hands That Built America" live at the Academy Awards – it had just won a Golden Globe.

June 21:U2 play live at the opening of 11th Special Olympics World Summer Games in Dublin; Nelson Mandela joins them on stage.

October: Things are not going well in the studio with Chris Thomas.

November 29: Bono and Edge perform at the 46664 concert honouring Nelson Mandela at Cape Town's Greenpoint Stadium.

2004

January: Steve Lillywhite arrives discreetly in Dublin to take over production from Chris Thomas.

March 25: *Rolling Stone* magazine puts U2 on the cover among a list of immortals of rock.

November 8:The new album's first single, "Vertigo", is released.

November 23: *How to Dismantle an Atomic Bomb* is released. The same day, *The Complete U2* digital box set is released on the iTunes Store. It is the first major release of a purely-digital online set by any artist.

December 13: Edge's daughter Sian is diagnosed with a serious illness which will have a major impact on the band over the next couple of years.

2005

February 13:"Vertigo" harvests three Grammys.

March 14: Bruce Springsteen inducts U2 into the Rock and Roll Hall of Fame.

March 28, 30:Vertigo tour sets out

with two dates in San Diego, Ca. The new stage set is more complex than the previous tour and uses a curtain backdrop composed of LED lights.

May 28: First leg of the Vertigo tour concludes in Boston

June 6: "City of Blinding Lights" is released as the fourth single from *How to Dismantle an Atomic Bomb*.

June 10: The European leg of the Vertigo Tour begins in Brussels.

July 2: U2 perform at Live 8, opening the show. The band plays "Sgt. Pepper's Lonely Hearts Club Band" with Paul McCartney.

November 17: Edge tours hurricane-devastated New Orleans; his Music Rising charity takes on the task of replacing 3,000 lost instruments.

December 19: Bono appears for the fourth time on the front cover of *Time* with Bill and Melinda Gates. The same day touring ends for the year in Portland, Oregon.

2006

January 26: At the World Economic Forum, Davos, Bono launches (Product) RED.

February 8: U2 collect 5 Grammys, while Steve Lillywhite also gets one for his work on *How to Dismantle An Atomic Bomb*.

February 12: An eight-date Latin American leg of the Vertigo tour commences in Monterrey, Mexico.

Early March: U2 arrive in Australia for the next leg of the Vertigo Tour but it is postponed until further notice due to Sian's illness.

September 25: U2 play with Green Day to open an NFL game in the Louisiana Superdome, New Orleans.

November 07: The postponed dates in Australia, New Zealand, Japan, and Hawaii commence in Brisbane: previously 10 dates, the number is increased to 13.

November 17: *U218 Singles* and *U218 Videos* are released.

December 9: The Vertigo tour ends in Honolulu – the second highest grossing tour in music history, next to Stones A Bigger Bang Tour.

2007

January 1: The "Window in the Skies" single is released.

May 22: The band move to Fez in Morocco with Eno and Lanois to write new album material.

November 20: *The Joshua Tree* is re-released as a 20th anniversary triple album.

2008

March 31: U2 sign a 12-year deal with Live Nation worth an estimated $100 million

Summer: *Boy, October, War,* and *Under a Blood Red Sky* are remastered and released.

November 6: Bono presents an Ultimate Legend Award to Paul McCartney at the 2008 MTV Europe Music Awards held at the Echo Arena Liverpool, England.

December: The band completed the new album *No Line on the Horizon*.

2009

January 23: "Get on Your Boots" is the first single release from the new album.

February 27: U2's 12th studio album, *No Line on the Horizon*, is released.

June 30: The U2 360° Tour sets out from Barcelona, Spain. The innovative stage set is an island surrounded on all sides by the audience.

November 5: In Berlin, Germany, they play an anniversary concert marking the fall of the Berlin Wall.

2010

May 21: Bono has emergency surgery on a back injury forcing postponement of the North American leg of the U2 360° Tour and their appearance at the Glastonbury Festival.

August 6: The second European leg of the U2 360° Tour starts on in Italy – their first performance since Bono recovered from his back injury.

December 19: Last touring date of U2 360° Tour 2010 in Perth, Australia. The cancelled gigs of 2010 have been rescheduled for 2011.

2011

February 13,18: The U2 360° Tour resumes with two dates in S Africa, Johannesburg and Cape Town: the last date of the tour will be in Moncton, Canada in July 2011.

April 1: Official release of *Killing Bono* the comedy film based on Neil McCormick's memoir *Killing Bono: I Was Bono's Doppelgänger*.

April 10:U2 smash the Rolling Stones' record for biggest grossing tour when they perform in Sao Paulo's Morumbi Stadium.

Discography

Studio Albums

1980: Boy: Island Records; 20 Oct

1981: October: Island Records; 12 Oct

1983: War: Island Records; 28 Feb

1984: The Unforgettable Fire: Island Records; 01 Oct

1987: The Joshua Tree: Island Records; 09 Mar

1988: Rattle and Hum: Island Records; 10 Oct

1991: Achtung Baby: Island Records; 19 Nov

1993: Zooropa: Island Records; 06 Jul

1997: Pop: Island Records; 04 Mar

2000: All That You Can't Leave Behind: Island Records/ Interscope Records; 3 Oct

2004: How to Dismantle an Atomic Bomb: Island Records/ Interscope Records; 19 Nov

2009: No Line on the Horizon: Interscope; 27 Feb

Live Albums

1983: Under a Blood Red Sky: Island Records; Nov

2004: Live from Boston 1981: Island Records; 23 Nov

Live from the Point Depot: Island Records; 23 Nov

2008: Live from Paris: iTunes; Jul

Compilation Albums

1998: The Best of 1980–1990: Island Records; 10 Nov

2002: The Best of 1990–2000: Island Records; 12 Nov

2004: Unreleased and Rare: Island Records; 23 Nov

2006: U218 Singles: Island Records; 17 Nov

Box Sets

2004: The Complete U2: Island Records; 23 Nov

EPs

1979: Three: Island Records; Sept

1985: Wide Awake in America: Island Records; May

1997: Please: PopHeart Live EP September 8/9, Island Records

2002: 7: Island Records; 22 Jan

2003: Exclusive: Island Records; 24 Apr

2004: Early Demos: Island Records; 23 Nov

Live from Under the Brooklyn Bridge: Island Records; 09 Dec

2010: Wide Awake in Europe: Island Records; 26 Nov

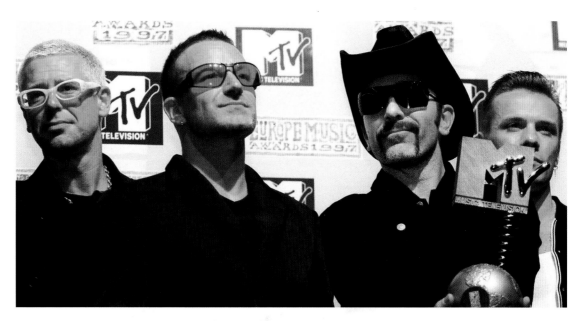